The spiritual nature of man

THE SPIRITUAL NATURE OF MAN

A study of contemporary religious experience

BY

SIR ALISTER HARDY, F.R.S.

Emeritus Professor of Zoology and Honorary Fellow of Exeter College and Merton College, Oxford

From the Religious Experience Research Unit, Manchester College, Oxford

CLARENDON PRESS · OXFORD
1979

Oxford University Press, Walton Street, Oxford OX2 6DP

OXFORD LONDON GLASGOW
NEW YORK TORONTO MELBOURNE WELLINGTON
KUALA LUMPUR SINGAPORE JAKARTA HONG KONG TOKYO
DELHI BOMBAY CALCUTTA MADRAS KARACHI
NAIROBI DAR ES SALAAM CAPE TOWN

Published in the United States
by Oxford University Press
New York

British Library Cataloguing in Publication Data
Hardy, *Sir* Alister
   The spiritual nature of man.
   1. Religious Experience Research Unit – History
   I. Title
   291.4'2   BL53   79–41143
   ISBN 0-19-824618-3

Set by Hope Services, Abingdon
and printed in Great Britain by
Lowe & Brydone (Printers) Limited,
Thetford, Norfolk

To Robert
—The Hon. E. R. H. Wills,
Founder and Chairman
of the Farmington Trust—
whose generosity and encouragement
so greatly helped the development
of the work here described.

PREFACE

This book is based upon the first eight years' work of the Religious Experience Research Unit set up at Manchester College, Oxford, in 1969. I wish to express my gratitude to the College and to thank all those people without whose help our work could never have developed.

I began fund-raising with lecture tours in this country and America in 1968 and so raised just over £10,000. With this we were able to make a modest start. We then received the most generous support from the Hon. Robert Wills, who had founded the Farmington Trust; not only did he second from his staff and pay the salary of Mr Timothy Beardsworth but then in the subsequent year he gave a grant of £2500 a year for seven years from a special charitable Trust, the Broadfield Trust, which he had set up; and subsequently he increased it. Other generous grants were made form the Dulverton Trust, the Hibbert Trust, the Instone Bloomfield Trust, the Moorgate Trust, the Phyllis Trust, and the Spalding Trust, whilst in addition we have received a large number of contributions from the general public, which either in form of seven-year covenants or single donations, have averaged some £1200 a year over our first eight years.

I would particularly like the name of the late Mrs Constance Ernest to be linked with our beginnings, for she had tremendous faith in what we were setting out to do. In addition to letting us have a most important account of her own religious experience, she was, although by no means well off, among the first to make contributions to our research fund and when she died, during the first year of our work, she left us a legacy of over £2000. She shared with us the vision of what we were striving for and did all she could to help in launching our quest.

At first I had the help of Timothy Beardsworth, an Oxford Greats man concerned with the philosophy of religion, who, being interested in our venture, was kindly lent half-time to me for a year by the Farmington Trust to get the work started. Then in 1970 I appointed Edward Robinson, another Oxford Greats man especially interested in the study of natural religion, to be my deputy; he had an additional qualification of being a botanist and so had the all important naturalist's approach to the exploration we were making. In 1976 he succeeded me as Director of the Unit on my reaching the age of 80.

Brian Carter joined the Unit for a year in 1970, one of the first graduates to come from the Department of Religious Studies of the University of Lancaster; he was followed in 1971 by Michael Walker who was a former Oxford pupil of mine in Zoology and so again one who combined the naturalist's approach with a keen interest in the study of religious experience, but he, too, unfortunately could only be with us for one year. In the meantime Beardsworth returned to make an examination of those very unusual so-called quasi-sensory experiences in which people felt convinced that they either saw lights or visions, or heard voices or felt themselves touched. For a short time Miss Joan Crewdson took part in the research after taking her B.D. for a theological thesis relating to our work. From 1973 to 1975 Mrs Vita Toon, an Oxford graduate in theology, did valuable work as Curator of Records; and recently we have been joined by Miss Carolyn Wilde, a philosopher from Cambridge and London.

David Hay, Lecturer in Biology in the Department of Education at the University of Nottingham, worked in co-operation with our unit, and we then appointed Miss Ann Morisy, a sociologist, as a member of our staff to work with him in Nottingham.

Under the editorship of Edward Robinson a series of smaller volumes with the general heading Studies in Religious Experience on different aspects of the Unit's work are now being published; four have already appeared as follows: *The Original Vision* by Robinson (1977); *A Sense of Presence* by Beardsworth (1977); *This Time-bound Ladder* edited by Robinson; and *Living the Questions* by Robinson (1978).

I have endeavoured to make my present book, in addition to describing the development of the work and the ideas behind it, a discussion of the whole range of religious experience as revealed by an examination of the first three thousand personal accounts sent in to the Unit. I hope the title will not be considered too ambitious or even pretentious; this book is intended as a contribution towards the study of this important, but still so little understood, part of our make-up made in the spirit of an inquiring naturalist.

It will be obvious throughout the book, I hope, how much of what I am describing is the work of my colleagues. I also owe much to our regular discussions on the progress of our research. Edward Robinson and Carolyn Wilde both read the manuscript before it finally went to press and made many helpful suggestions for its improvement; its faults, however, are all mine, for I did not always take their advice. Finally, I want especially to thank Mrs Venetia Pollock who has kindly taken a great interest in the book and, with her literary skill and experience, has helped me enormously in a rearrangement of the material to make it a more presentable volume for the general public. I am also most grateful for the encouragement and help given me by the Oxford University Press.

All quotations are acknowledged with references where they occur.

Oxford 1979   A.C.H.

CONTENTS

1

SPIRITUAL FEELING IN A SCIENTIFIC AGE

I have had, especially during my childhood, several experiences where I felt very strongly that a power in which I could be wholly confident was acting for and around me, even if at that time I was too little to give it a divine explanation.

One day as I was walking along Marylebone Road I was suddenly seized with an extraordinary sense of great joy and exaltation, as though a marvellous beam of spiritual power had shot through me linking me in a rapture with the world, the Universe, Life with a capital L, and all the beings around me. All delight and power, all things living, all time fused in a brief second.

Over the years my colleagues and I have collected together over four thousand first-hand accounts, such as the ones above, which show that a large number of people even today possess a deep awareness of a benevolent non-physical power. which appears to be partly or wholly beyond, and far greater than, the individual self.

At certain times in their lives many people have had specific, deeply felt, transcendental experiences which have made them all aware of the presence of this power. The experience when it comes has always been quite different from any other type of experience they have ever had. They do not necessarily call it a religious feeling, nor does it occur only to those who belong to an institutional religion or who indulge in corporate acts of worship. It often occurs to children, to atheists and agnostics, and it usually induces in the person concerned a conviction that the everyday world is not the whole of reality: that there is another dimension to life.

Some people feel a personal devotional relationship with the power after their experience; some call it God, some do not. Some see it as an aspect of their wider self through which such an experience has come, whilst others see it as part of man's general consciousness.

To some, the presence of this abstract non-physical power is strongest when contemplating natural beauty or listening to music: others feel it when they paint or create. Awareness of its presence affects the way man looks at the world, it alters behaviour and changes attitudes. Knowledge of this wider dimension to life may be seen by an individual as life-enhancing, or he may recognize it as a special force which gives him added confidence and courage. As a result of their experiences many are led to prayer and to religion.

People experience the abstract power in a wide variety of ways. Some may describe their feelings in terms of trust, awe, joy, or bliss; exceptionally they may reach the heights of ecstasy. Others may have sensory impressions, see lights, hear voices, or have the feeling of being touched. So far we have suggested ninety-two categories for the accounts given in this book alone; but, however diverse the kind of experience, spiritual awareness appears to be universal to human kind: it occurs equally among primitive and sophisticated peoples.

Apart from the work of James and Starbuck, to whom I shall come in a moment, there has been little organized knowledge of this phenomenon. Because of its importance I set up a research unit to find out more about it, and I have endeavoured in this book to explore the spiritual nature of man as systematically and objectively as possible. First, we have tried to build up a body of knowledge of actual experiences by collecting thousands of individual first-hand accounts which we have then collated under classificatory labels. Secondly, we have examined these examples in depth, looking at their development, their dynamic patterns, antecedents, and consequences. Thirdly, we have begun quantitative studies. Finally, I have tried to draw certain tentative conclusions. For only when we have collected, collated, examined, and counted a great many first-hand accounts can we hope to learn more about the essential part that man's spirituality plays in his make-up.

To clear away any possible misunderstanding, let me state at the outset that I am not in any way endeavouring to find support for this or that form of institutional religion, or indeed for the doctrines of any particular faith. It is not my desire to be doctrinaire in any way. I am essentially concerned with man's spiritual feelings in general: with increasing knowledge about this sense of awareness and with finding out more about the effect it may have upon a man's life.

In view of remarks sometimes heard it is perhaps also necessary that I should at once dispel the idea that I am trying to use the scientific method to 'prove' the existence of God. We cannot, of course, do that. I do not believe in a deity with an anthropomorphic image—an old gentleman 'out there'—but I take 'theism' to mean at least a belief in a contact with a power which *appears to be* greater than, and in part to lie beyond, the individual self. Towards this element, whatever it may be, those who are conscious of it may have a feeling as if towards a being. No doubt for good biological or psychological reasons, this feeling may be linked with the emotions of an early child–parent affection—indeed it may be a personal, devotional love relationship. Freud has taught us much about this personification, although I do not believe that his super-ego gives us the complete explanation of this feeling. But I do believe that by the continued collection of evidence we should in time have sufficient to demonstrate that a large proportion of people do have feelings towards a benign power. Studies of individual experience in depth should also tell us something of what people feel to be the nature of this power. Whether or not it exists beyond the subconscious of the persons concerned cannot be scientifically proved; we can, however, consider the problem in the light of experience.

I am sometimes asked what I really mean when I use the word 'religion'. While I hope what I have just said will provide part of the answer, it may be help-ful if I am more specific. My meaning is almost equivalent to that given in the *Concise Oxford Dictionary* (6th edition) which I shall now quote and then point out just where my personal interpretation may be thought by some to diverge from it. Apart from the more specialized connotations relating to monastic conditions and the practice of sacred rites, with which I am not concerned, it gives the following two main meanings. First, as 'Particular system of faith and worship (*the Christian, Muslim, Buddhist, religion*)'; I may, of course, at times speak of religion in this sense. And secondly as 'Human recognition of superhuman controlling power and esp. of a personal God or gods entitled to obedience and worship; effect of such recognition on conduct and mental attitude'; my use of the word religion is so similiar that I would say that it can be covered by this phrase if the points I have made in the preceding paragraphs are noted as variations in interpretation. For 'superhuman' I prefer 'transcendental' in the same way that I would prefer 'para-physical' to 'supernatural' in that I regard all these phenomena as part of the *natural world*; for me the 'personal God' is not a person *out there* but has none the less an equally important *personal* reality of a psycho-logical nature. All this, however, will, I hope, be better understood when we come to the final chapters *after* our examination of all the evidence of human experience.

Now let me briefly sketch the development of the main ideas which led to the start of the research, and mention some of the earlier writers on the scientific treatment of religious experience. I will then consider the validity of such an inquiry in relation to the canons of present-day science and follow this with a description of how the research was carried out.

The possibility of investigating man's transcendental experiences and of building up a body of knowledge about them from first-hand accounts has been a life-long interest which I have always regarded as part of my biological outlook. I began to collect material towards such a study more than fifty years ago: in September 1925 to be exact. I always regarded the planning of my research as an exercise in human ecology, for, to me, one of the greatest contributions biology could make to mankind would be to work out an ecological outlook which took into account not only man's economic and nutritional needs but also his emotional and spiritual behaviour (Hardy 1942).

It had always seemed to me that man was religious by nature, but that modern man's craving for a spiritual philosophy had become frustrated, making him restless and uncertain. I had felt for a long time that these unappeased religious desires could only be satisfied with spiritual philosophy which could be seen to be based upon a systematic study of recorded experience and which was not incompatible with modern biological theory.

If the true nature of religion is based upon a subjective feeling, many will ask how any such philosophy could be established in a world dominated by the scientific attitude. It is not, I believe, quite so difficult as many brought up in our twentieth-century culture might suppose. I have always emphasized that science itself can never deal with the real essence of religion any more than it can with the nature of art or the poetry of human love. Nevertheless science does not deny the reality of man's experience of beauty in nature, his sense of curiosity, or his love of adventure. Psychologists and biologists may seek to explain these feelings in rational terms, but they would never refuse to admit that they existed as important parts of human behaviour. In just the same way I believe we must recognize that a great many people have what we may call a spiritual side to their nature. What we have to do is to present such a weight of *objective* evidence in the form of *written records* of these subjective spiritual feelings and of their effects on the lives of the people concerned, that the intellectual world must come to see that they are in fact as real and as influential as are the forces of love.

It is true of course, that those who have these spiritual feelings find it exceedingly difficult to put them into words; the mystics have always protested that the experiences are ineffable. Nevertheless, however difficult and inadequate it may be to convert the elements of any single one of these subjective experiences into an account open to objective observation, if we have a sufficient number of records to study, then any fundamental patterns that may exist—such, for example, as a commonly recurring feeling of being in touch with what *appears to the person concerned* to be a benign power beyond the self—should eventually reveal their presence to systematic study.

EARLIER WRITERS ON THE SCIENTIFIC TREATMENT
OF RELIGIOUS EXPERIENCES

The great pioneer in the study of religious feeling was William James. In his classic and profound study *The Varieties of Religious Experience*, written in 1902, he points to the reality of man's contact with a power beyond the conscious self, which affects his actions; and of which James gives innumerable examples. In his final philosophical postscript to the volume he says:

I am so impressed by the importance of these phenomena that I adopt the hypothesis which they so naturally suggest. At these places at least, I say, it would seem as though transmundane energies, God, if you will, produce immediate effects within the natural world to which the rest of our experience belongs.

Then in his final chapter of conclusions he writes of the elements of religious experience:

treating these as purely subjective phenomena, without regard to the question of their 'truth', we are obliged, on account of their extraordinary influence upon action and endurance, to class them amongst the most important biological functions of mankind.

His contemporary Edwin Starbuck with his *Psychology of Religion* of 1899 also illustrates exactly the scientific treatment of religion for which I am arguing. Starbuck opens his book boldly with the following words:

Science has conquered one field after another, until now it is entering the most complex, the most inaccessible, and, of all, the most sacred domain—that of religion. The Psychology of religion has for its work to carry the well-established methods of science into the analysis and organisation of the facts of the religious consciousness, and to ascertain the laws which determine its growth and character.

A third writer on the psychology of religion of the same period should also be mentioned, James H. Leuba, who also used the empirical method of examining case histories but not to anything like the same extent as the other two; in his first two articles (1896, 1901) and in subsequent books (1912, 1929) he took a less idealistic attitude. Whether we agree with his attitude or not, he certainly recognized, as James acknowledges in referring to him, the great importance of the concept of God to mankind; James gives an abridged quotation from Leuba's 1901 article as follows:

God is not known, he is not understood; he is used—sometimes as meat-purveyor, sometimes as moral support, sometimes as friend, sometimes as an object of love. If he proves himself useful, the religious consciousness asked for no more than that. Does God really exist? How does he exist? What is he? are so many irrelevant questions. Not God, but life, more life, a larger, richer, more satisfying life, is in the last analysis, the end of religion. The love of life, at any and every level of development, is the religious impulse.

Two important volumes of the same period, but written from a religious rather than a psychological standpoint, are A. Poulain's *Des Grâces d'Oraison* (1901) translated as *The Graces of Interior Prayer* (1910) and E. Underhill's *Mysticism: a Study in the Nature and Development of Man's Spiritual Conscious-ness* (1911). They, with their enormous collection and discussion of records of the past, are both most valuable for comparision with the experiences of today; indeed Poulain emphasizes the importance of this: 'the two kinds of information', he says, 'are indispensable, each one throws light upon the other. There are many passages in the old writers, the real sense of which is only grasped when it is commented on by the living voice of a person who has passed through similar states, and the converse is true'. I hope that the material which we have collected may serve such a purpose.*

SOCIAL ANTHROPOLOGISTS

The lead of these pioneers was not followed for close on sixty years, except

*Since I wrote this J. M. Cohen and J.-F. Phipps have published *The Common Experience* (1979) using many of our records for just such a purpose.

by social anthropologists. For years anthropologists have been collecting accounts of religious attitudes, ideas, and feelings from primitive peoples. As a result we know much more about the religious feelings of Polynesians, North American Indians, and various tribes in Africa than we do about those of our fellow-citizens in Western society.

The anthropologist R. R. Marett pointed out in his book *Psychology and Folk-Lore* in 1920:

Put very shortly, the moral of the history of primitive religion would seem to be this—that religion is all along vital to man as a striving and progressive being . . . Enough has been said to show that, corresponding to the anthropologist's wide use of the term 'religion', there is a real sameness, felt all along, if expressed with no great clearness at first, in the characteristic manifestations of the religious consciousness at all times and in all places. It is the common experience of man that he can draw on a power that makes for, and in its most typical form wills, righteousness, the sole condition being that a certain fear, a certain shyness and humility, accompany the effort so to do. That such a universal belief exists amongst all mankind, and that it is no less universally helpful in the highest degree, is the abiding impression left on my mind by the study of religion in its historico-scientific aspect.

A few years earlier, Emile Durkheim in France had come to much the same conclusion. In his *Elementary Forms of Religious Life* (1915) he writes:

The believer, who has communicated with his god, is not merely a man who sees new truths of which the unbeliever is ignorant; he is a man who is *stronger*. He feels within him more force, either to endure the trials of existence or to conquer them. It is as though he were raised above the miseries of the world, because he is raised above his condition as a mere man; he believes that he is saved from evil, under whatever form he may conceive this evil. The first article in every creed is the belief in salvation by faith.

In another passage in the same book he writes:

Our entire study rests upon this postulate that the unanimous sentiment of the believers of all times cannot be purely illusory. Together with a recent apologist of the faith [he is referring here to William James] we admit that these religious beliefs rest upon a specific experience whose demonstrative value is, in one sense, not one bit inferior to that of scientific experiments, though different from them.

Here we see him agreeing that the reality of religion rests upon the evidence of experience. He goes on to say much more about the development of religion as a social force. Many, who perhaps have not read Durkheim sufficiently carefully, have thought, I believe, that his theory of religion is one linking it simply to a *mechanistic* interpretation of the evolution of man as a social animal. Nothing could be further from the truth, as is clearly shown when he says, 'it is necessary to avoid seeing in this theory of religion a simple restatement of historical materialism: that would be mistaking our thought to an extreme degree'. He then explains that whilst he regards religion as something essentially social, and believes that social life depends upon its material foundation, just as an individual's mental life depends upon his nervous system, there is what he calls a *collective consciousness* which is, he says, 'something more than a mere epiphenomenon of its morphological basis, just as individual consciousness is something more than a simple efflorescence of the nervous system'. This indeed is his idea of God, and he makes it clear in one of the last paragraphs of his book that he considers it to be a power which is beyond the individual.

the collective consciousness is the highest form of psychic life, since it is the consciousness of the consciousnesses. Being placed outside of and above individual and local contingencies, it sees things only in their permanent and essential aspects, which it crystallizes into communicable ideas.

More recent studies of the religious feelings of members of individual tribes are those by the late Professor Sir Edward Evans-Pritchard in his book on *Nuer Religion* (1956) and by Dr Godfrey Lienhardt in his *Divinity and Experience: the Religion of the Dinka* (1961). Both are remarkable accounts of spiritual awareness among most primitive communities and they tell the same story.

MODERN STUDIES

Apart from the social anthropologists, there was for many years a dearth of scientific interest in man's spiritual awareness. There are, I believe, several reasons for this relative neglect: one is that it is difficult to reconcile religious concepts with the materialistic interpretation of life which tends to prevail in the modern intellectual world. Another reason is that a good deal of what has been regarded as 'religion' has elements in it of superstition on the one hand and wishful thinking on the other. A further reason is that some so-called 'religions' have been concerned with a variety of concepts each proclaimed to be true by rival theological doctrines but which most clearly can be seen to contradict one another in regard to a number of points thought by the different sects to be vitally important. When theological scholars of the highest distinction are divided in their views it tends to deter would-be investigators from researching into the subject of religious experience. When all is said and done, however, who can doubt that a systematic examination of religious experience, when all theological speculation is set on one side, must contribute towards a better understanding of human life and living?

This neglect of a systematic study of religious feelings in the modern world is particularly surprising in view of the widespread recognition of the part religion has played in the development of past civilizations and in the history of our own culture. Many indeed have been the wars of religion. Little is more emotionally powerful in human behaviour than the bitter antagonism of rival beliefs. We see the truth of this when we look at the appalling clashes between Hindus and Moslems in India and Pakistan, between Moslems and Jews in the Middle East, and alas between Catholics and Protestants in a part of Great Britain.

At last, however, we have a revival of interest. In America we have the psychological studies of Maslow (1964) emphasizing the importance of what he calls 'peak' (i.e. ecstatic) experience; the work of Glock and Stark (1965), who made a questionnaire survey of religious experience in California and also attempted to apply a form of classification; and then the opinion-poll surveys of Back and Bourque (1970) and those of Greeley and McCready (1974). In Sweden there are the theoretical psychological studies of Sunden (1954–74) which I know only through a discussion of them by Unger (1976) of Uppsala, who also writes on the psychology of religious experience but in a more philosophical manner, and his empirical examples are few. Then in Britain we have the sociological studies of religious behaviour of Argyle (1958) and Argyle and Beit-Hallahmi (1975), and the work from our own research unit to be described in the present volume: Robinson (1977, 1978), Beardsworth (1977), and in co-operation with us Hay (1974, 1979) and Hay and Morisy (1978).

RELIGION'S RELATIONSHIP WITH SCIENCE

Whilst I cannot here explore in detail the relation of our work to modern scientific theory, I need to discuss the theme in order to show how it may be accepted into the prevailing climate of intellectual thought today. The bringing of the elements of religion into the realm of scientific thought may prove to be a vital issue: unless this can be done, religion as a moral force may disappear, and we cannot be sure that our civilization will survive without it.

There have grown up certain ideas about science which, I believe, may be most damaging to its very spirit as well as to man's peace of mind. One of these proclaims that all that is truly scientific will ultimately be explained in terms of physics and chemistry. There are many biologists who hold such views and often express them with so much conviction that the general public may come to accept them as a true part of science. I am sure, of course, that all the physical and mechanical actions of the animal body—and the human too—can be described in physical and chemical terms; there can be no doubt that physically speaking we are chemical machines. It now seems certain that the modern geneticists and embryologists are right: the building of the material body of each person is accomplished by a most elaborate series of chemical reactions initiated by the genes which form the coded 'instructions' laid down in the molecular 'plans' within the chromosomes of each individual. This, however, is not the whole story; I believe, with those great neurologists Sir Charles Sherrington, Sir John Eccles, and Lord Brain, that mental events may belong to a different order which somehow, in a way we do not *yet* understand, is linked with the physical system. The mystery of the mind–body relationship is still unsolved; no doubt in time the two elements will be united in a single philosophy. Sherrington, perhaps the greatest investigator of our nervous action, in his Gifford Lectures *Man on his Nature* (1940) said: 'mental phenomena on examination do not seem amenable to understanding under physics and chemistry. I have therefore to think of the brain as an organ of liaison between energy and mind, but not as a converter of energy into mind or vice versa'. Nearing the end of his life in 1947 he wrote 'that our being should consist of *two* fundamental elements offers I suppose no greater inherent improbability than that it should rest on only one'.[1]

We can apply the scientific method to the study of certain aspects of living things quite independently of physics and chemistry. Just as important as the physico-chemical analysis of the animal's internal mechanism is the science of the living animal, looked at as a whole, in relation to its natural surroundings: this is done by those branches of biology which we call ecology and ethology (the study of animal behaviour). Physics and chemistry are sciences because they are based upon statistical laws and experiment; so also ecology and ethology are part of true science *in their own right*, being based upon a quantitative treatment and an experimental analysis of the interactions and behaviour of animals as *living wholes*. There is no need for these latter studies to be wedded to the unproven hypothesis or *dogma* of materialism; animal bodies may, as I have said, be completely described in physico-chemical statements, but it is merely a pretence to suggest that we understand their mental side in similar terms.

On account of this mechanistic dogma an increasing number of people today regard the idea of a spiritual or transcendental side of the universe as a pleasant illusion, as a myth remaining from a pre-scientific age which civilization must grow out of. This is the view of the new humanism which typically had its expression in the voice of my old friend the late Sir Julian Huxley (1962):

It is a monistic vision showing us all reality as a unitary and continuous process, with no dualistic split between soul and body, between matter and mind, between life and non-life, no cleavage between natural and super-natural; it reveals that all phenomena from worms to women, from radiation to religion are natural.

I readily grant that all phenomena, including religion, may be called *natural* and I am certain that man is a part of the evolutionary process; to assert, however, that matter and mind are of the same order of nature is as yet a quite unwarranted assumption. Sir Julian Huxley was not in fact so dogmatic a monist as he often appeared to be. Having been asked in a letter what meaning he attached to the terms 'monism' and 'dualism', he replied that he had always been very careful to point out that he was not a materialist, but a monist in the sense that he believed that we and the rest of life are products of—and agents in—a single process. He then said, 'but the products have two aspects—material when observed from outside, subjective when viewed from inside . . . I think I am right in saying that there is still a great deal of mystery about the relation between the two aspects; but we are getting to know more all the time'.

[1]When the international Congress of Physiology met in Oxford in 1947 they published, as a compliment to Sherrington, his great book *The Integrative Action of the Nervous System* which was first published in 1906: my quotation is taken from the remarkable foreword he wrote for this 1947 edition published by Cambridge University Press.

This is indeed the mystery we are here concerned with. What is it that both perceives the material world and at the same time subjectively knows of its own existence? Clearly, as I have said, it is closely linked with the physical system and I agree, of course, that in the living evolutionary stream this element combines with the matter–energy complex to form a single process.

RELIGION AND DARWINIAN EVOLUTION

I am a convinced Darwinian. Indeed it was the need to reconcile fully the Darwinian doctrine of natural selection with the spiritual side of man which postponed my active attack upon the problems in this book for thirty-five years. But after much hard thinking and searching of the literature I did eventually become satisfied that the two concepts were not contradictory. I am convinced of the truth of the selection theory but, as I shall explain, I do not believe that all selection is just chance. Nor do I agree with the unwarranted dogma that belief in modern evolutionary theory shows that the whole process is an entirely materialistic one leaving no room for the possibility of a spiritual side to man. Unfortunately many biologists do tell this story. I will quote just one example. Dr G. G. Simpson, late Director of the American Museum of Natural History, in his Terry Lectures delivered in 1949 at Yale University and published as *The Meaning of Evolution* (1950) says on p. 230:

It would be brash, indeed, to claim complete understanding of this extraordinarily intricate process, but it does seem that the problem is now essentially solved and that the mechanism of adaptation is known. It turns out to be basically materialistic ... [and later, on p. 277] ... In fact, as the geneticists' studies progressed they were providing the last major piece of the truth so long sought regarding the causes of evolution.

It is always rash to speak of the last major piece of truth. His book had not been printed for more than five years before Crick and Watson discovered the nature of the remarkable DNA molecule (deoxyribonucleic acid) and how it forms the chemical genetic code I have just referred to. This code determines the structural variations of animals and plants, upon which Darwinian selection works. Crick and Watson showed how these differences are caused by the random changes in the links between the two sides of the double spiral arrangement of this complex molecule; their theoretical model has been fully proved by X-ray diffraction analysis and many other experimental methods. In an article (*Scientific American,* September 1957) written for the more general public Crick ended with these words:

From every point of view biology is getting nearer and nearer to the molecular level. Here in the realm of heredity we now find ourselves dealing with polymers [i.e. chain molecules] and reducing the decisive controls of life to a matter of the precise order in which monomers [i.e. the units in a chain] are arranged in a giant molecule.

'*The decisive controls of life*' says Crick, but is it really true? An increasing number of people follow him in this belief. It all appears at first sight like a soul-less automatic process; I believe, however, that this is only a superficial view. I am, as I have already said, a true Darwinian and I grant that the DNA code almost certainly determines the *physical* nature of the individual organism; I do not, however, believe that this gives us a complete account of the evolutionary process. It is a fallacy to suppose that chance random changes in the DNA molecules control the course of evolution; they provide the almost infinite range of variation among members of any population of animals and plants for natural selection to act upon, but it is *selection* that guides the process and selection is far from random. Much of selection is certainly due to factors outside the organism such as the physical environment and the action of predators and competitors in the struggle for life, but these are not everything; so many biologists are so impressed by the remarkable adaptations that these factors produce that they become blind to other possibilities. It is not, of course, just lines of individuals that are evolving; it is whole populations. In the higher ranges of evolution, as I have explained in *The Living Stream* (1965), new patterns of behaviour can exert important selective forces within populations of animals to bring about better adaptational changes. Thus the *mental* side of life turns out to be a factor of cardinal importance within the process of Darwinian evolution. I will not deny that the *manifestation* of this side of life itself must to a considerable extent be facilitated by the genetic code governing the forms of the nerve and brain mechanism, as seen, for instance, in the inheritance of mathematical or musical ability and other such qualities in man, which are seen to run in families; this, however, is not to say that we are any nearer to an understanding of the fundamental nature of this mental side.

THE IMPORTANCE OF NON-GENETIC INFORMATION

Although the process of evolution has been a continuous one, there has come about, in a remarkably short period of time—that is geologically speaking—as great, or perhaps an even greater, change in the nature of life between man and his animal ancestors as that which distinguishes animals from plants. Man is an animal with a difference. This difference in his constitution is the result of the extraordinarily rapid evolution of the brain, making possible a reasoning mind and the development of speech: the two faculties have indeed evolved hand in hand together as one process. Now here comes something even more surprising: the resulting powers of linguistic communication have altered the very mechanism of evolution itself. We are now within a different system from that governed simply by Darwinian natural selection. Whilst we are still prone to the selective effects of pathogenic organisms and the effects of the physical environment, the force of these is continually being reduced by the progress of medicine and technology; far more important now, in the evolution of human society, are the effects of tradition. We have reached what Sir Julian Huxley called, in his Darwin

Centennial address at the University of Chicago in 1959, the new psycho-social phase of evolution.

The significance of this great change for humanity at large was so well expressed in the same year by Sir Peter Medawar in his Reith Lectures *The Future of Man* (published 1960) in which he brought home to us how relevant is a true knowledge of our own evolution for a proper understanding of human affairs.

In their hunger for synthesis and systematisation, the evolutionary philosophers of the nineteenth century and some of their modern counterparts have missed the point: they thought that great lessons were to be learnt from similarities between Darwinian and social evolution; but it is from the differences that all the great lessons are to be learnt. For one thing, our newer style of evolution is Lamarckian in nature. The environment cannot imprint genetical information upon us, but it can and does imprint non-genetical information which we can and do pass on. Acquired characters are indeed inherited. The blacksmith was under an illusion if he supposed that his habits of life could impress themselves upon the genetic makeup of his children; but there is no doubting his ability to teach his children his trade, so that they can grow up to be as stalwart and skilful as himself.

It is important to realize that while Sir Peter says that our 'newer syle of evolution is Lamarckian in nature' he does not believe, as Lamarck did, that acquired characters are inherited by the physical genetical system; this he makes clear in his next sentence 'The environment cannot imprint genetical information upon us'. I find it necessary to point this out for I find that some people have misunderstood him.

Earlier in his volume of essays *The Uniqueness of the Individual* (1957) he discusses the fundamental distinction between the 'Springs of Action' in mice and men. He points out that mice have no traditions, or at most very few, as can be shown by breeding them in such a way that each individual in successive generations is separated from its parents from the moment of birth; when this is done there is 'no loss of their mouse-like ways'. He then makes his most telling point. 'The entire structure of human society as we know it', he says, 'would be destroyed in a single generation if anything of the kind were to be done with man.' Tradition, he emphasizes, is 'a biological instrument, by means of which human beings conserve, propagate and enlarge upon those properties to which they owe their present biological fitness, and their hope of becoming fitter still'. The future of the human race now lies in the behaviour of man himself; in the kind of traditions he is handing on to the coming generations.

THE SURVIVAL OF IDEAS

Richard Dawkins in his book *The Selfish Gene* (1976) discusses the handing on of the mental ideas to the next generation; and Peter Medawar in reviewing the book described him as 'one of the most brilliant of the rising generation of biologists'. Dawkins begins with the origin of living material becoming possible by the formation, within the primeval chemical soup of some three thousand million years ago, of stable complex molecules which were able, from the surrounding atoms and molecules, to make copies of themselves. These were the forerunners of the DNA molecules—the genes—around which all life from bacteria to man has been evolved by the process of Darwinian selection. The selfish genes are those which give rise to the bodily and behavioural characteristics which tend to enable their particular types of animals and plants to have a better chance of survival. However, it is not with the greater part of this book that I am here concerned, except to note with pleasure that he regards the evolution of subjective consciousness as 'the most profound mystery facing modern biology'; I am only going to refer to his last chapter.

Here, after pointing out the fundamental change in human evolution already emphasized by Medawar, Julian Huxley, Waddington, and others, he compares the new evolution with the old in the following terms:

I think we have got to start again and go right back to first principles. The argument I shall advance, surprising as it may seem coming from the author of the earlier chapters, is that, for an understanding of the evolution of modern man we must begin by throwing out the gene as the sole basis of our ideas on evolution. I am an enthusiastic Darwinian, but I think Darwinism is too big a theory to be confined to the narrow context of the gene. The gene will enter my thesis as an analogy, nothing more.

What, after all, is so special about genes? The answer is that they are replicators.

He now goes on with his analogy to compare the handing-on of mental ideas to the replication of the genes and, just as the genes arose as the replicating molecules in the primeval chemical soup, so he talks of the replicating ideas, passed on from one person to another, as new units of evolution developed in the 'soup of human culture'. We need a name for the new replicator, he says, and for comparison with the gene he suggests, somewhat whimsically, the term *meme* (pronounced to rhyme with 'cream'). Thus he writes:

Examples of memes are tunes, ideas, catch-phrases, clothes fashions, ways of making pots or of building arches. Just as genes propagate themselves in the gene pool by leaping from body to body via sperms or eggs, so memes propagate themselves in the meme pool by leaping from brain to brain via a process which, in the broad sense, can be called imitation . . .

Consider the idea of God. We do not know how it arose in the meme pool. Probably it originated many times by independent 'mutation'. In any case, it is very old indeed. How does it replicate itself? By the spoken and written word, aided by great music and great art. Why does it have such high survival value? Remember that 'survival value' here does not mean value for a gene in a gene pool, but value for a meme in a meme pool. The question really means: What is it about the idea of a god which gives it its stability and penetrance in the cultural environment? The survival value of the god meme in the meme pool results from its great psychological appeal. It provides a superficially plausible answer to deep and troubling questions about existence. It suggests that injustices in this world may be rectified in the next. The 'everlasting arms' hold out a cushion against our own inadequacies which, like a doctor's placebo, is none the less effective for being imaginary. These are some of the reasons why the idea of God is copied so readily by successive generations of individual brains. God exists, if only in the form of a meme with high survival value, or infective power, in the environment provided by human culture.

Is it not possible that there are other things in the universe that are just as real and remarkable as the replicating molecules, the genes, upon which the evolution of those physico-chemical machines—the bodies of plants, animals, and man—depend? Is it not possible that some of Dawkins's so-called memes relate to other profound realities: that what we call God may be as real, and as mysterious, as is the nature of consciousness? That, indeed, has always been my view.

CONSCIOUS BEHAVIOUR

Very often changes in behaviour may be caused by changes in the environment, but not always; they may also be due to the restless, inquisitive, exploratory nature of the animals themselves as they discover new ways of life. I cannot believe that some terrestrial animals like the ancestor of the otters first got webbed feet by chance and then took to the water to use them; this is nonsense. The more enterprising and more adventurous otters found they got more food by hunting in the water and so changed their habits; this new behaviour, copied by others and taught to the young, would then act as a selective force conserving such genetic variations in DNA that occurred by chance in the population to produce more efficient feet for swimming. I believe that most adaptations for running, climbing, digging, flying, and so on have come about in this way. In other words I think it likely that *conscious behaviour* plays an increasing role in true Darwinian evolution as we come to the higher forms of life.

We have no right to assume that the higher animals, at least, are not conscious beings. Can anyone who has kept and become fond of a dog, a cat, or a horse believe that they are unconscious organic machines? Can we really believe that consciousness is but an epiphenomenon—a by-product—of an entirely physico-chemical brain? It is the fundamental nature of this consciousness that we do not yet understand. In the field of consciousness, as we experience it, lie all our feelings of purpose, love, joy, sorrow, the sense of the sacred, the sense of right and wrong, the appreciation of beauty, indeed all that really matters in life.

Is it not remarkable that so many today either regard consciousness as a pleasant illusion or completely ignore the problem? I was delighted when the late Sir Cyril Hinshelwood gave such prominence to the matter in his Presidential Address to the Royal Society in 1959:

It is surprising that biological discussions often underestimate human consciousness as a fundamental experimental datum. In science we attach no value to unverifiable deductions, or to empty qualitative statements, but nobody defends the neglect of experimental data. Among these we cannot validly disregard those of our own consciousness except by a deliberate abstraction for which we must assume responsibility, and which we should not forget having made . . . There is at present no obvious answer to the question of what kind of advance can possibly be hoped for in this problem of psycho-physical concomitance. This, however, is no reason for giving up thought which at least helps to avoid the kind of errors so easily made both about physics and about biology when the problem is ignored.

Is it not possible that modern humanistic man, excited by the success of the scientific method, and exalted by his liberation from the absurdities of medieval thought, has been carried away into a new period of dogmatic folly only a little less absurd than that which preceded it? Could he be making a gigantic mistake?

It is clear that man, supposedly intelligent man, can be so mistaken. He has only comparatively recently, since the Renaissance, escaped from an appalling mental nightmare: a fantasy held as gospel truth by nearly all the leading minds of Europe. It was a belief in the world as seen by medieval theology, based upon Adam and his Fall, a personal Devil, and a localized Hell. It was, as the late Lord Samuel said in his address to the Royal Institute of Philosophy in 1948, 'accepted not a symbolism but literally; it was pictured in the churches and preached from the pulpits. It was the cosmos of Dante, Milton and Michaelangelo'.

It is not, of course, science itself which is creating a new dogmatism, for science by its very nature cannot be dogmatic. I passionately believe in the validity of science and the scientific method, yet just as strongly do I deplore the unproven assertions so often made by those who call themselves scientists that *science* has now reduced the mystery of life to a matter of molecular biology. Such dogmatic materialistic statements could lead to a world even more horrific than that created by the medieval mind, a future of which Aldous Huxley warned us, or it could lead to our complete destruction, a possibility that was not even on the horizon when he wrote *Brave New World*.

Why is consciousness, which is the seat of all our values, ignored in the equation of life? How can the concept of perception be held without a recognition of the apparent dualism of perceiver and perceived? Why is the mind–body relationship consistently ignored? I have called this dualism an *apparent* one and have already said that I believe that in time the two elements will be united in a single philosophy; but why, as Hinshelwood has said, is not more thought given to the matter by scientists? It is because such questions raise awkward problems for those who accept only a materialistic system.

The time has come to use the scientific method to demonstrate whether or not a belief in the spiritual side of man may be regarded as reasonable or not. Could we not go back to an earlier attitude? As Langdon-Davies pointed out in his book *Man and his Universe* (1930) 'the whole history of science had been a direct search for God, deliberate and conscious, until well into the eighteenth century . . . Copernicus, Kepler, Galileo, Newton, Leibnitz and the rest did not merely believe in God in an orthodox sort of way: they believed that their work told humanity more about God than had been known before'.

THE IMPORTANCE OF WRITTEN RECORDS

It may not be inappropriate that I should interpolate a comment upon the expression of an attitude towards our work which was given in a review of my book *The Biology of God* (1975), for this may be a misunderstanding widely held among scientists. Dr Bernard Dixon wrote in the *New Scientist* 1975:

Perhaps the one conclusion that one *can* draw from some of the types of experience recorded during Sir Alister's researches is that they appear to be entirely self-vindicating, primary experiences whose reality for their subject lies beyond question. Yet it is in part this very certainty that makes them well nigh impossible to communicate to others. That being so, it is difficult to see how even the mass of data collected at Manchester College will take us much further. As the late Ian Ramsey was fond of pointing out, third person experience, however extensive, can never replace experience in the first person. Whatever we come to believe as individuals, science and religion as categories for intellectual discussion must surely remain distinct, immiscible, irreconcilable.

It is indeed good to have scientists' recognition that the experiences we are recording 'appear to be entirely self-vindicating, primary experiences whose reality for the subject lies beyond question'; however, while I accept that science and religion are immiscible categories I certainly *cannot* agree that *for intellectual discussion* they must remain irreconcilable. Whilst love and art are equally immiscible with science, a consideration of their existence cannot surely be irreconcilable with the scientific outlook in any philosophical examination of reality. Of course, the late Ian Ramsey was right; no accumulation of accounts of third-person experience can equal for any *individual* his own spiritual awareness, but that is not the point under discussion.

We wish to know whether our objective study of a large number of *written* personal accounts can demonstrate that many people do find this kind of experience of the highest value as an influence in their lives. While it does not *as yet* constitute a contribution *to science* in the strict sense, this is coming, although it can never, of course, be a science of the inner essence of spirituality, but a quantitative, sociological survey of man's behaviour and reactions in relation to his experience of this inner awareness. Such numerical studies are important in that they lend themselves to repetition and confirmation by other workers and so give confidence as to the validity of the results. It is, however, the study of the inner sense of spirituality in the lives of individuals, as revealed in the written records, which, while not a part of quantitative science, must be the more profound aspect of our work.

In this introductory discussion, the reader, if he has read some of my earlier books, will have found in places some of the same ideas expressed here in very much the same words, and so also will he find some in the concluding chapter; I feel that they form an essential background to the subject of the book, but find it impossible to express them adequately or as clearly if I try to put them into very different words.

2

RESEARCH

RESEARCH METHODS

In September 1925 my attention had been arrested by a description of a religious experience in the daily press. How often, I wondered, did such reports occur and pass unnoticed? By the use of a press-cutting agency I tried to find out. Although the material collected proved to be quite unsatisfactory for research purposes, it provided an interesting reflection of public religious opinion at the time.

It was this original attempt which led me to use the press, although in quite a different way, as a means of appealing to individual readers to send in accounts of their own personal experiences. My first idea was to ask the editors of every religious journal in Great Britain to publish a short article appealing for such records to be sent to me together with relevant information concerning age, sex, and religious upbringing, promising that all such material would be treated as strictly confidential. Some thirty journals accepted these articles, but the result was most disappointing in that we received barely two hundred replies and these came from a narrow age range; a high percentage of replies were from the elderly and a very large proportion of these were female. Perhaps the readers of denominational papers, being so concerned with their own particular practices and doctrines, did not understand the reason for, or the significance of, our research.

In the summer of 1968 I asked Manchester College, of whose Council I was already a member, if I might have two rooms there in which to begin my researches and they most kindly placed at my disposal, at an economic rent, one of their College houses in the centre of Oxford. A wide variety of private charitable trusts mentioned in my preface gave most generous support and in addition the general public were extremely helpful. This book is based upon the first eight years' work of the Unit, which I have called The Religious Experience Research Unit.

(1) Newspaper appeals

In 1969 the editor of the *Guardian* asked me to give an interview to Geoffrey

Moorhouse for an article on the Unit's work, to which I agreed, on condition
that it would include an appeal for accounts of experience. This appeal appeared
on 20 September 1969; it attracted considerable attention and brought in a very
good crop of records covering a wide range of both sexes from sixth-form boys
and girls upwards. A similar request came from the editor of the *Observer*, and
and here again the response was splendid; later I was invited to contribute two
articles to *The Times* which also included an appeal. It was then said by some,
rightly I think, that our samples on the whole were being drawn from one
particular stratum of society; two later articles in the *Daily Mail*, however,
remedied this and produced over a thousand records for us.

In the early appeals there was some definition of the type of experience
which specially interested us, and for which I used a particular illustration; I
give as an example that from the *Observer* article of 8 March 1970:

To further his research . . . Professor Hardy is seeking the help of *Observer* readers.
He is not at present studying the more ecstatic or mystical states, but more general
feelings exemplified in this following quotation from an address by Baroness
Mary Stocks to the World Congress of Faiths:
'Beatrice Webb,' she said, in discussing her autobiography, 'was conscious of
experiencing a sense of reverence or awe—an apprehension of a power and purpose outside herself—which she called "feeling" and which was sometimes induced
by appreciation of great music or corporate worship. But her experience went
further than this nebulous, fleeting "feeling"—because as a result of it she achieved
a religious interpretation of the universe which satisfied and upheld her and
enabled her to seek continuous guidance in prayer—and this without comprom-
ising her intellectual integrity.'
Professor Hardy proposes, if readers will kindly cooperate, to study and compare as many personal records of such experiences as possible. He invites all
who have been conscious of, and perhaps influenced by, some such power,
whether they call it the power of God or not, to write a simple and brief account
of these feelings and their effects. They should include particulars of age, sex,
nationality, religious upbringing and other factors thought to be relevant and
should be sent with name and address to: The Director, Religious Experience
Research Unit, Manchester College, Oxford, OX1 3TD. They will be regarded as
strictly confidential and names will be suppressed in any published accounts of
the research.

In spite of our saying this, examples of the more ecstatic, dramatic types of
experience were sent in in fair numbers from the very beginning. Perhaps the
use of the term 'religious experience' in the name of our Unit tended to give the
impression that we were only concerned with particular isolated unusual experiences rather than with a continuing feeling of a transcendental reality or of a
divine presence. Some people use the expression 'an experience' to signify something exceptional—'quite an experience' they may say—and it has been suggested
that perhaps it would have been better if we had called our project the unit for
the study of spiritual awareness. The term religious experience, however, was
chosen with thought, partly in recognition of William James's pioneering study,
The Varieties of Religious Experience (1902), but, more importantly, our whole

study was in the technical sense, based upon the examination of records of human *experience*—religious experience in *all* its forms. We were dealing essentially with the experiential element in religion. Even if some stressed their greater interest in what might be called a continuing spiritual awareness, it was the accounts of the *experience* of such an awareness, or of any other kind of religious phenomen, with which we were most concerned.

Since people were sending in accounts of the more ecstatic experiences as well as those of a more general spiritual awareness we decided subsequently in our requests not to specify any particular types but to leave it to people to send in whatever they decided had been an experience of a religious nature.

2. Pamphlets

In addition to the articles in newspapers we also had printed and widely circulated our own special appeal entitled 'Research into Religious Experience—How You Can Take Part'. In this we were able to answer some of the queries and criticisms about what we were doing as well as to point out that we were not only concerned with the more isolated, exceptional experiences. I will now quote some sections from this general appeal.

It would appear from many letters which we have received that a number of people have at first refrained from sending in such accounts either because they were not quite clear what we really require or because they may have had reservations as to the desirability of our research. I hope I may now resolve these difficulties. Some people may have felt that there is nothing particularly remarkable about their own experiences and that we would not be interested in them. The very reverse is true. We do indeed want accounts of these seemingly more ordinary but deeply felt experiences. Again, some may have been misled by the very term 'religious experience', thinking that it must only refer to the more dramatic isolated experiences; I want to make it quite clear that we are just as interested in accounts of that continuing sense of spiritual awareness which many people feel makes a difference to their lives . . . There is, as Professor C. C. J. Webb said [1945], 'a serious danger of overlooking the existence of a genuine religious experience which, although taking forms perhaps less strange and striking [i.e. than those of some mystics], is not therefore less real and significant'.

We further realize that there are people who feel that their religious experience is altogether too sacred and personal a matter to be exposed to any examination, even though their names will never be made known in relation to it. We respect their attitude but hope they may be persuaded to co-operate, because we are sure that a study of these experiences is of the utmost importance in providing the evidence to show the intellectual world of today that these feelings form some fundamental part of man's nature which may indeed help him in his actions. Others again may fear that our methods may obscure the essential spiritual quality of their experiences; I hope, however, that any who have read my Gifford Lectures, *The Divine Flame*, in which I foreshadowed this research, will know that we will do our best to overcome this difficulty.

Now let me come to those who may have disapproved of what we are trying to do: I believe it is because they do not really understand our motives. I sometimes get letters indignantly asking 'Are you not satisfied with the evidence of spiritual experience provided for us in the Bible or in the works of the mystics? Why need you seek for more?' I fully agree, of course, that the scriptures and writings of the mystics contain some of the most profound examples of such experience. What is also important, however, is to demonstrate that these experiences are just as real and vital to modern man as they were in the lives of those of long ago . . .

With these explanations we hope that many more may be able to help us in our work. All those who feel that they have been conscious of, and perhaps influenced by, some Power, whether they call it God or not, which may either appear to be beyond their individual selves or partly, or even entirely, within their being, are asked to write a simple account of these feelings and their effects. . . . [Then follows the request for personal particulars, etc.]

This specially printed appeal ended with a selection of short extracts from the first thousand accounts of experience received both to show something of their wide range of variety and to indicate to readers that we wished to receive records of *all kinds* of different experiences of a religious or spiritual nature. I reproduce a selection here for the same reason: it shows the kind of material we are dealing with. A systematic review of this variety forms the subject of later chapters.

(786) As far back as I can remember I have never had a sense of separation from the spiritual force I now choose to call God. . . . From the age of about 6 to 12 in places of quiet and desolation this feeling of 'oneness' often passed to a state of 'listening'. I mean by 'listening' that I was suddenly alerted to something that was going to happen. What followed was a feeling of tremendous exaltation in which time stood still.

(183) I heard nothing, yet it was as if I were *surrounded by golden light* and as if I only had to reach out my hand to touch God himself who was so surrounding me with his compassion.

(651) I think from my childhood I have always had the feeling that the true reality is not to be found in the world as the average person sees it. There seems to be a constant force at work from the inside trying to push its way to the surface of consciousness. The mind is continually trying to create a symbol sufficiently comprehensive to contain it, but this always ends in failure. There are moments of pure joy with a heightened awareness of one's surroundings, as if a great truth had been passed across.

(854) About ten years later I began to pray for my children's safety, and this became a habit which I have never lost, and often the answer to such a prayer is spectacular. Now I've evolved a belief which is identical with Beatrice Webb's: 'I find it best to live as if the soul of man were in communion with a superhuman force which makes for righteousness' . . . May I add that since this belief grew in me I feel as if I had grown, as if my mind had stretched to take in the vast universe and be part of it.

(663) I find it difficult to describe my experience, only to say that it seems to be outside of me and enormous and yet at the same time I am part of it, everything is. It is purely personal and helps me to live and to love others. It is difficult to describe, but in some way because of this feeling I feel united to all people, to all living things. Of recent years the feeling has become so strong that I am now training to become a social worker because I find that I must help people: in some way I feel their unhappiness as my own.

(712) It seemed to me that, in some way, I was extending into my surroundings and was becoming one with them. At the same time I felt a sense of lightness, exhilaration and power as if I was beginning to understand the true meaning of the whole Universe.

(680) When I was on holiday, aged about 17, I glanced down and watched an ant striving to drag a bit of twig through a patch of sun on a wall in the graveyard of a Greek church, while chanting came from within the white building. The feeling aroused in me was quite unanticipated, welling up from some great depth, and essentially timeless. The concentration of simplicity and innocence was intensely of some vital present. I've had similar experiences on buses, suddenly watching people and being aware how *right* everything essentially is.

(843) I have a growing sense of reality, and personal identity, which comes from being united to something more powerful than myself, something that is helping me to be what I want to be.

3. Questionnaires

Our method of collecting these records of personal experience has been criticized by some social psychologists who have thought that we should at the very outset have started with a definite questionnaire. With this I disagree. For one thing these experiences are so precious and personal to the people who have them that many are likely to be put off by being asked to fill in such a form about them; secondly, and still more important, the very manner of asking the questions would be apt, I believe, to give a slant to the content of the replies. The specimens we are hunting are shy and delicate ones which we want to secure in as natural a condition as possible; we must at all costs avoid damaging or distorting them by trying to trap them within an artificial framework. In the first instance we prefer a description set down in the words and manner thought most fitting by those who have had the experiences; these tell us so much more about the personality of the sender than any replies given to a series of questions on a form like an income-tax return.

In the second stage of our work we did use the questionnaire technique. After the examination and classification of our records, various members of staff who were specially interested in this or that particular type of experience selected these for special study; they wrote back to the respondents concerned and asked if they would kindly reply to a series of questions designed to enable us the better to compare and contrast the different varieties. We have been most encouraged by the large proportion of those so approached who have sent back helpful answers.

What steps have we taken, we are frequently asked, to test the honesty or validity of the accounts sent in? Apart from a small proportion from those who clearly were mentally ill, some were no doubt emotionally exaggerated and others may have been written to give a swollen importance to the self, but no one with an unbiased mind, I believe, can read the majority of the accounts without being impressed by a feeling of their deep sincerity. Our stressing the confidential treatment of the material has I am sure been an important factor; we have received many very moving and intimate personal accounts, sometimes describing experiences related to tragic bereavement or broken lives, and others of religious feelings that the writers say they have never spoken of to any other person. I am convinced that the vast majority of these are indeed sincere and important human documents. It is conceivable that some records are false or designed as a deliberate hoax, but if so, I believe, they form a quite insignificant minority which among the large number of records we are dealing with can have no real bearing on the results.

The possibility, even the certainty, that some of these experiences may be accounted for by bodily rather than mental pathological conditions has not, of course, escaped us. There are, indeed, examples such as those from people with brain tumours which demonstrate this; these, however, do not, I believe destroy the significance of the feelings that such a condition may give rise to—they illustrate the remarkable resilience of the human spirit.

RESEARCH PROGRAMME

The plans for our programme of research were first outlined in a lecture I gave at the Royal Institution in 1969 (Hardy 1970*b*) and reports on the progress of the work have been published each year in *Faith and Freedom* (Hardy 1970-5; Robinson 1976-8).

The work so far outlined has been designed to give us firstly a better knowledge of the different kinds of spiritual feelings as experienced by the public at large based upon the examination of several thousand examples and secondly, by examining those of particular kinds in depth, to learn more about the nature of such experiences. While the latter is, I believe, the more fundamental part of our work, it was realized in the very beginning that the kind of sampling already described could never tell us the relative number of individuals in different populations who have had this or that kind of religious feeling and, particularly important, the proportions of those who say they have *never* had anything they could call such an experience. This could only be discovered by using the 'opinion research' random sampling methods which might also show differences in the results say from the south of England and from Scotland, or between persons living in the country and those brought up in the big cities. We were beginning to make arrangements for such a survey when, quite independently, David Hay, Lecturer in Biology in the Department of Education at the University of Nottingham, developed a keen interest in a similar line of research. We were delighted when he wrote expressing the hope that his work could be done in co-operation with ours; this indeed has come about and we appointed Miss Ann Morisy, a sociologist, as a member of our staff to work with him in Nottingham. The beginning and development of this work is described in Chapter 8.

It must be realized, of course, that our work is only just beginning and should develop in many different directions; at present its field is largely confined to the Western world of Christian tradition but we would hope eventually, if funds should become available, to extend such studies to the East and so to members of other faiths.

Classification

How was our large collection of material to be catalogued? At first, with my biological background, I had thought that we might classify the records with a system not unlike that used by the naturalists; perhaps to begin with we could divide them into two main kinds (almost like the division between the plant and animal kingdoms) with, on the one hand, those describing a more general sense of spiritual awareness and, on the other, those which were of a more dramatic, ecstatic, mystical character. Then I had imagined that the various individual examples within each of these major divisions could be classed in a hierarchical system like biological specimens: those of the same kind might form a labelled unit corresponding to a species, and such units whose members were slightly different from those of other units, yet had many points in common, would be grouped together into a higher category, and these again into yet higher ones and so on. We very soon found, however, that such a system could not work, for the situation was much more complex.

Very few of the accounts of experience could be put, as a whole, into just one particular classificatory compartment. So many of them were a mixture of widely different items. Indeed some of them combined together features characteristic of the two main classes into which I had first thought to divide them. For example a person who for long had been either an agnostic or an atheist might suddenly have an entirely unexpected ecstatic mystical type of experience; and then, having come to feel that the universe was not at all the sort of place he had imagined it to be, he begins to develop a general sense of spiritual awareness. It soon became evident that any system which could cover such a variety of elements must be one distinguishing all the different characteristics which in varying combinations went to make up the accounts of the experiences rather than being one which attempted to classify the individual examples themselves of which hardly any two offered exactly the same set of ingredients. It was for these reasons that we did not adopt any such system of classification as that put forward in Glock and Stark (1965).

We have drawn up a list of twelve main divisions, each of which is then subdivided to give a number of subsidiary categories denoting the various ways in which such items may be found in any particular experience. It must always be remembered that we are studying and classifying the written *accounts* of such experiences which are as near as we can get to the subjective feelings themselves; the initial statements, however, may be supplemented by further statements elicited in the second-stage questionnaire procedure and these may bring us nearer to the actual experience than did the original records. The broad outline of the classification was first made by Beardsworth and then added to and modified in discussions at various staff meetings. The main elements are given numbers and the first four are all in the field of what we call sensory or quasi-sensory experiences: 1 visual; 2 auditory; 3 touch; and 4 (very rare) smell. Then follow the experiences we classify as 5 supposed extra-sensory perception; 6 behavioural changes; 7 cognitive and affective elements. Next, under 8, development of experience, we classify all those accounts describing the different ways in which the writer's religious feelings arose and expanded with the course of time, and followed by 9 dynamic patterns of experience and 10 dream experiences. Then we have 11 the antecedents or 'triggers' of experience, in which the writers give accounts of the many different factors that have given rise to their own states of spiritual awareness, and finally 12 the consequences of experience, to include the records in which are described the effects the experiences may have had on the lives of those concerned.

The subdivisions of each of these main elements are now given distinguishing letters: (a), (b), (c), (d), etc. so that each particular experience can then be given a descriptive label which will indicate its nature; some may just have only one character, say, $1(c)$ or $7(b)$ or, as is more usual, have several components and so be designated for example as $1(d)7(b)(e)$ or $6(a)7(a)8(c)$, to cite but two of the hundreds of possible combinations. Such classificatory labels tell us the main items to be found in any particular account of an experience, just as in chemistry the formula H_2SO_4 tells us the different elements involved in the composition of sulphuric acid. In mentioning such an analogy I hope it will not be thought that we regard the recorded experiences as made up in any such way as is a chemical compound; the comparison is merely to indicate a somewhat similar method of labelling. Any experience is, of course, not just the adding together of a number of different components; it is very much a case of the whole being greater than the sum of the parts.

Before examining the present form of our classification it will be as well to say a little more about the nature of the material we are classifying. It is very uneven both in quantity and quality. In quantity the range is great: one account (in an extreme case) may be written on a postcard, while the next may run to twenty pages of typescript. These variations naturally make any *quantitative* study of the raw material as a whole virtually impossible, and any numerical results that appear to emerge may well be misleading; especially is this so when some of the briefer accounts hint at other forms of experience which are not described, although this can sometimes, but not always, be remedied by further correspondence with the writer. It has never been our intention that any mathematical treatment should be made of this essentially observational material except to give mere indications of possible trends; I may stress again that this stage is one of natural history and not of quantitative science. The statistical treatment is reserved for those special investigations of random samples which I have already referred to (p. 22).

Qualitatively, as well, the material is heterogeneous. Variations in educational and cultural background mean that while in some accounts there is no difficulty in understanding the delicate differences in the writer's feelings; in others it is extremely hard to know how much one may legitimately read into a description which may be largely inarticulate or incoherent but which nevertheless does indicate some genuine and deeply felt experience. In such cases, it must be frankly admitted, much is left to the subjective judgement or sympathetic imagination of the researcher; and we have ourselves had practical experience of how two different observers may reach widely divergent judgements on a given sample. While, of course, these disagreements are disconcerting in any such investigation, I would point out that they present just the same kind of difficulties that have always confronted naturalists exploring new territory; in the early observational natural history phase differences of opinion regarding identification and other features may well occur which are later cleared up either by better observation or in the more scientific ecological study which may follow. In our own work this can be done by the researcher going back to the respondent for more detailed information.

Coming now to the classification itself, we must once more emphasize that it is essentially provisional and practical both in origin and purpose. It is one which, as I have already said, has grown and been modified as the investigation has developed, partly by the addition of new material continually coming in but also as different members of staff have become more interested in this or that particular field than in others and so surveyed them in greater detail. No doubt it will be modified further as the work goes on; it is a progressive process. In some areas there are obvious overlappings and it may be a matter of personal judgement into which of two divisions in some main section a particular example should be placed; if there is any doubt, however, there is no need to make such a choice, for any particular example may be put into *both* sections where they tend to overlap. Here is the scheme as at present evolved:

A PROVISIONAL CLASSIFICATION OF THE VARIOUS ELEMENTS FOUND IN THE ACCOUNTS OF RELIGIOUS EXPERIENCE SO FAR EXAMINED

Against each sub-division is placed (in brackets) the number of occurrences of that category which have been found in a thousand accounts, based on an average of the first three thousand received; the numbers in each separate thousand are given in Table 1 of Appendix I. All the figures for the number of occurrences given here and in the rest of the chapter are kindly provided by Mrs Vita Toon, an Oxford graduate in Theology, who was with us for two years as Curator of Records.

1. Sensory or quasi-sensory experience: visual

(*a*) Visions (181.3)
(*b*) Illuminations (45)
(*c*) A particular light (88)
(*d*) Feeling of unity with surroundings and/or with other people (59.3)
(*e*) 'Out-of-the-body' (59.7)
(*f*) *'Déjà vu'* (5.3)
(*g*) Transformation of surroundings (24.3)

2. Sensory or quasi-sensory experience: auditory

(*a*) 'Voices', calming (73.7)
(*b*) 'Voices', guiding (70)
(*c*) 'Being spoken through', gift of tongues (31)
(*d*) 'Music' and other sounds (23)

3. Sensory or quasi-sensory experience: touch

(*a*) Healing (15.3)
(*b*) Comforting (29)
(*c*) Feelings of warmth, etc. (53.7)
(*d*) Being hit, shocked, etc. (18.3)
(*e*) Guiding (5.3)

4. Sensory or quasi-sensory experience: smell (11)

5. Supposed extra-sensory perception

(*a*) Telepathy (36.7)
(*b*) Precognition (69.3)
(*c*) Clairvoyance (15.3)
(*d*) Supposed contact with the dead (79.7)
(*e*) Apparitions (34)

6. Behavioural changes: enhanced or 'superhuman' power displayed by man

(*a*) Comforting, guiding (27)
(*b*) Healing (34.3)
(*c*) Exorcism (3.7)
(*d*) Heroism (6.3)

7. Cognitive and affective elements

(*a*) Sense of security, protection, peace (253)
(*b*) Sense of joy, happiness, well-being (212)

7. Cognitive and affective elements *Continued*

(*c*) Sense of new strength in oneself (65)
(*d*) Sense of guidance, vocation, inspiration (157.7)
(*e*) Awe, reverence, wonder (66)
(*f*) Sense of certainty, clarity, enlightenment (194.7)
(*g*) Exaltation, excitement, ecstasy (47.3)
(*h*) Sense of being at a loss for words (25.3)
(*i*) Sense of harmony, order, unity (66.7)
(*j*) Sense of timelessness (37.7)
(*k*) Feeling of love, affection (in oneself) (56.7)
(*l*) Yearning, desire, nostalgia (14.3)
(*m*) Sense of forgiveness, restoration, renewal (40)
(*n*) Sense of integration, wholeness, fulfilment (12.7)
(*o*) Hope, optimism (15.3)
(*p*) Sense of release from fear of death (36.3)
(*q*) Fear, horror (41.7)
(*r*) Remorse, sense of guilt (23.7)
(*s*) Sense of indifference, detachment (11.3)
(*t*) Sense of purpose behind events (113.7)
(*u*) Sense of prayer answered in events (138.3)
(*v*) Sense of presence (not human) (202.3)

8. Development of experience

(i) Within the individual

(*a*) Steady disposition; little or no development recorded (1.3)
(*b*) Gradual growth of sense of awareness: experience more or less continuous (91.3)
(*c*) Sudden change to a new sense of awareness, conversion, the 'moment of truth' (175.3)
(*d*) Particular experiences, no growth recorded (13.7)
(*e*) Particular experiences, each contributing to growth of sense of awareness (145.7)

(ii) In relation to others

(*k*) Identification with ideal human figure, discipleship, hero-worship (6)
(*l*) Development by personal encounter (113)
(*m*) Participation in church, institutional, or corporate life (29.7)
(*n*) Development through contact with literature or the arts (117.7)
(*o*) Experience essentially individualistic, involving isolation from or rejection of others (27)

(iii) Periods of significant development

- (*r*) In childhood (117.7)
- (*s*) In adolescence (123.7)
- (*t*) In middle age (70.3)
- (*u*) In old age (7.7)

9. Dynamic patterns in experience

(i) Positive or constructive

- (*a*) Initiative felt to be beyond the self, coming 'out of the blue', grace (124)
- (*b*) Initiative felt to lie within the self, but response from beyond; prayers answered (322.7)
- (*c*) Initiative and response both felt as within the self; the result seen as 'individuation' (Jung), 'self-actualization' (Maslow) (4.7)
- (*d*) Differentiation between initiative and response felt as illusory; merging of the self into the All; the unitive experience (22.3)

(ii) Negative or destructive

- (*m*) Sense of external evil force as having initiative (44.7)

10. Dream experiences (87.7)

11. Antecedents or 'triggers' of experience

- (i) (*a*) Natural beauty (122.7)
- (*b*) Sacred places (26)
- (*c*) Participation in religious worship (117.7)
- (*d*) Prayer, meditation (135.7)
- (*e*) Music (56.7)
- (*f*) Visual art (24.7)
- (*g*) Literature, drama, film (82)
- (*h*) Creative work (20.7)
- (*i*) Physical activity (9.7)
- (*j*) Relaxation (16.7)
- (*k*) Sexual relations (4)
- (*l*) Happiness (7.3)
- (*m*) Depression, despair (183.7)
- (*n*) Illness (80)
- (*o*) Childbirth (8.7)
- (*p*) The prospect of death (15.3)
- (*q*) The death of others (28)
- (*r*) Crises in personal relations (37.3)
- (*s*) Silence, solitude (15.3)

(ii) (*w*) Drugs: anaesthetic (10.7)
   (*x*) Drugs: psychedelic (6.7)

12. Consequences of experience

   (*a*) Sense of purpose or new meaning to life (184.7)
   (*b*) Changes in religious belief (38.7)
   (*c*) Changes in attitude to others (77)

As explained in the paragraph introducing the classification, the figures given against each category represent the average occurrence per thousand of that particular element as found in the first three thousand records. They are taken from Table 1 in Appendix I (p. 143) where the figures of their occurrence in each of the thousand records are also shown separately. This separate treatment shows some interesting points. It may be recalled that in making our appeals for records of experience we had said that at first we should not be studying the more ecstatic or mystical states, but rather those accounts which described a sense of spiritual awareness which many feel make such a difference to their lives; in spite of this, however, we had nevertheless received a number of these, more dramatic examples from the very beginning and so we soon dropped any distinction between different types and asked for accounts of any experience which those concerned would regard as of a religious nature. The effect of this change in policy is well shown in this Appendix Table 1 by the progressive increase in the number of examples of these more dramatic experiences as we pass from the first thousand, through the second, to the third thousand records received; such changes are seen in the following sub-divisions: 1(*a*) accounts of visions; 1(*b*) accounts of illumination; 1(*c*) of those who described a particular light; 1(*e*) those remarkable out-of-the-body experiences; and 2(*b*) the hearing of guiding voices. As a result of these increases it is to be expected that there should be some corresponding reduction in the proportions of other types of experience per thousand; while such progressive decreases are shown in categories 7(*f*), 8(*n*), 8(*s*), 8(*t*), 11(*a*), 11(*e*), and 12(*a*), it is difficult to suggest why it should be these particular items that show it more than others.

To enable one to see at a glance which are the more common elements in the collection I have picked out all those categories which have occurred more than a hundred times per thousand records received and arranged them as follows in decreasing numerical order:

9(*b*), 7(*a*), 7(*b*), 7(*v*), 12(*a*), 11(*m*), 1(*a*), 8(*c*), 7(*d*), 8(*e*), 7(*u*), 11(*d*), 9(*a*), 8(*s*), 11(*a*), 8(*n*), 8(*r*), 11(*c*), 7(*c*), and 8(*l*).

They range in frequency from 322.7 per thousand for 9(*b*) which is among the dynamic patterns in experience (i.e. initiative felt to lie within the self, but response coming from beyond—prayers answered) to 113 per thousand for 8(*l*) which is one of the categories describing the development of experience (i.e. by personal encounter).

With the exception of the seeing of visions $(1(a))$ there are no examples of supposed extra-sensory perception or behavioural changes among the more frequent items recorded; the ones that are really abundant, apart from $9(b)$ just mentioned, are either those among the cognitive and affective elements—such as sense of security $(7(a))$, sense of joy $(7(b))$, of a new strength $(7(c))$, of guidance or inspiration $(7(d))$, or of certainty $(7(f))$, of prayer answered in events $(7(u))$, or a sense of presence $(7(v))$—or those items relating to the development of an experience $(8(c), 8(e), 8(l), 8(n), 8(r),$ and $8(s))$. Also among the very common items are those which describe the factors giving rise to a particular experience such as natural beauty $(11(a))$, participation in worship $(11(c))$, prayer or meditation $(11(d))$, or despair $(11(m))$, together with, among the more frequent, a sense of purpose or new meaning to life, as a consequence of experience $(12(a))$.

To show the rarer categories I have now picked out all those that have occurred less than twenty times per thousand and arranged them as before in decreasing numerical order:

$7(o), 8(d), 7(n), 7(s), 4, 11(a), 11(o), 8(a), 11(e), 11(x), 6(d) 8(k), 1(f), 3(e),$ $9(c), 11(k), 6(c),$ and $8(a)$

They range from 15.3 per thousand for $7(o)$–and I find it surprising that this figure should be so low when this category represents 'hope and optimism'—to that of 1.3 per thousand for that of $8(a)$ which is not so unexpected when we see that it represents, within the 'development of experience' series, that of 'steady disposition—little or no development recorded' which may perhaps be usually thought to be not worth recording.

The age range of the respondents is shown in Table 2 of Appendix I (p. 146) where we see that it extends from those in their teens, of whom there is a total of 54, to those of 90 and over of whom there are 18; the greater number lie in the ranges of 50-59 years with 494 and 60-69 years with 391. As will be seen from the table we have not been successful in obtaining the ages of much more than two-thirds of the writers for the total of the last column is only 2187 instead of 3000.

There are more than twice as many females among the respondents as males: the figures for the first three thousand being 2080 females and 895 males, with 25 not giving their sex. This, however, should not necessarily be taken to indicate that the former are so much more religious than the latter, for it may be that the men, being perhaps more fully occupied with other matters may not be so inclined to spend their time in writing accounts of their experiences; indeed it is most likely that some such cause may contribute to our results, for the indications from the nation-wide sampling survey carried out by the National Opinion Poll for Hay and Morisy described in Chapter 8 show a much smaller difference with 41 per cent of females giving a positive response compared with 31 per cent of males (p. 127). In the next chapters I will make an attempt to review the whole range of the different kinds of experience which our collection of accounts has shown us in the course of these opening years; they indeed present us with a great variety. Each category in our classificatory scheme will be considered in turn and illustrated by just one or two examples.

3

VARIETIES OF SPIRITUAL AWARENESS

(1) Sensory and behavioural elements

In this and the next three chapters we look at the various features distinguishing the different kinds of experience that have seemed to be of a religious nature to those who have written about them. This is the criterion on which we include them; it is, with certain exceptions, what the members of the general public themselves have felt to be of religious significance. The few exceptions are those which, for example, appear to lie within the field of parapsychology without having the religious content which would allow them to be included. The quoted extracts which illustrate our account are taken mainly from the first two thousand records received, with a few from the third thousand.

The elements we shall deal with in this chapter are those which make up the first six major divisions of our classification (p. 26) and range from what we have termed the sensory and quasi-sensory experiences, through the examples of supposed extra-sensory perception to those of behavioural changes; in the next chapter we shall discuss the variations in the very large Division 7 concerned with the cognitive and affective experiences. Together all these make up the essential varieties of spiritual awareness. The other elements in the accounts, those in the remaining divisions of our classification, are concerned more with the development of such experiences, their dynamic patterns, their antecedents, and their consequences than with actual kinds of awareness themselves; these are reserved for discussion in Chapters 5 and 6.

While our examples in these chapters illustrate each of the 92 categories recognized in our classification and follow the same order, the purpose of their review here is not just to exemplify this system but to show what our early studies have revealed about the nature of these experiences, which clearly move many people in our present-day society to religious feelings. They provide the material for our later discussion as to their possible significance. Although we cannot, for reasons of space, choose more than one or two examples of each kind, they should, I believe, be sufficient to portray a general picture of this remarkable side to man's nature and indicate the richness of the collection we have gathered.

We may perhaps give a somewhat different impression from that presented by William James in his classic study *The Varieties of Religious Experience* in that he deliberately tended to select the more exceptional, and at times the truly abnormal, examples in order to illustrate his psychological arguments concerning different aspects of the subject. We indeed include many extraordinary cases, but they are to be seen as a limited number of items among a much larger array of more normal patterns of feeling and behaviour. Some idea, but only a rough idea, of their relative numerical importance may be gained from the number of occurrences of each kind that we have found in our first three thousand records and which is given against each category; this, however, can only be a rough indication because, as we have pointed out earlier (p. 19), many people who have had the more normal types of experience may not have thought them sufficiently interesting to submit to us. The real knowledge of the relative numerical importance of the different kinds will be seen when we have the results from our random sampling of the population.

We begin our survey with those experiences which make up the first four main divisions of our classification and to which we give the general name of 'sensory or quasi-sensory' experiences; the four divisions cover respectively those examples whose nature may be termed (1) visual; (2) auditory; (3) 'sensations' of being touched; and (4) impressions of smell.

Because these quasi-sensory experiences are placed first in our survey it does not mean that we attach any greater significance to them than we do to those perhaps less spectacular kinds which follow. My personal view is that the reverse is true; while the former phenomena are indeed interesting as they appear to illustrate some very unusual states of consciousness, they are, to my way of thinking, nothing like so profound as the states of spiritual awareness which are described in the later accounts, particularly those under Section 7 in the next chapter.

It is not easy to assess such experiences if they are judged solely in terms of subjective/objective polarity. It would be, for example, just as unwise to accept all accounts of 'visions' as referring to events as publicly verifiable as those of our normal sense experience, as it would be to dismiss them altogether as *mere* hallucinations, fantasies, or delusions.

1. SENSORY OR QUASI-SENSORY EXPERIENCES: VISUAL

1(a) Visions

Visions, apparitions, or, as they are sometimes called, hallucinations, in themselves by no means always have a religious significance for those who experience them. However, among our first three thousand records received there were no fewer than 544 examples of visions sent in by those who felt them to be of a religious nature (and it is likely that the number would have been higher but for the reason given on p. 18). There can be no doubt that such experiences are more common than many people suppose. Professor H. H. Price, when Wykeham Professor of Logic at Oxford, wrote a preface to Tyrrell's book *Apparitions* (1943) in which he sums up the situation as follows:

The tea-party question, 'Do you believe in ghosts?' is one of the most ambiguous which can be asked. But if we take it to mean, 'Do you believe that people some-times experience apparitions?' the answer is that they certainly do. No one who examines the evidence can come to any other conclusion. Instead of disputing the facts, we must try to explain them. But whatever explanation we offer, we soon find ourselves in very deep waters indeed.

It is well known among psychologists that, with suitable subjects, apparitions can be produced at the will of the experimenter using hypnotic suggestion. Under these conditions a subject can be made to experience a hallucination, in some cases an apparition of a person who is not present but which appears to be as solid as in normal visual perception. The whole field of vision appears to be men-tally reconstructed in detail just as is the imagined scene in a vivid dream. Brief general accounts of the phenomena are given in books on hypnosis such as that by Marcuse (1959), but those who are specially interested should consult the research papers in the *British Journal of Medical Hypnotism* (especially Vol. 10, pp. 35-42 and Vol. 11, pp. 41-7). To what extent visions may be produced in a similar way without hypnosis but under high emotional stress, such as may be engendered by a particularly vivid religious experience, or in the case of apparitions by a harrowing bereavement, will not be discussed here, as I am not qualified to do so. I do *not* however wish to imply that, because such visions may eventually be fitted into a framework of psychological knowledge, they may in time be dis-missed from consideration as experiences of religious value. On the contrary, such understanding may indeed enhance their importance as vehicles of spiritual awareness.

I give two examples. In each case, as in all those given in this and the following chapter, the quotations will have their reference number, the sex (M or F) of the sender, and his or her age, if known. In nearly all examples the part given is but a small extract from the original account picked out to illustrate the particular category of experience considered.

I decided to go away from those who could bring pressure to bear and for a week stayed with an elderly and wise friend in the Lake District. My question was whether or not I should be confirmed and so become an Anglican. Every day throughout the week I prayed and thought. My major prayer was 'Dear Lord, what do you want me to do?' It was a week of coldness and darkness with no indication of any kind—UNTIL on the evening before I was due to return to London I spent several hours by myself sitting on a sofa. I was unaware of time. I then saw with great vividness the FEET OF OUR LORD some twelve feet from the floor and with that vision was the overwhelming thought of ORDINATION, which hitherto had never entered my head.

That was the answer to my prayer and in consequence I was ordained . . . The clarity of this 'vision' was to me unmistakable and I owe my vocation to it . . .

To me there is no doubt about the validity of this spiritual experience and the turning point and sign-post that it was.

(2166, M, 58)

One morning early I sat up in bed in my mission caravan and read a prayer from a book by the late Archbishop Temple. The prayer began with the words 'Help me, O Lord, to see myself as Thou seest me.' I had often read this prayer before but on this particular morning these words seemed to strike me specially and I wondered how Christ saw me, and I whispered, 'Am I like Mary Magdalene of old who knelt weeping at His feet, or am I what the prophet saw—the righteousness which is but filthy rags? How dost Thou see me O Christ?' Then I looked up and a few feet away between wardrobe and window there flashed a picture. It showed a narrow dusty, uphill road, and along the road came a child, a little girl. She was not a happy child; she looked very, very tired as she toiled along, and her little face was tear-stained . . . As she wiped away her tears she did not see the beautiful figure waiting for her at the end of the road, the figure of Christ. He was bending forward with hands and arms outstretched and the little girl would walk right into them. He had the loveliest smile and was robed in shimmering white. The picture faded but the message came to me—'You are that child still travelling on life's way—My child, I shall wipe away the soil and dust of sin, and all the tears.'

(358, F, Age ?)

1(b) Illuminations

There were 135 instances in our first 3000 records of persons feeling themselves bathed in a general glowing light which, as Beardsworth (1977) relates in his special study is often described as a 'golden light'. In the following example no mention is made of the colour of the light, although a 'sense of warmth' is mentioned:

On the first night I knelt to say my prayers, which I had now made a constant practice, I was aware of a glowing light which seemed to envelop me and which was accompanied by a sense of warmth all round me.

(73, M, Age ?)

1(c) A particular light

Slightly more common (264 examples in the first 3000) than the sense of general illumination is the impression of seeing some particular pattern of light, often of a symbolic character. The experience, as in the case about to be quoted, may be accompanied by a deep feeling of emotion, which may suggest that it is not unlike a hallucinatory vision; however, as I have already said in relation to such visions, this does not destoy their spiritual significance for the person concerned. I give just one example:

I was in Scotland and had been to the cubicle in my hut and walking back to the Mess when suddenly a light shone on the wall of the passage with a cross clearly displayed, as though intense sunlight was coming through a window with the cross casting an intense shadow. There was in fact no window or source of light to account for what I saw. The curious factor to me was that although in those days I was nervous of the dark and very impressionable, I had a curious feeling of comfort and a deep feeling of intense emotion.

(192, M, 65)

1(d) Feeling of unity with surroundings

Among this class of experience, of which we have 178 in our first 3000, we have the elements of ecstatic mysticism: the sense of fusion with a greater whole. While for convenience we have classed these cases as a category in our *visual* series of quasi-sensory experiences, they may often be accompanied by a heightened sense of auditory and olfactory sensation as well as that of vision; this general sense of heightened awareness is well illustrated in our example.

The phenomenon invariably occurs out of doors, more often than not when I am alone, although it has occurred when I have been in company with others. It is generally prefaced by a general feeling of 'gladness to be alive'. I am never aware of how long this feeling persists but after a period I am conscious of an awakening of my senses. Everything becomes suddenly more clearly defined, sights, sounds and smells take on a whole new meaning. I become aware of the goodness of everything. Then, as though a light were switched off, everything becomes still, and I actually feel as though I were part of the scene around me.

(615, M, 37)

1(e) 'Out-of-the-body' experiences

Here is another kind of experience which is now being realized to be much more common than it was thought to be in the past. There are actually 179 examples of it among our first 3000. Our knowledge of these extraordinary experiences has been much increased in the last decade or two by the researches of Dr Robert Crookall (1966, 1970), Celia Green (1968), and the experiences of Professor Michael Whiteman (1961); their significance is particularly well discussed by the late Professor C. D. Broad (1962) who compares them with the so-called 'lucid dreams' which we discuss on p. 79. The experience is usually recorded by people who have been very near to death but then recovered, either from illness, especially in a critical operation, or from injury in an accident; most of the examples submitted to us, however, are of a more spontaneous nature, coming unexpectedly 'out of the blue' to some one in normal good health. I am told that it has also been known to occur under conditions of low blood pressure, or in acute psychological states, or even that it can intentionally be brought on by yoga training; some experiences under an anaesthetic have been said to be of a similar nature, but I think they should rather be regarded as examples of the lucid dream.

When a person has the sensation of being outside his or her own body, their abandoned body appears to the person to be 'clearly seen' from a point some little distance away and often above the body left behind. It is because these cases involve the apparent seeing of the body that we class them among the visual experiences, and yet the eyes that are said 'to see' the body cannot, of course, be the physical eyes of the body itself; and this brings us to a most remarkable feature of so many of these surprising descriptions which are so consistent with one another, and so numerous, that they can no longer be lightly dismissed as unworthy of serious consideration. It is this—the conviction of the person concerned that while the 'discarded' body is seen to have every appearance of reality, he or she has the feeling of being in a second body identical with the other one and *equally real*; it is this aspect of the phenomenon which has been held by some to support the belief that there is a so-called 'astral' non-material body which is an exact duplicate of the physical one, and further that it is this 'astral body' which leaves the physical body at death. Such a belief is held by many theosophists.

I will give four examples of this phenomenon. Most of these experiences are not in themselves of a religious character yet they so often induce in the person concerned, as in the first two examples I am about to give, a conviction that the material everyday world is not the whole of reality and that there is another part of life in which the essence of religion lies.

In 1948 I had an out-of-the-body experience spontaneously, in broad daylight, for no obvious reason, and being in perfect health. (At the time I did not know that such experiences were fairly frequent and well documented.) The experience itself was unsensational—for a while I contemplated my body, which was lying on a divan, from under the ceiling; I felt splendidly liberated, light and only a little surprised, and it became amply clear that the 'I' was not the body on the divan but the consciousness which contemplated it. 'I' returned into my body with the greatest reluctance—I knew I had to return—and since then I have been quite unable to fear physical death.

(505, F, 46)

At the age of twelve, I was quite ill in bed, I found myself floating up from my body into a ray of sunshine. At the time I thought quite consciously that I was dying, and I remember that the feeling of liberation was joyful beyond anything I have ever known. I didn't die, of course, but returned quite gently to my body. From that time on I've never been afraid of death.

(802, F, 21)

Now for examples of the more unusual kinds, of which one is just a short extract:

Later, when in my early twenties, as a lay preacher, I was taking a service in a tiny village chapel, I had another experience that remains both unusual and unique. Quite without any unusual context as I carried on the worship I ceased to be aware of my taking any active part, let alone conduct the service myself. My only experience was that of sitting *behind* myself in the pulpit (noting that I had very square shoulders) whilst I wondered how it came about that I was watching myself conducting the service.

(147, M, 89)

The next and last example is one of the most remarkable accounts I have ever read and deserves to be quoted at some length; the lady concerned was a highly intelligent person who had been secretary to a famous scientist. She was personally known to me and up to the last—she died in her ninety-first year—she was mentally wonderfully alert and anxious to discuss the latest views in philosophy and theology. The long accounts of her experiences, which contain so much other material of a more religious character, although deposited with us when she was 89, were written out long before and relate to earlier stages in her life. Now here is the relevant part of her account; if I had not known her and had a number of long talks with her I might well have thought that this was no more than a highly imaginative piece of writing.

In June 1915 I went to stay at Tintagel with my children, aged 4 and 5; we lodged half a mile away from the little town. I knew no-one there. The weather was warm and sunny. Almost every afternoon I took them to the church cliff, where they played and I read devotional literature (all I had taken with me: the Bible, the *Imitation*, Prayer Book, etc.) and attended church. It was peaceful. The cliffs face west. The sun shone over the sea. I got up about 4 p.m. to collect the chicks and their toys to go back for tea, and looked about us. The old church behind us was, I saw outlined by a stream of golden light. Looking inland, I saw every hedge giving off golden flames, quivering. I stared. Was it my eyesight? For the June sun was blazing its glittering path across the sea towards us. Then I turned and saw my double, my body, getting up and busying herself with the children, putting them in their little push-chair. 'She' did not see me. I was bewildered. I was her exact duplicate, to her watch-bracelet. I felt myself; I was warm and solid. 'She' presently went off, dawdling and talking to the tinies, and they did not see me either. I went along too, walking independently of them, and trying to understand what had happened. They stopped to watch a hedgehog: picked flowers; and I waited nearby for them to go on again. I watched 'her' closely. I felt some vague jealousy of her, the chicks not missing me; but, at the same time, I was realising an extraordinary happiness, as if all sadness and weariness with our altered circumstances simply did not matter any more. A great peace filled my mind.

We arrived. Mrs. B. had laid tea. 'She' took the chicks upstairs to tidy, and I waited at the foot, hearing it all going on. They came down, sat at the table, and Mrs. B. came in with the tray. I hoped that she would see me, for it worried me a little not to be seen by them. But she didn't. I stood, my back to the empty fire-place, and found I was standing a foot or so above floor level. I could return to the floor. Was I dead? *I* couldn't be dead; 'she' looked as well as usual. So was I, who felt well as never before. I felt very curious. Routine continued. By 7 p.m. she had put them to bed, I looking on, and had come down stairs.

I always went out again, across some fields, by a short cut to the same cliff to watch the sun set and the glorious afterglow over the Atlantic; to a stile, where I would sit. A rough slate and turf wall had been passed. 'She' climbed it. I sailed over it, but otherwise walked. 'She' perched on the stile, and, there being a bit of broken brick wall some way away, I went and leaned up against it. I could do that!

By 9 p.m. 'we' were back at our digs again, in the sitting-room, where Mrs. B. had lighted an oil lamp. 'She' as usual went out to the kitchen for a glass of milk and a chat with the B.'s. But I had had time to think, and stayed in our parlour, and sat down. I wondered, am I dying? Will 'she' die in her sleep? If so, I must write three letters.

I wrote them, and must evidently have been in my body again, without remarking on it? I don't know. What I do know is that when 'she' went presently up to bed, I had those letters in my hand. While 'she' prepared for bed I leant against the window, watching her, and watching the night roll slowly up from behind Kingsdown—my last recollection.

Next morning Mrs. B. woke me with early morning tea, and I was in bed. Hastily I covered the letters, which I saw on the night-table, and that was that! I was not dead: 'she' was not dead.

It was not the end. Half way through dressing 'we' separated again. The condition continued all day, so that I grew used to it. Eventually we were spending the afternoon again on the cliff. The hedges still flickered with little live golden flames. All was serene. At no time did any persons appear; we had it all to ourselves. It came to 4 p.m. I was standing near them, 'she' busy as on the day before, and I looking out to sea, when the glorious light slowly changed and began to dim, and it grew ever darker and darker, as if the sun had ceased to shine and night were coming on. But the June sun was still shining out of an unclouded sky, its brilliant path shining over the sea, and 'she' and I were one again. But the sunlight was as a weak candle-glimmer to the light in which I must have been living without knowing it. Back came sadness and human 'trouble'—things gone that could never come again.

It never happened again.

(124, F, 89)

If we take it at its face value—and it only really differs from other examples in its wealth of detail, its literary expression, and its unusual complexity and duration—what are we to make of it, or indeed all the other examples of this phenomenon? What psychological explanation is there? There are I believe only vague hypotheses. Here is a field which calls for so much further study.

1(f) Déjà-vu

These experiences cannot usually be considered as in any way religious and no doubt for this reason we received only sixteen in our first 3000. The one selected is typical. They are generally thought, I believe, to have a simple psychological explanation; some of those who experience them, however, seem to feel that, like the out-of-the-body experiences, they may indicate a non-material side of the everyday world, and so, for them at least, have religious significance.

Often I have the feeling of having 'lived' an experience of 'feeling' previously, and the other oddity is that of thinking I see someone on the street or avenue several times and later actually seeing this person. Usually, but not always, it is someone I haven't seen in years . . .

(454, F, Age ?)

1(g) Transformation of surroundings

Here are ecstatic experiences which verge on the mystical; we have 73 examples in our first 3000 that we can include in this category. Some of them, like the one here quoted, overlap with other experiences, in this case with some of those classed as 1(*b*)—illuminations—in that there was the sensation of the scene being lit up with a bright light, being accompanied by auditory experiences.

When I was about 8 years old we were living in the country. At the foot of our garden was a very old large pear tree, which at the time was crammed with white blossom and at its summit a blackbird was singing, while beyond the tree a meadow sloped up to a marvellous sunrise. As I looked at this someone or something said to me: 'That is beautiful', and immediately the whole scene lit up as though a bright light had been turned on, irradiating everything. The meadow was a more vivid green, the pear tree glowed and the blackbird's song was more loud and sweet. A curious thrill ran down my spine.

(98, M, 78)

2. AUDITORY EXPERIENCES

Hearing voices is only a little less infrequent than seeing visions, and at times both visions and voices may be seen and heard together. Among the first 3000 experiences reported to us, 544 were accompanied by visions, whilst 431 described the hearing of voices (221 in our subcategory (a) and 210 under (b)). Again, as in the case of visions, such phenomena are not by any means confined to those who are religious. As Bernard Shaw points out in the preface to *Saint Joan*, our criminal lunatic asylums contain many whose acts of homicide have been committed in obedience to voices they claim to have heard; this, however, does not lead him to dismiss the Maid's voices as irrelevant as we see in the following quotation from the same preface (p.xiv).

Joan's voices and visions have played many tricks with her reputation. They have been held to prove that she was mad, that she was a liar and imposter, that she was a sorceress (she was burned for this), and finally that she was a saint. They do not prove any of these things; but the variety of the conclusions reached show how little our matter-of-fact historians know about other people's minds, or even about their own. There are people in the world whose imagination is so vivid that when they have an idea it comes to them as an audible voice, sometimes uttered by a visible figure.

Socrates, Saint Francis, Saint Joan, Luther, Swedenborg, and Blake are prominent examples from history of those whose vivid religious imagination caused them to see visions and hear voices. In our own day we have had the striking testimony of both phenomena in the remarkable life of the founder of the Burrswood centre for spiritual healing, the late Miss Dorothy Kerin, in *The Living Touch* (1914) and *Fulfilling* (1960). Whatever the psychological causes for such phenomena may be, there can be no doubt that they often make a most profound impression upon those who experience them, and their religious significance may be great.

We give here examples from each of the two categories relating to voices:

2(a) 'Voices' calming

Gradually I became aware of this power and began really to court it. It has come to me often—once in a dream—as light, warmth, comfort and love past understanding. It has walked with me and sometimes I hear something or someone calling my name.

(393, F, 55)

2(b) 'Voices' guiding

But the great experience that led me to be ordained was when I was about 17 . . . I went on a lonely walking tour with a sheep dog on the Whitby and Scarborough Moors which have a wonderful and spiritual atmosphere . . . It was towards the end of this tour that one morning I was drawing near the ruins of Rievaulx Abbey . . . and I sensed a wonderful atmosphere of quiet peace, and then heard a most entrancing voice which in one way seemed external and yet in another from deep down within me, calling me to be ordained, I saw nothing, yet I was convinced it was Christ Himself and he desired me like Andrew and Peter to rise up and follow Him and be ordained. With the voice came the Inner Conviction that Christ would make all things possible. . . .

(432, M, 87)

2(c) 'Being spoken through', and the gift of tongues

In view of the revival of pentecostal and charismatic services in various Christian churches it is perhaps surprising that we have not received more examples of this type of experience, only 93 out of the first 3000; and most of them are not of a pentecostal nature. I give two examples.

About six years ago there occurred a series of events unique in my life. For a period of days—even weeks—I felt strangely 'withdrawn' from my surroundings, but at the same time elated and excited. One evening, while visiting friends (who later described my behaviour as 'like one drugged') I found myself uttering the following words: 'Everything's relative . . . It's all a matter of degree . . . love without touching; don't touch without loving.' These words puzzled me at the time, and still do. It was as if I was repeating without understanding something that was being said to me.

(711, M, 38)

I was working in a British Army camp running a youth club for the children under the auspices of the YMCA. . . . After three months, one of the Army lads who was helping me at the Youth Club went out and murdered a taxi-driver, and this rather shook me. From that time onwards God seemed to become less and less real. . . . Prayer in particular was a real grind, as God did not seem to be there . . . This time came to a very dramatic and sudden end on the night of July 1, 1966. I was 22 at the time. I discovered afterwards that one of my friends had been praying for me all that day. Somewhere between 10 and 10.30 that evening it seemed that God Himself filled my little room where I was kneeling in prayer. I spoke in tongues on that occasion, and feeling of the presence of Jesus was quite amazing, unlike anything I had ever known before. I believe the speaking in tongues was an important part of the feeling, as, when I did it, it was almost as if I was sitting back watching it happening. There was an extraordinary sensation that Someone Else was moving my lips, and yet it was most definitely my own lips that were moving. In a sense it was ecstatic, but in another sense it was not, as I discovered that I was completely in control of myself, and could stop or start speaking in tongues whenever I wished to—and I still can. However, the long-term results of this experience are the most important. As a result of all this God and Jesus really became real to me.

(922, M, 31)

2(d) Music and other sounds

We have placed 69 accounts in this category out of the first 3000 received, and a very miscellaneous group they are. I give two examples, the first of which is an experience from the First World War written by an officer well known to me.

I walked eastward for about two miles along the towpath and then turned about. The nearer I drew to the village, the more alive my surroundings seemed to become. It was as if something which had been dormant when I was in the wood were coming to life. I must have drifted into an exalted state. The moon, when I looked up at it, seemed to have become personalised and observant, as if it were aware of my presence on the tow-path. A sweet scent pervaded the air. Early shoots were breaking from the sticky buds of the balsam poplars which bordered the canal; their pleasant resinous odour conveyed good-will. The slowly moving waters of the canal, which was winding its unhurried way from the battlefields to the sea, acquired a 'numen' which endorsed the intimations of the burgeoning trees. . . . A feeling that I was being absorbed into the living surroundings gained in intensity and was working up to a climax. Something was going to happen. Then it happened. The experience lasted, I should say, about thirty seconds and seemed to come out of the sky in which were resounding harmonies. The thought: 'That is the music of the spheres' was immediately followed by a glimpse of luminous bodies—meteors or stars—circulating in predestined courses emitting both light and music. I stood still on the tow-path and wondered if I was going to fall down. I dropped on to one knee and thought: 'How wonderful to die at this moment!'

(283, M, 74)

About 20 odd years ago I was rather poorly and one evening felt so ill that I decided to go to bed. While in my room preparing I suddenly felt all round me a beautiful warm Presence so comforting that I said out loud 'Well Father if I have to be ill to feel *you* like that—I will be ill.' Then the room filled with triumphant music—so beautiful it conveyed to me that I had chosen aright and that there was rejoicing—then across the room came in large letters of gold LOVE. It all faded leaving a sense of wonderful peace.

The most important part is that ever since then I have a sense of Peace—sometimes more, sometimes less, but I feel cared for and led. To pray is easy I relax into the Presence (as I call it) and tell my problems or make requests and leave them there—the answer comes by events or leadings—petty jealousies and hurt feelings disappear—my little self is less important. Love and service is a joy.

(614, F, 84)

3. EXPERIENCE OF TOUCH

Among the first 3000 records there are 365 from people who have felt that they were physically touched in some unaccountable fashion. No doubt a number of these sensations may be due to some unsuspected physical or physiological cause and others may be purely psychological; nevertheless, whatever the actual cause, they had, in most cases, a very moving effect upon the person concerned. We have made the following five sub-categories represented by 46, 87, 161, 55, and 16 examples respectively in the first 3000 records.

3(*a*) *Healing*

I was in a very weak state at home having lost 1½ stone in a fortnight's illness . . . It seemed to me that my forehead was very swiftly touched and from that moment I took courage.

(964, F, Age ?)

3(*b*) *Comforting*

Then something very strange and very wonderful happened, something that stays with me to this day. I felt pressure as if someone were touching me. There definitely was pressure on my right side. I felt lifted up. My whole being was filled with ecstasy . . . All cares were taken away . . . nothing of this world mattered. I knew there was another.

(55, F, Age ?)

My daughter Joan was killed by a car when she was 7 years old. She and I were very close and I was grief-stricken. She was lying in her coffin in her bedroom. I fell on my knees by the bedside. Suddenly I felt as if something a bit behind me was so overcome with pity that it was consolidating itself. Then I felt a touch on my shoulder lasting only an instant, and I knew there was another world.

(165, M, 77)

3(*c*) *Feeling of warmth*

All at once I felt someone near me, a Presence entered this little room, of which I became immediately conscious. Dazed, I knelt by the nearest chair and here is the physical phenomenon that has recurred many times since. Into my heart there came a great warmth. The only way I can describe it is in the words of the disciples on their way to Emmaus: 'Our hearts burned within us'.

(657, F, Age ?)

3(*d*) *Being struck*

My father would not attend my confirmation service. The service was held in a cold red-brick building, but to me it was full of golden light and was beautiful! When we arrived home, my father was furious because we were late and he wanted his supper, but for once I was not afraid and felt like singing and dancing round the room. Gradually I became accustomed to attending the Holy Communion service, which was quite an effort because I worked long hours during the week. One morning as I knelt at the altar rail, I felt as if I had been struck by lightning—I wanted to get up and run away—but I was unable to do so. This could only have lasted for a second or so, but it was something I could not forget, and was too shy to talk about.

(474, F, 60+)

3(e) Guiding

It occurred when I was about 6 or 7 years old. I attended a Day Nursery at the time. One day I left a building to go home at the usual departure hour, but there was a terrible thunder and lightning storm just then, and although I was terrified I knew my mother expected me home, and so ventured forth amongst the fallen trees, poles and electric wires. As I passed a doorway, on my right side, I felt a hand firmly but gently on my left arm just above the elbow and I was guided into this sheltered spot.

(146, F, 34)

4. QUASI-SENSORY EXPERIENCE OF SMELL

While there are only 33 examples of people experiencing smell in the first 3000 records we have received, the phenomenon may possibly be more common than this number would suggest; I say this because during the course of our investigation we have received a most interesting privately printed booklet, entitled *The Odour of Sanctity*, containing 58 modern examples of such scenting mainly from various letters sent to Mrs. Enid Case* and published in various journals such as *Light, Woman's Journal, The Church Times,* and *Psychic News.* The example given below is from our own collection:

After the sudden death of a four and a half year old son I found no comfort in anything or anyone, the Church seemed powerless to help me as did the medical profession. I could not go out of the flat I was living in at that time and although I tried very hard I could see nothing but blackness and an intense longing to die. One morning I was dusting—tidying, the usual household chores, when I smelled the most wonderful garden flowers, it is difficult to describe the smell I mean— rather like a garden after rain, being of a somewhat practical mind in such things I looked around for the source of the smell, there were no flowers in the flat, certainly none outside, no perfumed polishes or toilet things in use, then I sat down and for the first time since my son died I felt peaceful inside. I believe this was God's comfort, my son felt very near and I no longer felt alone.

(2674, F, Age ?)

5. SUPPOSED EXTRA-SENSORY PERCEPTION

A fair number of those who have written to us have described experiences which might broadly be classed as psychical. Without attempting a precise definition of the word, it may be said to denote, in addition to those forms of supposed

---

The Odour of Sanctity may be obtained from Mrs. Case, Red Rock, Bramford Speke, Exeter, price £1 (including postage).

extra-sensory perception dealt with below such as telepathy, precognition, and clairvoyance, the so-called mediumistic practices which are regarded by a considerable number of people (particularly by those who belong to the cult of spiritualism) as indicative of communication with deceased personalities whom they believe may be contacted by these means. We do not include in our survey any of these different kinds of experience that appear to be purely psychic in nature, although it must be admitted that it is often very difficult to draw a hard-and-fast line between them and those that might be classed as religious; the psychic or extra-sensory experiences which we include are only those that appear to have given rise to religious feelings in the persons concerned.

A closer study of the relationship between the psychic and spiritual experiences is clearly desirable, and for such an inquiry our files would offer copious material of great variety, some of it of the most unusual kind. Such a project might well lead to an elaboration of the sub-divisions of this section. The separation of these elements in any classification is notoriously difficult, since in some examples two of them may be combined, such as telepathy and clairvoyance, or clairvoyance and precognition; indeed these elements in themselves are not always easy in practice to distinguish.

5(a) Telepathy

Many scientists will still not accept at its face value the evidence that has been put forward for what has been called telepathy: the supposed communication between one mind and another by means other than those of the physical sense organs. The reasons for this reluctance I have discussed at length elsewhere (Hardy 1965, 1975) and we need not go into them here. I have also in these books expressed my doubts as to whether the well known card-guessing experiments (the results of which can, I believe, no longer be denied) are really demonstrating telepathy, but are in fact revealing something very different yet no less remarkable about the nature of our universe.

If experimental scientific evidence for the existence of telepathy could be established, I believe that it would help people to accept a spiritual philosophy which is greatly needed in our modern materialistic society; it would show that there was a mental extension of the individual's psyche beyond the physico-chemical structure of the brain and so would lend plausibility to the concept of there being a spiritual dimension outside that of the strictly physical, material world. The difficulties of such experimentation are great; my own attempts in this direction, described in the volume *The Challenge of Chance* (Hardy, Harvie, and Koestler 1974), showed that a larger part is played in these matters by chance coincidence than is generally realized. Nevertheless there were, as I have described in the same volume, experiments by others which did, to my mind, demonstrate experimentally the reality of telepathy.

Apart from experimental tests there have been a vast number of spontaneous cases of supposed telepathy investigated and reported in the *Proceedings of the Society for Psychical Research*; many of the earlier ones were collected in the classic two volumes of *Phantasies of the Living* edited by Gurney, Myers, and Podmore, 1886 (abridged edition, 1918). The cases in our collection are all of this anecdotal kind; there are 110 of them in the first 3000 records received. I give two examples:

On May 26th 1918 the Battalion was in the line not far from Rheims. That evening I went to Battalion H.Q. and was told by the C.O. that the French on our right expected an enemy attack or raid. We did not take the information seriously. I remember looking at the sinking sun and being filled with a feeling of complete unreality. I had no foreboding of death or wounds. I just felt that things were incomprehensible. At dawn on the 27th the attack came. I was wounded, taken prisoner, and put to bed in the church (used as a hospital) of the village of Chateau Porcien on the Aisne. I naturally expected to be reported missing and was afraid that my Mother (quite recently widowed) would worry about me. I knew that she believed in telepathy, so I made a determined attempt to let her know telepathically that I was alive, wounded and a P.O.W. Unfortunately I was reported killed, so definitely that my name was inscribed on the temporary Roll of Honour in —— College Chapel. My mother never believed the official report, which was later corrected. In her first letter to me thereafter (I was by then in prison-camp in Germany) she wrote as follows (the underlinings are mine):– 'Aug. 15th 1918 . . . I knew the first week what had happened to you and told [my sister and a friend] but then came the awful news . . . That made it awkward, but telepathy worked, and though sometimes doubtful during the day, I could at night-time swear to your being living . . . People looked askance at my unbelief, but it helped.'

(1108, M, Age ?)

One of these [supernatural] incidents concerned a married friend who had problems which had brought him to a point nearing breakdown. During a telephone conversaion he spoke suddenly of his distress and misery and I longed to help him. Hugh thought that if I could give any comfort I should go to see him but I was quite certain that, as a married woman, this was something I could not do in the present circumstances and instead I went on my knees saying, 'I know I may not go to him, but if I could go, this is what I'd say'—and I said to God all that was in my heart to give comfort to our friend.

Some days later I met him unexpectedly and he said, 'I'm feeling better. If you ever get as low as that, remember this' and he proceeded to tell me, almost word for word, what I said on my knees. I have no doubt that we had met on some different plane and God has used me to bring him the comfort it would have been entirely wrong to give in any other way.

(2023, F, Age ?)

5(*b*) Precognition

There were 208 accounts which could be placed in this category among the first 3000, but, as in so many examples of telepathy, it is not always obvious to see how some of the cases described can be regarded in themselves as experience of a religious nature, except that they led the persons concerned to feel either that the material world was not the whole of existence or that it was a direct act of Providence. Again, of course, I am not claiming that these accounts do in fact provide proof of an extra-sensory gift of foretelling future events; they add to the great many anecdotal cases which suggest it. I give just one example.

In 1952 when out at work on a polio patient—my mind entirely taken up with work in hand—suddenly my mind seemed to go blank and I then saw 'in my mind' my son lying in a road run over—it was quite impossible to remove this from my mind and so I excused myself, went out to my husband who was waiting to drive me home, via his office. I insisted on going directly, very quickly, my husband being very annoyed but realising that something was really upsetting me—we arrived home in 25 minutes, but on arrival I said 'No, not here, take me to the market place—as we drew up—the school bus drove into the market place and my young son (who was standing by the door) opened the door and fell out of the bus, it hitting him and he lay *exactly* as I had seen him—How did I see something before it happened? My husband was speechless and will verify that this happened as I have said here.

(1360, F, 59)

5(c) Clairvoyance

There are only 46 accounts in the first 3000 which may be placed in this category. I again give just one example:

I was a young married woman with a 6 month old baby daughter. My husband and I got an evening off to see a film at K___ about 6 miles away. One of the hotel staff had volunteered to baby sit and we set off . . . We had not been long seated in the cinema when a terrible uneasiness overcame me. I could distinctly smell burning. I fidgeted a lot and my husband asked what was the matter. I told him I could smell burning. He said I'd probably dropped a bit of my cigarette. I stooped and had a look on the carpet but no sign of any glow. The smell persisted and eventually I told my husband I was leaving. He followed me reluctantly, muttering something derogatory about women.
As we boarded the bus for home I prayed for it to go faster; at each stop I almost died. At last we were sprinting down the lane leading to the cottage. The smell of burning was now very definite to me though my husband could not smell a thing. We reached the door which I literally burst in. As I did so the dense smoke poured out and a chair by the fire burst into flames. I rushed through to the bedroom and got the baby out while my husband dragged out the unconscious girl. She had fallen asleep in the armchair and dropped her lighted cigarette into the chair which had smouldered for hours. Yes, God sent me home to save my baby. God was with me telling me to hurry home; of that I am convinced and also my husband.

(1929, F, Age ?)

5(d) Supposed contact with the dead

As explained on p. 44 we are not including in our collection of experiences supposed evidence of human survival of death obtained by messages purporting to come through a spiritualist medium *unless* such a message was a means of giving rise to some significant religious feeling. Apart from the many purely psychical experiences reported (and filed separately from our main collection) there are 239 among the first 3000 records which contain a religious element. The following single example must suffice:

After the sudden death of my husband about nine years ago, I had several exper-iences, which proved to *me* that there is a life after death. I am not a Spiritualist, nor a Churchgoer, but I try to follow Jesus, and I am a great believer in meditation, as a way to God. After his passing, I both saw and spoke to my husband and held his hand. This hand was strong and not at all ghost-like, nor was his appear-ance. I was alone at the time, so no medium there to act as a link. Probably this is not a detail to prove God's existence, but to me, it indeed did.

(1615, F, Age ?)

5(e) Apparitions

There is clearly a similarity between the experiences which may be classed under this heading among examples of supposed extra-sensory perception and those placed under 'visions' among the quasi-sensory experiences. The intro-ductory remarks made on p. 32 in regard to the latter apply equally well here and need not be repeated. Among the first 3000 accounts received there were 102 that we classed as apparitions; I will give just one example.

Not long afterwards [i.e. following a different type of experience she had when she was with her husband as he died in hospital], I awoke shaking violently from head to foot. He had appeared to me, radiant, smiling, his usual happy self. I had impulsively gone forward to greet him, saying, 'Do you know—I've just been having a dream.' Something stooped me before I touched him—he was there, completely himself, but of a different 'substance'. I drew back, as it were, looking in through a frame, to another dimension. I stopped, and said to him, 'I know, I understand'. This experience, following his death, has given me great comfort . . .

(4, F, Age ?)

6. BEHAVIOURAL CHANGES

Where an experience appears to have been accompanied or followed by an actual alteration in behaviour, either of the person describing the experience or in others, it is noted in this section. Some of these accounts will also, of course, be classified under Section 7 in the next chapter: feelings and behaviour cannot always be separated. For a proper study of such behavioural changes a special investigation will clearly be necessary, and more information would naturally enable us to place a larger number of accounts in this section. At present I have divided it into the following four categories which are represented by 81 examples of comforting, 103 of healing, 11 examples of exorcism, and 19 of heroism in the first 3000 records. I give only one example of each.

6(a) Comforting, guiding

The experience of being filled with the Spirit is different for each person, but in all cases something happens to make you know it . . . I now find I am enabled to help those who are sick in body, mind and spirit because I know the power of God working through me and my only desire is to be that sort of channel.

(200, F, 55)

6(*b*) *Healing*

The example I give under this heading consists of four excerpts taken from a very long account sent in by a clergyman:

Eventually, and after months of reluctance—for I am by nature a sceptic! or more accurately, want to know why and how and I am indeed sceptical of sudden emotional decisions and overwhelming spiritual certainties; I was pushed into the practice of the ministry of healing. It was not another human being that pushed me; I was merely faced by a situation in which I could only do one of two things, either show a visitor the door, regretfully declining to do as asked, lay my hands on the person in the name of Jesus, or do just that. I chose the second course. For some years after this, I kept a strict record of every person with whom I had more than a passing contact; in other words, I kept notes on what happened to the whole person to whom I ministered. . . .

I do not look upon myself as, like Time, the Great Healer, but with a certain shyness and humility—more than that, with a grateful certainty that it is not I who heal, but a power outside me, using me as an instrument—I have called again and again on this power that makes for and wills righteousness. . . .

Healing comes to people in a bewildering variety of ways; after one ministry; only after many such acts; a year after one laying on of hands; nothing at all happens physically but a person is made whole and never ceases giving thanks to God etc. etc. etc. The one constant factor is a serenity of spirit that, as is commonly said, can almost be felt; it can be seen even in those whose physical ailment has not been healed, seen as a physical as well as a spiritual glow of health. Death is not always defeated—I mean even temporarily, for of course death will always come—but people with cancer die without pain or drugs and in such serenity of mind and spirit that their passing is a triumph. It seems to me that it is impossible for one human being to do this for another *unaided*. I have comforted, and have been comforted, by another, but always the comfort waned. This awareness of a power, beyond us humans, remains and grows and wholeness or, if you like, righteousness, increases. I have not found any human ailment too trivial or too large for this healing power. . . .

I have not given you a long list of people and ailments that have been cured, for you do not want this, but I would quote the words of one woman who was healed, in a week, of a vast varicose ulcer; on being told by some friends that she seemed remarkably casual about it, she said: 'I'm not casual or ungrateful, but the much more important fact than my healed ulcer and the freedom from pain and discomfort is that whereas I was a worrier and built all my bridges before I came to them, now I pray and trust and have lost anxiety and fear.'

(270, M, 67)

6(*c*) *Exorcism*

Here is a reported phenomenon that would seem to call for more study and particularly psychological investigation. The example I give is a remarkable one submitted to us by a clergyman. I tried, with his permission, to get corroborative evidence from 'T', one of the two other people concerned; the third person 'N' was no longer alive, the instance having occurred some thirty years ago. 'T', also a priest, did not deny the experience, but refused to say anything about it, implying that he did not approve of us making any study of the matter; the tone of his letter did in fact suggest that something very extraordinary had taken place. Whatever construction is placed upon it, it is, I believe, a record of what the writer really thought had taken place; if it had been a fanciful invention he would hardly have given me 'T's', address. The following is a slightly abridged extract from the account:

On the last evening of the ——— Convention three of us set out, about 10.15 p.m. for a walk through a small wood which led to a village on the other side. N., one of the party, started to tell the story of his life . . . He had missed the influence of home, and fell into bad company, unable to resist temptation. As N. finished his story there was a silence. I sat with my eyes closed, wondering how I, as one of the convention leaders, could help the young fellow. What happened next was over in a very short space of time. Breaking through the silence, and crashing through the darkness with tremendous power came my voice: 'IN THE NAME OF THE LORD JESUS CHRIST DEPART'. Immediately N. let out a half-shout, and fell towards me. He said afterwards, 'At those words "In the name of the Lord Jesus Christ" I saw a black form appear from somewhere at my feet and vanish into the wood, and, at the same time, something indescribable left me' . . . It seemed as if horrifying pandemonium had been let loose; as if all the powers of Hell were concentrated in that spot in the wood. I saw numbers of black shapes, blacker than the night, moving about and seeking to come between myself and N. who I was gripping hard. I saw three demon spirits, perhaps more, between N. and myself. . . . 'Pray, N.' I called to him, but the poor fellow could do nothing but sob. With my hands on his shoulders I cried: 'The blood of Jesus Christ cleanseth from all sin.' Again and again I repeated the phrase. I did not notice T. was silent until he said: 'What a horrible atmosphere'. 'Pray, T.' I commanded, 'pray with us.' Together we cried with a loud voice 'The blood of Jesus Christ cleanseth from all sin.' Then, after a pause, in a colossal voice, such as I have never heard before or since, came a verse from scripture through my lips in terrifying power. The words forced out of my mouth: 'I give to my sheep eternal life, they shall never perish, neither shall any pluck them out of my hand' . . . the feeling of power was immense; the atmosphere was charged with a living presence, impossible to describe. Then everything grew quiet. The air seemed soft and pleasant, as if angel voices were singing, as if a battle had ended, or a great storm had blown itself out . . . Quite independently, N. told of how he had seen seven black forms emerge from the trees in the wood, and how he felt power pushing him forward out of my grip.

(248, M, 45+)

6(*d*) Heroism

I have very few examples under this heading, which may perhaps be accounted for by a natural modesty preventing many claiming heroism for themselves. I mention just one:

Many times during the long years since that date [1897] I have been aware of a

Presence helping me to overcome obstacles which would have threatened my contact with God:

The clearest and greatest example of this awareness of what I believe was the Presence of God came to me during the night of August 7th 1915—the landing of thousands of troops at Suvla Bay. Under fire for the first time was very trying, and at first I was as afraid as most men were. As man after man went down, however, a Presence came to me which took away all my fears and replaced them with a feeling of ecstasy. Everything was overwhelmed with this feeling and I was for the time a brave man, without a fear or anxiety in the world. During that night I was severely wounded and disabled in consequence . . . The memory of this night however and the few other occasions when I have been favoured with this nearness of God, have been the outstanding experiences of my long life . . .

(15, M, 81)

The next chapter is concerned with those accounts which illustrate the cognitive and affective elements of religious experience.

4

VARIETIES OF SPIRITUAL AWARENESS

(2) Cognitive and affective elements

The cognitive and affective examples cover a very wide field so we have divided them up into twenty-two sub-categories. The experiences here described include all those feelings which are most generally associated with the spiritual side of man: the sense of joy, peace, security, awe, reverence, and wonder; the feelings of exaltation and ecstasy, of harmony and unity, of hope and fulfilment; the sense of timelessness, the sense of presence, the sense of purpose, and the sense of prayer answered in events. There is also the darker side: feelings of remorse and guilt, of fear and horror. In this chapter the essential elements of the subject are encountered.

Originally I had thought it reasonable to make a distinction between the cognitive and the affective elements by placing them in separate sections. Experience could lead to new forms of awareness, an individual might feel that he had learnt something from his experience, and this cognitive aspect could surely be distinguished from the emotive element associated with or resulting from the experience. In practice, however, any such distinction breaks down.

Then again, as the examples show, there can be no precise analysis of such 'feelings'. Some cases quoted could be used to illustrate half a dozen of these categories. Overlaps abound. Once more I would emphasize that the purpose of this classification is only to act as an index, to facilitate subsequent study of particular aspects of experience rather than to record the relative frequency of this or that 'feeling'—though such records may sometimes be not without interest in themselves.

Overlaps occur not only within this section but with other sections. Section 7(i), for example ('Sense of harmony, order, unity'), has much in common with 1(d) ('Feeling of unity with surroundings and/or other people'), and the examples quoted here might have been used to illustrate that section. Why do we need two? It may be as artificial to attempt to separate sensation from emotion as it is to distinguish cognition; it is evident, however, that for some people sensation in some form plays a significant part in their religious experience, and the categories of Sections 1 to 4 represent an attempt to isolate such cases for comparative study. In practice it will probably be found that there are cases that can be listed under 7(*i*) that cannot be included in 1(*d*), as no sensory element is involved.

7(*a*) Sense of security, protection, peace

A great variety of different kinds of experience could be included in this section, but it would have made our classification too unwieldy if we had separated them into several distinct sub-categories. We received no fewer than 759 accounts from the first 3000 records. Here is one example:

In 1939 . . . I was appointed to a post I had always wanted . . . but in 1945 I had to resign for personal reasons . . . This was a great disappointment and I had no idea what else I should do . . . After wrestling with this problem for some weeks, I was sitting one summer afternoon under a weeping willow tree in a Cambridge garden. Time seemed to stand still. The quiet seclusion calmed the turmoil in my mind; I was able to stand back from it and clearly place the whole situation before God committing the future entirely to Him. Plans took shape and seemed entirely right and appropriate and with them was given the confidence that I should be helped through any difficulties that might arise. The peace and strength and support from this encounter has never left me and has slowly grown as other opportunities have developed.

(522, F, 62)

7(*b*) Sense of joy, happiness, well-being

Extraordinary ecstatic feelings of joy may be experienced under the most unlikely conditions. They may occur at times of crisis, but perhaps more often under the most mundane circumstances, like walking down the Marylebone Road, as in the example with which I open this book.

However, experiences of intense joy, while so often leading to a profound realization of the spiritual side of life, need not invariably have such a result. The student of the subject must take very seriously the careful studies of Marghanita Laski in her book *Ecstasy: a Study of some Secular and Religious Experiences* (1961); here she applies the systematic, almost ecological method to compare the records of subjective feelings experienced by members of three different groups of people. She calls herself an atheist and is certainly as much opposed to any concept of God as a human-like figure 'out there' as she is to institutional religion; nevertheless I have a feeling that she is not really as anti-religious as most people (perhaps indeed including herself) imagine.

However we may interpret these remarkable moments of joy, it cannot be denied that they form a significant element in many of the experiences which people regard as being of a spiritual nature. They occur in 636 accounts out of 3000: just over 21 per cent of the records sent in. The example I have chosen to give here need not be considered as confidential, for although it was sent in to me personally, it was published by the sender, the late Rev. Dr Leslie Weatherhead, in his book *The Christian Agnostic* (1965).

I could not call myself a mystic, but on half-a-dozen occasions I have had experiences which *for me* made me certain of the reality of some supernatural Entity which, or whom, I label 'God'. One was among the foothills of the Himalayas near Simla, one at Vauxhall Station, one on a railway bridge at Woolwich, one in the lounge at a Swanwick Conference, one during the writing of a sermon in my own study, and once at a Holy Communion service when the bombs were falling near us, and we (the members of the City Temple Friday Fellowship) knelt on the rough boards of an upper room off Fleet Street lent to us by the Vicar of St. Bride's Church, the City Temple having been burned to the ground by incendiary bombs.

It would be boring to describe them all, but they all had similar characteristics. I will try to describe one. Vauxhall Station on a murky November Saturday evening is not the setting one would choose for a revelation of God! I was a young theological student aged nineteen, being sent from Richmond Theological College (London University) to take the services somewhere—I cannot remember where—for some minister in a Greater London church who had fallen ill. The third-class compartment was full. I cannot remember any particular thought processes which may have led up to the great moment. It is possible that I was ruminating over the sermons I had prepared, and feeling—what I have always felt—how inadequate they were to 'get over' to others what I really felt about the Christian religion and its glorious message.

But the great moment came and when, years later, I read C. S. Lewis's *Surprised by Joy* I thought, 'Yes, I know exactly how he felt. I felt like that.' For a few seconds only, I suppose, the whole compartment was filled with light. This is the only way I know in which to describe the moment, for there was nothing to *see* at all. I felt caught up into some tremendous sense of being within a loving, triumphant and shining purpose. I never felt more humble. I never felt more exalted. A most curious, but overwhelming sense possessed me and filled me with ecstasy. I felt that all was well for mankind—how poor the words seem! The word 'well' is so poverty stricken. All men were shining and glorious beings who in the end would enter incredible joy. Beauty, music, joy, love immeasurable and a glory unspeakable, all this they would inherit. Of this they were heirs. My puny message, if I passed my exams and qualified as a minister, would contribute only an infinitesimal drop to the ocean of love and truth which God wanted men to enjoy, but my message was of the same *nature* as that ocean. I was right to want to be a minister. I had wanted to be a doctor and the conflict had been intense, but in that hour I knew the ministry was the right path for me. For me it was right, right, right . . . An indescribable joy possessed me . . .

All this happened over fifty years ago but even now I can see myself in the corner of that dingy, third-class compartment with the feeble lights of inverted gas mantles overhead and the Vauxhall Station platform outside with milk cans standing there. In a few moments the glory departed—all but one curious, lingering feeling. I loved everybody in that compartment. It sounds silly now, and indeed I blush to write it, but at that moment I think I would have died for any one of the people in that compartment. . . .

(385, M, 80+)

7(c) Sense of new strength in oneself

Here are examples of that feature so commonly found in the religious experience of all kinds of people, whether from primitive tribes or from Western society. On page 6 I quoted Durkheim's suggestion that the man 'who has communicated with his god ... is a man who is stronger. He feels within him more force either to endure the trials of existence or to conquer them ... he is raised above his condition as a mere man ... 'A modern psychologist, the late Professor Sir Frederic Bartlett, said (1950) that there were many people, whom he had met and respected, who 'have done, effectively and consistently, many things which all ordinary sources of evidence seem to set outside the range of unassisted humanity. When they say "it is God working through me" I cannot see that I have either the right or the knowledge to reject their testimony.'

I give two examples:

For some time I have experienced myself an extraordinary contact with what I may call some 'power' or guidance outside my ordinary day-to-day life. To solve the many problems that we all have to face I find that 'organized' religion is useless, but in some quite unexplainable way my long search for 'light' seems to be leading me towards what I most need. I can now contact the vast storehouse of power that comprises the universe. By concentrated, voiceless prayer and, in a way, relaxation, I may feel my whole spirit filled with this power, and my whole being recharged. When this happens, then I know that anxiety, troubles and so forth will be solved; and indeed they are.

(271, F, Age ?)

Several times in my life I have been either very frightened or very unhappy or have been unable to see how my life could continue. At those times I have been able to put my trust in this calm love and sense of God, concentrate on what little I could do, and though it wasn't always pleasant and I certainly didn't go around in a bland euphoria, I was given strength I didn't have and things were accomplished and righted with a great kindness that had my gratitude, because I knew it was God's help, and not something I had done or something that would have come about anyway in the way the world works.

(491, F, 32)

7(d) Sense of guidance, vocation, inspiration

The feeling of being guided is certainly very strong in the lives of many people. Examples abound in literature from the Old Testament onwards and among our records there are 473 in the first 3000 received. I suspect that there are many who feel that their lives are being guided towards a particular goal and yet shrink from admitting it, entirely for reasons of modesty which I will discuss under a similar category 7(t), *Sense of purpose behind events*, on p. 64; indeed it would have been better to place these two sub-sections next to one another. These curious feelings certainly require a great deal more study and a beginning has been made by Michael Walker as reported in Chapter 7 (p. 114). Since he quotes several examples I will here give only one.

Among the most vivid experiences I have had occurred when I was 63 and on the retiring list. I received a call to go out and teach in Nigeria. Nothing was further from my mind. However, in accordance with my commitment, I submitted the proposal to God and waited for an answer. But like Moses I spent the time thinking of other teachers who would do better. They all had good reasons for not going! I continued listening for an answer and God said clearly to me, 'I want *you* to go.' I eventually said I would go if that was what He wanted. As soon as I had said it, back came the answer, 'I will give you all you need.' At that moment all fear left me and never came back throughout two glorious years teaching in Lagos. God fulfilled that promise more abundantly than I could have asked or thought and I love Him for it.

(16, M, 78)

7(e) *Awe, reverence, wonder*

Here are other relatively frequent elements in religious experience which we have classed together although each of the three might well form a category on its own; they together occur in some 7 per cent of our records (198 out of the first 3000).

The first also illustrates another and quite different phnomenon: that intense religious feelings may come for a period and then wane, but later return. In the particular example quoted, the periods of intensity came in stretches of one or two weeks at a time. Such an ebb and flow of spiritual feeling, or of a person's confidence in their faith, has often been recorded in the annals of devotional religion. What does it mean? To the biologist it may well suggest a connection with some physiological rhythm; now in saying this I am *not* intending in any way to denigrate the spiritual reality of the experience, but to point out the possibility of a profound relationship between it and the very nature of the living system.

Through one period of my life I experienced a greatly intensified feeling of hunger for God which usually lasted about one to two weeks without any let-up at all, day or night, and then suddenly ceased. During these periods I could not describe my feelings: it was like a pain which radiated through every part of me; yet at the same time I was aware of God's reality and nearness. It usually became almost unbearable after a few days. One evening during one of these periods I was trying to pray when I suddenly found I could express myself no longer; not that words failed me, but I seemed to come to the end of myself. A few seconds passed and I became aware that although I was no longer able to pray or even think, yet the state of prayer continued most positively, and at a deep level. It flashed through my conscious mind, 'This is the Holy Spirit.' I knew something of what St. Paul meant when he said, 'The Holy Spirit maketh intercession for us.' This I knew was happening at that very moment and I was in its presence. I was conscious of no emotion, no joy or fear, only interest, and what I can only describe as a strange pulling sensation. It was as though I was deliberately being allowed to see and know something private and holy. As the awareness faded I was filled with awe and wonder that all the power and love of God was concerned with me.

(54, F, 50)

Waking one morning to watch the 1910 comet, I found something other than myself looking at the sky through, or with, my eyes. It knew something about the Universe which I didn't know. I connected 'It', as I called it, with other inexpressible feelings, and decided that there was a power behind the visible universe with which one could come in contact if one knew how. Later in life I was shown how. *'It'* was beneficent, but awful, could bring me to a state of bliss, obliterating even the thought of life's miseries. 'It' could also be stern when approached in the wrong way.

(849, F, 78)

7(f) Sense of certainty, clarity, enlightenment

Towards the end of his life, Jung was said to have been asked in an interview: 'Do you believe in God?' He is reported to have replied at once, 'I don't believe, *I know!*'*

This feeling of conviction is well represented in our collection: there are 584 examples in our first 3000 records. I must mention, however, that this sudden sense of certainty does not always apply only to a conviction as to a divine reality; but sometimes, as in the first example here, the respondent may report that he has suddenly obtained a feeling of general omniscience which must clearly be a delusion.

Suddenly everything became crystal clear, clearer, more definite, than anything in normal existence. There was also an amazing 'knowingness' rather than 'knowledgeableness': that is, I knew, not by application to study, but because it was in my mind from the beginning and had so existed as an attribute, a primary possession. There was no 'I think', 'I understand', 'I believe', 'I reason', but simply I KNOW. I knew that I was capable of answering any question or problem put to me, no matter how abstruse. . . .

(189, M, Age ?)

In 1966 I was one day alone in the house when quite suddenly I became aware of my own attitude to life. I realised that I was wrapped up in deep self pity, that my thoughts were all for myself and my own sorrows, that I had not thought of others. I thought how others in the world suffered too. I was rather shocked at my selfish attitude and was filled with compassion for others; then, as if without thinking, I knelt down in the room and made a vow to God that from then on for the rest of my life I would love and serve mankind. The following morning when I awoke I had a sudden experience, for into my mind poured knowledge (which knowledge has remained with me ever since); I knew that the love and service of mankind was the will of God for mankind. That we are to love all.

---

*Whilst I cannot give a reference which confirms these exact words so often quoted, I have a copy of notes given me by the late Leonard Elmhirst taken from an interview with C. G. Jung by Frederick Sands published in the *Daily Mail* on Monday 25 April 1955. I expect these were the real words used which have become shortened in quotation:

"All that I have learned has led me step by step to an unshakable conviction of the existence of God."

"I only believe in what I know. That eliminates believing. Therefore I do not take His existence on belief—I know that He exists."

That we serve God by serving his purpose and by our service of others, that God is manifest in all living things . . . My whole outlook on life changed from that time. To explain my experience figuratively, it was as if all my life I had been in a darkened room and then I had suddenly walked out of it into the sunlight of day.

(2, F, 41)

7(g) Exaltation, excitement, ecstasy

Here are more examples of that intense sense of joy that characterized those of the former sub-division of this section, 7(b); so similar are they that one may indeed doubt whether they should be separated from each other except for an almost physical agitation accompanying the experiences here which links them with those quasi-sensory experiences included in our first four main divisions. The first example shows a joyousness 'sweeping round and through' the person, but 'not like a wind'; the second example is likewise linked to another category in this main division, that of 7(v), a sense of presence. From our first 3000 records 142 accounts have been placed in this exaltation category; if these are added to the 636 people who felt a sense of joy (7b) we see what an important feature ecstasy is in man's spiritual experience.

Suddenly I felt a great joyousness sweeping over me. I use the word 'sweeping' because this feeling seemed to do just that. I actually felt it as coming from my left and sweeping round and through me, completely engulfing me. I do not know how to describe it. It was not like a wind. But suddenly it was there, and I felt it move around and through me. Great joy was in it. Exaltation might be a better word.

(297, F, Age ?)

I can never adequately describe the experience which came upon me. I had found the Pivot of Life. It was Jesus Christ Himself. No one told me—I just knew. I wanted only to read the Bible, which lit up in a marvellous fashion and had a message to me in all my needs and queries. Overnight, literally, I became changed. All anguish, all fretfulness, seeking and querying were gone. This light, this Some-one was so close with an unspeakable glory and joy that I could scarcely speak. I constantly fell to my knees in worshipping adoration, sometimes having to ask that the 'experience' be lifted for a while, so intense was the burden of the joy and liberation. For liberation it was: my old nature, with its temper and unpre-dictable moods, was gone. In place was a constant light, equanimity and peace.

(401, F, 64)

7(h) Sense of being at a loss for words

Again and again the mystics throughout the ages have declared that their experiences were ineffable, too great or deep to be put into words. It is perhaps surprising that more of our respondents have not written specifically of the impossibility of adequately describing their feelings; only 76 in our first 3000 did so. For it is easy enough to describe concrete objective phenomena in words, but quite another matter to try to explain an overwhelming experience of beauty, either in nature or art, and the same is surely true of personal love. There can be little doubt, I think, that the root of it lies in that fundamental difference between the two forms of knowledge that Michael Polanyi (1958) called *tacit* and *explicit* knowledge; the former, knowing without words, being the more fundamental in that it is infinitely older in the animal kingdom, whereas the latter, dependent upon language, is, in terms of evolutionary history, a very recent invention of man. The example here illustrates Polanyi's tacit knowledge.

I cannot say how long it took to develop, but the ecstasy lasted over roughly three weeks. The main sensation was of being loved, a flood of sweetness of great strength, without any element of sentimentality or anything but itself. The description is quite inadequate. I also felt a unification of myself with the external world: I did not lose my own identity, yet all things and I somehow entered into each other; all things seemed to 'speak' to me. Something was communicated to me, not in words or images, but in another form of knowing.

(793, M, 47)

7(i) Sense of harmony, order, unity

The experiences in this section have *no* quasi-sensory element in them, which distinguishes them from those placed in sub-section 1(d) where people felt at unity with their surroundings in a visual sense. I have chosen to give just one example from the 200 accounts we possess of this sense of unity:

About 1962 I spent 4 hours standing at a busy road centre in Birmingham (a city I hardly knew) with 5 or 6 others in a Peace Vigil. At the 3 previous vigils in which I had taken part, I felt cut off from—perhaps a little superior to—the general public hurrying past, and had spent much of my time trying to pray for them, for those at war and for world peace. On this occasion I found instead that I was overtaken by an intense feeling of affection for and unity with everyone around as they ran to catch buses, took children shopping or joyfully met their friends. The feeling was so strong that I wanted to leave my silent vigil and join them in their urgent living.
This sense of 'oneness' is basic to what I understand of religion. Hitherto I think I had only experienced it so irresistably towards a few individuals, sometimes towards my children, or when in love.
The Effect of the Experience has been, I think, a permanent increase in my awareness that we are 'members one of another', a consequent greater openness towards all and a widening of my concern for others.

(504, F, 56)

7(j) Sense of timelessness

It is perhaps not surprising that an absence of the element of time appears not infrequently to be associated with experiences felt to have religious significance (there are 113 such examples in our first 3000), for indeed disassociations with time are similarly a feature of many other intense emotional experiences such as love or fear.

I felt he (my dying husband) might be aware of my presence although unconscious, and took his hand and closed my eyes. Immediately my surroundings disappeared from my conscious mind and I was aware of two distinct things at once: reverence for the presence of God on my left hand side, powerful in its effect, and then I was swiftly being propelled into a vast current into space that is almost indescribable. It resembled the ecstasy of a beautiful symphony. It was out of this world of feeling. Love was its force. The speed of it was as though I were travelling a million miles a second. I felt this involved my husband's being as it did my own, and I was closer in love and spirit with him than ever in our actual lives. The energy of this vast stream of upward and outward spatial experience finally frightened me as I was aware that if I held on to my husband's hand too long I should be unable to return. I dropped it and opened my eyes to look for God. But he wasn't there. I looked at the officers in the room, and my son, and asked them if they had seen anything; they had not. When I closed my eyes my son was in the act of putting the telephone back on the receiver: when I opened them his hand had just placed it there.

(517, F, Age ?)

7(k) *Feeling of love, affection (in oneself)*

The feeling of the love of God, and for God, naturally figures frequently in the accounts sent to us and may be expressed in many forms and be included in a number of different categories. Linked with this divine love and included in this section is expression of love for other people. There are 190 such examples among our first 3000 records. I give just one example from our collection which illustrates the extraordinary exuberance of the young caught up in a movement like that of the so-called Jesus People. I should mention, however, that just the same enthusiastic spirit of love is manifest in the youthful adherents of other cults such as those who followed the Guru Maharaj-ji. I went to a great rally at Alexandra Palace to hear him speak. The exuberance shown is for the Divine Light, as they call it, and for the spirit of 'Satsang' which as one of them explained to me 'is the sharing of the love that is very deep within every human being'. I can only describe the emotional euphoria of the thousands who packed the vast hall as the nearest thing I have seen in real life to those documentary films which portray the fanatical behaviour of Hitler Youth at rallies in Germany in the 1930s. Now for my example:

The guys still wear their hair long, but we're all like children when we talk about Jesus, we love him so much! I'm not scared of anything, I look forward to death if that is what my Lord wants. There's a love in me that's supernatural. I never could love people as I do now with Jesus in my heart. The kids are all finding Jesus, and man, there's gonna be a revolution about him, you can't imagine until you accept him how he can change your heart.

(59, F, 17)

7(l) *Yearning, desire, nostalgia*

Here we have a small number of examples, only 43 out of the first 3000, combining joy with a yearning or a feeling of nostalgia.

From time to time I have again experienced these wonderful ecstasies, always at completely unexpected times, sometimes while washing up and doing daily chores about the house. There is always this same feeling, leaving me weeping with a great joy and feeling of deep reverence and worship and love. I think it best described as a sort of homesickness, a 'nostalgia for some other where', almost as if I had known an existence of such beauty and indescribable happiness and am yearning and homesick for it again . . . Even when everything seems to have fallen away and troubles pile up and I've used to everybody; even then this yearning for rock-bottom of despair, as comes to everybody; even then this yearning for something I had known somewhere sustains and brings me through. Could it be a self-evident sort of truth? One can't be homesick for something one has never known.

(975, F, 55)

7(m) Sense of forgiveness, restoration, renewal

The accounts in this sub-section will I think be found to be deeply moving; there are 120 in our first 3000; I give just one example.

Gradually I had become psychotic, and attempted suicide. I had done something which I considered utterly dreadful, and I was being driven to self-destruction because of an intense feeling of guilt. I had only one desire—to be forgiven . . . I was visited by the psychiatrists, my husband, my brother and the hospital chaplain, but I was unable to communicate sensibly with any of them. Then quite dramatically the whole picture changed overnight. The weight of guilt had been lifted and I was myself again, quite rational and ready to go home again. This recovery was not due to any medical aid at all. Both psychiatrists and clergy were at a loss to understand this sudden change; but it was quite simple to me: I believed that God had forgiven me . . . It was not a temporary healing: I never needed treatment since that time. Looking back I still know that there was a divine intervention in my life at that point.

(210, F, 40)

7(n) Sense of integration, wholeness, fulfilment

There can be little doubt that some of the experiences recorded in the accounts sent in are caused by a pathological condition; in some cases this is definitely stated to be so, as in the first of the two examples given to illustrate this category. Whilst there is this background behind the experience, it does not, to my mind, destroy the significance of the feelings that come to the person concerned; such examples illustrate the resilience of the human spirit—a factor which should indeed be recognized in any study of these aspects of human life. There were 38 accounts in our first 3000 that we placed in this category. Two examples follow:

I was drifting; and I knew it was becoming serious, and I was full of disgust and loathing for this 'bad' part of me which was taking such a firm hold. All this time I was becoming ill, and when at last at the age of 38 I found myself in hospital with a brain tumour to be removed, I felt a strange sense of inevitability, and was glad that at last a crisis had been reached . . . I felt rather like a rat caught in a trap; and yet all the time the 'good' part of me was happy because I did not want to live any more saddled with the 'bad' part . . . I had the impression that, while unconscious, I was in communication with beings whom I can only describe as beloved companions. It seemed I asked to be released from something; and as if with the utmost love that they replied that I was free to finish the particular life-cycle but that I had not accomplished what I set out to do. They implied that I still could if I would. They implied that it would be very hard going. I seemed to get the impression that I would be somehow letting them down, and so I said YES, I will go back . . .I was next aware of the deepest, most unutterable lone-liness and fear . . . Many ghastly weeks later I felt utterly overcome, ground into the earth by some tremendous cosmic power . . . The next morning . . . I felt full of gratitude, and I sat down and wrote to the surgeon to thank him for using his skill on me. The extent of my disfigurement was such that children ran away, and people averted their gaze. And yet, he had given me the opportunity to try again to fulfil my potential in service to the Purpose . . . Some years later . . . the most marvellous realization flashed upon me: I felt I had been given back my now (relatively) purified personality. It was so great a conviction that I cried out 'Oh thank you, thank you.' I know it was important because it seemed to mark the point of no return. There had been a shattering of the old personality, followed by months and years of painstaking effort to piece together a new one.

(336, F, 49)

When alone in deep meditation I 'reach God', tears fill my eyes and a great sense of peace and wholeness seems to possess me. It is a kind of catharsis, I suppose. It is not based on emotion as far as I can tell. It is an intellectual exercise which nearly always has physical results, in the feeling of freshness and restored vitality after the experience.

(438, F, 33)

7(o) Hope, optimism

The feelings of hope and optimism in spiritual experience may be found in accounts written by those who have widely different views as to the nature of deity, as the two examples given here will show. The first is reminiscent of the feelings of Richard Jeffries expressed in his remarkable autobiography *The Story of My Heart* (1883); Jeffries sometimes called himself an atheist (thinking no doubt of a god in human form 'out there'), yet he prayed, and prayed with intense joy. He wrote in the last paragraph of this book, 'As the sky extends beyond the valley, so I know that there are ideas beyond the valley of my thought; I know there is something infinitely higher than deity'.

There are 46 accounts in our first 3000 records which I have placed in this sub-category of hope.

I feel that the country can provide all I need, both in the way of food and also intellectually and artistically by its complexity and beauty. I feel that it is greater than I am, that I cannot harm it, nor can mankind itself. I have the belief that mankind may wipe itself out by ignoring nature, but that nature will survive . . .

Being in the country gives me a tremendous feeling of hope and exhilaration, which I never feel about Christianity.

(932, F, 25)

The eternal nature of God as perfect love filled me with an inexpressible sense of joy and complete reassurance that above all our storms is tranquillity and wholeness. I now know that anxiety has no place, and discouragement cannot be more than a temporary setback. In the face of this, what can one do but worship? It adds a new dimension to 'living in hope'.

(195, F, 52)

7(p) Sense of release from fear of death

Expressions of this release occur in 109 out of 3000 records. I give two examples. In the first it will be seen that this feeling came to the same person in three different ways: this single excerpt illustrates features shown separately in a number of other records. In addition to these examples we may refer back to two cases of out-of-the-body experiences (505, F, 46) and (802, F, 21) given on page 36 in each of which the feeling of separation from the physical body provides a release from the fear of death.

About 9 years ago my mother died after a short illness at home—my father and I looking after her with a little outside help. She died one evening and when I finally went to bed, exhausted and in considerable distress, suddenly the distress left me and I became aware 'There is no death'. It seemed a laughable impossibility. The intensity of awareness did not last long but after that I could not grieve with the same intensity, although I felt almost guilty about this.

Last summer when walking on Hampstead Heath alone, feeling calm and at peace with the world, suddenly I became aware that there was no separateness between myself and other people, there was no such thing as death, and I was pervaded by a feeling of great peace and joy. Though the experience was transitory I felt my life had been changed by it.

In January this year I attended a talk on Transcendental Meditation, and as a result became initiated into the Maharishi's method of meditation by the use of mantra. The effect was immediate and bewildering from the first meditation, and two days after I had been initiated, just after the evening meditation I experienced what Stace in his 'Mysticism and Philosophy' calls an extravertive mystical experience. This was a perception of oneness, all was a manifestation of Being. Through all the objects in the room glowed a radiance. All problems dissolved or rather, there were no problems, there was no death and no 'I-ness'; it was a feeling of absolute bliss. This was followed as I gradually 'came back into the world' by a feeling of intoxication, so great was the happiness.

. . . This experience was of the nature of the ones earlier described but much fuller and clearer. I do not interpret it as becoming united with a separate Being, God. It is rather a becoming aware of the Universal Self, the Absolute. Perhaps one could interpret this as God.

(502, F, Age ?)

Life has been a continual struggle towards the light as recorded in diaries. . .
I have had a certain amount of vague mental illness (never official) and still suffer very uncomfortably at times but I know where my strength is—in God the

Father and our Lord Jesus Christ, who is with me every moment of the day and night.

I once had a so-called religious experience. During a bad bout and sleeping badly I saw a blue light accompanied by an indescribable sense of peace and wholeness which, if I live to be a hundred, I shall never forget. I knew I would *never* be alone again.

Life now is more wonderful than I could ever have hoped, for I have no fear of death. In fact I am looking forward. I attend Holy Communion at Church regularly.

(228, F, 63)

7(q) Fear, horror

Among our first 3000 records there were 125 which described the appalling sense of fear that people may experience. The possible causes of these horrific conditions probably lie in part within the field of psychology, of which I am not qualified to write: maybe these distressing experiences may be overcome by turning the mind to religious ideas.

Suddenly I became aware of a sense of the uttermost evil, so much so that I became awake. I could feel this sense of evil enveloping me. I had the terrifying impression that this evil force of presence was bent upon taking possession of me. How does one describe evil? I only knew that I was enveloped by this revolting force, so vile and rotting I could almost taste the evil. I was in terror, so much so I could not call out or move. A part of my mind told me I must at all costs act or I would be lost. I recall that I managed by a great effort to stretch out my right hand and with my index finger I traced the shape of the Cross in the air. Immediately on my doing this the evil enveloping me fell away completely, and I felt a wonderful sense of peace and safety.

(667, M, 54)

I was very nervous of being left alone. Fear gripped me in a great grip; I think I never had such fear. Then it came to remembrance the story of Elisha revealing to his servant the Host of Angels, and I accepted that as being true now. The fear left me and I was 'still'. But directly I let my thoughts fall from that Vision, that awful fear returned—so I would quickly renew my 'vision'.

(314, F, 83)

7(r) Remorse, sense of guilt

It is perhaps surprising that only 71 respondents among the first 3000 write of this sense of guilt or remorse, since feelings of guilt figure so prominently in the case books of the psychiatrists; it may well be that those who have these feelings have a strong disinclination to write of them. One example will suffice:

We may experience the conviction of wrongdoing. 'We have left undone those things which we ought to have done; and we have done those things which we ought not to have done.' The occasions when this must have been true of me would be too numerous to mention. On all these occasions—and many more—I had a sudden and profound sense of sorrow at having injured, or failed to help, another person. Where did this come from? A deeper level of myself—a power outside myself?

(424, F, 70)

7(s) Sense of indifference, detachment

This is a sub-category that cannot be easily defined and into it I have placed only 34 of the first 3000 records; I have some doubt as to whether it should be retained because so often these expressions of indifference are only a part of some other much more important experience which as a whole could not be described as indifference in the ordinary sense of the word. It may be useful, however, to retain it merely to indicate the presence of this element in a wide variety of different kinds of experience. I give two examples to show how disparate they can be; in the first one the experience is described as 'a sort of glorious indifference' which illustrates the point I have just made about it not really being indifference as generally understood, but a special form of detachment:

The feeling itself is very objective in that it is impersonal and, apparently, has little connection with my personal situation. I am filled with a warm glow that connects me with the external universe with which I seem to become as one. I transcend the trivia of everyday life and accept everything, good and evil, rich and poor, ugly and beautiful without any irritation. It is a sort of glorious indifference. Also these moods give a feeling of tremendous fertility, although I have never, to my knowledge, received any inspiration for creative activity from them. However, the feeling is similar to what I have felt whilst writing poetry, but far less active. It is an overwhelming potential which does not necessitate, indeed would be prostituted by, any specific action or thought. It is more the suppression of the senses or the complete coalition of them into a new and more complete sense.

(443, M, 22)

The simplest way in which I can describe it, is as if one had been enormously absorbed in a television programme (play) to the extent that one had come to feel and believe in the reality of the people, and then, suddenly, one becomes aware for some reason that it is, after all, only a play on television. For the word 'play' use the word 'life'. Increasingly I find that at moments of complete absorption with what is happening in my life, something 'clicks' and I know it all to be a play only. Whilst I can still watch, and even partake in the 'play', something in me is aware of a far greater significance, and despite even the most harrowing and difficult happenings, there is within me, a peace which defies understanding, and knowledge that what is occurring is only the appearance. Behind this appearance, something beyond my present comprehension is slowly unfolding itself to my view. As it comes into view, I see why it had to appear in the way it did appear.

(1267, F, 47)

7(t) Sense of purpose behind events

We have placed in this category 341 accounts out of the first 3000 received. I think it likely that many more people than like to admit it have a curious feeling that there is a sense of purpose behind the arrangement of their lives—as if a benevolent Providence was in charge of their affairs—yet shrink from saying so for fear of seeming arrogant. It is the same feeling of modesty as I have suggested in my brief discussion of a sense of guidance under 7(*d*) on p. 54. Indeed some of the examples included here approach closely some of those placed under 7(*d*) and may well also be included there. I know some one who has told me (what he says he has told no one else) that he had this feeling of arrangement in his life most strongly, yet dared not bring himself to accept that it was true because such belief would imply the appalling presumption that he could be the object of preferential treatment; he tried, he said, to persuade himself, against his real feeling, that it could only *appear* to be so and that it must either be lucky chance or have some deep psychological cause which he could not fathom. Another friend, a lady of over 80, in a personal letter which was not a response to our request for accounts of experience, wrote to me as follows:

When I was about 16, or perhaps a little earlier, I began to have what I called 'A Sense of Destiny'. It was only long afterwards that I realized that Napoleon and Hitler were the supreme examples of 'men of destiny' and that no good came of it. Though it explains nothing I consoled myself with the thought that this was an example of the polarities of life.
  This 'Sense of Destiny' is still with me—I suppose some people would call it 'guidance' but that implies a personal 'guide' which is no part of the experience.

I need only give one example from our collection here, for I give several others in a discussion of Michael Walker's work on p. 114.

I have been aware of this feeling for a number of years, and have frequently had the impression that I have been manoeuvred or even exploited for the carrying through of what I have come to regard as the Divine Purpose. I cannot offer a rational explanation for this, other than to say that I perceive in my life something of the sort of spirit that permeates 'The Cloud of Unknowing'. The net result is that I have been called upon to do many strange things that I would not at one time have thought myself capable or suitably qualified to undertake.
                                                      (43, M, Age ?)

7(*u*) Sense of prayer answered in events

I give one example of each of two kinds of events considered to be the result of prayer (415 accounts were sent in). The first illustrates changes in the person's sense of well-being and mental balance, whereas the second deals with what at first sight seems to be the more mundane matter of raising funds, yet the real issue, of course, is—in the words of the account—'our *ability* to raise the money' (italics mine). In both there is a new power generated from the process of devout prayer.

Crying out in despair one night, praying as I have never prayed before or since, utterly dejected and miserable, a condition brought upon myself by my own stupid folly and woeful ignorance; nevertheless, developments showed quite plainly that prayer was answered. From that time forward I felt new power; an inexpressible joy flowed through my whole being, and a certain sense of forgiveness anew. Mental balance restored, I became aware of moral obligation, and the urge to start life afresh.

(135, M, 76)

At last, after 6 years of pressure, the West C ——— Hospital Management Committee invited us to provide the necessary money to erect a centre at T ——— Hospital in conjunction with the Physiotherapy Department which would be run by them for observation and treatment of our spastic and disabled children. Some of us regarded this as an impossibility; I reminded them that Jesus Christ said 'Whatever you ask, in prayer, believing, you shall receive.' For I never doubted our ability to raise the money. So now it is available and early next year the Centre will be erected at a cost of £22,000. All these things have been accomplished in a miraculous manner.

(373, M, Age ?)

7(*v*) *Sense of presence (not human)*

In this, the last of the sub-categories in our large division of combined cognitive and affective experiences we had 607 splendid examples of what Rudolf Otto termed the numinous (*Das Heilige* 1917, translated as *The Idea of the Holy* 1923). It is interesting to note that the sense of a presence usually takes precedence over the secondary phenomena of voice, vision, or touch. I find the first example particularly interesting because it relates this sense of presence as felt 'strongly in old churches' with that experienced in the 'wild countryside' and also because it shows how occasionally this sense may be intensified into an almost ecstatic state in which there appears 'a pinkish golden light which was in everything'. The relation of this sense of presence to those 'as if visual' quasi-sensory phenomena to be found in category 1(*b*) has been specially pointed out by Beardsworth in *A Sense of Presence* (1977). I will, with his permission, quote from his final chapter:

These various kinds of experience . . . are essentially personal; you feel the voice or presence or whatever as a second person, a 'you'; and you experience the Other purely in relation to yourself, as comforting, benevolent, malignant or whatever; it is an affective relation, and the response is an emotional one,—warmth, a feeling of being loved, shame, awe, and so on. What I think might be true to say is this: the sense of presence, the sense that somebody is 'there' without any sensory manifestations, seems to be if anything the primary thing, and the rest (voice, vision, etc.) comes as a sensory elaboration of it. Take, for instance, those cases of being touched—if I felt a light pressure on my arm, I don't think I would infer from that, unless under very particular circumstances, that this was anything benevolent or punishing, that it was a 'presence', a Being of some kind; it would just be rather an odd nervous sensation, I think the feeling of somebody being near, of their having a certain *attitude* towards you, is the basic thing, from which the rest follows.

After all, if we add to the sense of 'presence' a 'voice', 'appearance', 'touch' or whatever, nothing crucially different results: the 'presence' is simply filled out for us. It makes no great difference whether the Other looks at me, speaks to me, touches me, or I simply sense his 'presence', these are just so many ways of expressing an affective relation, and that is the primary thing.

It would seem, however, from the first of the two examples I am about to give, that not everyone who feels the sense of presence as *personal* to him or her, would actually attribute the presence felt to that of a *person*—this is curious, for the writer says, 'It is in me, *it knows* about me, and I belong to it, but it is *not a Person* . . . ' (the italics are mine).

As far back as I can remember there has been a sweet, cool presence in and around me,—someone called it a Dazzling Darkness. This varies in intensity. It is in everything and is always there. On the rare occasions when it *has* receded I've felt frightened and alone. It is in me, it knows about me and I belong to it, but it is not a Person, so that praying in words seems crude. I prefer to 'inhale it' at prayer time, or at quiet moments in the day. I find the presence strongly in old churches, some old houses, in wild countryside, music, and in a few people. About 3 times it has intensified into what I suppose could be the mystical experience—a pinkish golden light which was in everything, was love, and made everything look beautiful, even Council Houses and a Corporation bus.

(489, M, 33)

Then, without any conscious seeking on my part, the Presence I knew and loved came most unmistakably to me—the same Presence I had first known as a child in the wood, and at other times as I grew older. I had come to recognize the reality of that Presence, for, not being a naturally loving person, the effect of it was always to awaken a spirit of love in me for those I found it difficult to love.

(64, F, 84)

We shall now pass on in the next two chapters to consider examples from the remaining divisions of our scheme of classification. These are the records which, apart from describing different kinds of experience, dwell on their development, describe their various dynamic patters, discuss what may trigger them off and show the consequences of these experiences in the lives of the persons involved.

5

DYNAMIC PATTERNS OF EXPERIENCE

If the examples in the last two chapters have impressed with their variety, an examination of those accounts which show something of an individual's development during his lifetime, the dynamic pattern and its effect, will, I believe provide a deeper insight into the nature of those driving powers which form the essence of man's religious life. In this and in the next chapter are seen forces at work which move men and women to higher levels of idealism and endeavour.

Sections 1 to 7 dealt with different kinds of experience so I felt that it was useful to give the exact numbers of examples of each kind which we had received out of the first 3000 records. Now, however, I feel the corresponding numbers are less important because the figures will show only the proportion of respondents who felt it worthwhile to write in and discuss these questions of development, patterns, causes, and effects. Therefore the relative quantities are not significant in this part of the book. What various people have to say about antecedents and consequences is more important.

8. DEVELOPMENT OF EXPERIENCE

The more I study the significant features in the development of man's spiritual life, the more apparent it becomes that there are no 'normal' patterns: each individual must find his own and it is the discovery of such a personal pattern that appears to be an essential part of all experience truly to be called religious.

We have split this section into three main divisions:

(i)   deals with development within the individual;
(ii) deals with development in relation to other people; and
(iii) is concerned with the different periods of life which were felt to be significant.

I have further sub-divided this last section into childhood, adolescence, middle age, and old age. Each of these smaller categories does not represent a distinctive type of experience but has merely been sub-divided as a matter of convenience in order to see more clearly whether any one form of experience is more frequent in, or more characteristic of, a certain period of life, than another.

I have left gaps between the letters used to distinguish one sub-category from another on purpose so that there is plenty of room for the addition of further categories as the work expands without having to renumber the whole classification again from the beginning. As a result there are gaps between (*e*) and (*k*), and between (*o*) and (*r*). These are deliberate.

The first division deals with the development of individual experience. There were a great number of such accounts, all of which would have illustrated William James's celebrated definition of religion in his *Varieties*.

Religion, therefore, as I now ask you arbitrarily to take it, shall mean for us *the feelings, acts and experiences of individual men in their solitude, so far as they apprehend themselves to stand in relation to whatever they may consider the divine* [italics as in original].

The importance of inter-personal and social relationship, in the development of experience is the subject of our second division; this was for Durkheim, in contrast to James, the heart, or at least the origin, of all religion. It must be admitted that the manner in which our material has been collected (by personal appeal) may have accounted for there being a larger number of examples in the first division than in the second. To do justice to the latter we perhaps need a rather different approach or different methods of sampling; nevertheless we have a fair range and quantity of examples to illustrate this more social side.

(i) Development within the individual

8(*a*) *Steady disposition: little or no development recorded*

It is convenient to have the first accounts which record no actual development placed alongside the others which do. I suspect that many others who have written to us may well experience this lasting feeling of the spiritual in their lives without specifically calling attention to its continuity. Little need be said in introducing the two examples I give beyond emphasizing their marked sense of reality.

I would like to go on record as one to whom the power beyond the visible world is a reality and has been for many years . . . My sense of conscious contact with the power at the heart of the universe dates from the age of 11 or 12 when I used to run as quickly as possible through the prayers I had been taught to say in order to get on to the real business of talking to someone who was 'there' . . . After all these years I still feel myself very much in the early stages.

(56, F, 58)

The real justification of religion is in personal spiritual and mystical experience. Without the spiritual apprehension of Him I call 'the living Christ' I could never have ventured to live alone. On the verifiable reality of that experience I would stake all that I have. All my life I have found God true.

(485, M, 70)

8(b) Gradual growth of sense of awareness: experience more or less continuous

Here no comment is needed for the examples speak for themselves.

All my life seems to have been a gradual unfolding of understanding, a slow development. Only in the last year or two has this seemed to reach religious experience. . . . I now feel purpose in life. I must become 'better'. From time to time I realize I am becoming slightly more aware. This immense drive I feel pushing me to deepen my knowledge of self—this I know to reach towards the whole meaning of the universe.

(820, F, 38)

There has been a growing sense of personal encounter with a power at the same time within and outside me, that has never left me since the original relationship began. However much I betray the relationship in feeling, thought and action, it remains with me. I no longer think of God in the anthropomorphic sense that I used to do. . . . . It is as if some power quite beyond my understanding has been doing continuous sorting of spiritual luggage, leaving me with the few basic certainties and helping me to travel light so far as theological problems are concerned.

(144, F, 58)

As I look back it seems that my whole life has been a religious experience, in the sense that my religious consciousness has grown and developed as inevitably as my body and mind.

(238, F, 75)

8(c) Sudden change to new sense of awareness: conversion, the moment of truth

In sharp contrast to the examples just considered come these in which there is a sudden realization—a revelation—of a side to the universe, whether called, as in our first example, 'the presence of God', or as in the second, 'a deep-down certainty that what I had heard was true'. Each example reveals the feeling of intense emotion expressed in terms of love or joy: 'I knew . . .', says the first, 'that he [God] loved me with a love beyond imagination' and the second, of her new life which resulted from the experience, says 'I only know that it's something that gives me tremendous joy and satisfaction'.

I had an experience seven years ago that changed my whole life. I had lost my husband six months before and my courage at the same time. I felt life would be useless if fear were allowed to govern me. One evening, with no preparation, as sudden and dynamic as the revelation to Saul of Tarsus, I knew that I was in the presence of God, and that he would never leave me nor forsake me and that he loved me with a love beyond imagination—no matter what I did. In that minute of time my life was changed. I feared nothing, and knew he was always with me.

(676, F, Age ?)

Until I was 21 I was in the 'I'm as good a Christian as any of that hypocritical mob' school of thought, until one evening the now Bishop of Woolwich, David

Shepherd, came to the hospital where I was in training as a nurse. I went to hear him, hoping I'd hear some good cricket stories. But instead I heard for the first time (consciously at least) what it meant to be a Christian. I can remember going out in a daze to my own rooms saying to myself, 'If this is true something in my life has to change.' I was clueless as to what one did on the occasion of being 'converted', and there was no Billy Graham advisers and counsellors around, so I started to read a New Testament which I had. At about 1 a.m. I knew something had happened: no voices from heaven but this kind of deep-down certainty that what I had heard was true, and that there had already been a change in me. . . . I now *am* a missionary. . . . I only know that it's something that gives me tremendous joy and satisfaction. I know that nothing except a superhuman power could have got me out here, or having got me here could keep me here.

(225, F, Age ?)

8(*d*) *Particular experiences, no growth recorded*

In contrast to the experiences described in earlier sub-categories of this section we must record some in which the effects were neither lasting nor developed. Two examples will serve as illustrations.

I was visited by such a feeling of peace, a sort of light, a feeling of joy and warmth, such as I have never ever before experienced. I am still confused and full of doubt and searching for some faith, I suppose, as much as ever . . . There have been moments when I have approached again this feeling—moments in the middle of periods of anxiety and doubt when I have wakened in the night and felt a strange sort of peace—though nothing so vivid as the one I have described.

(14, F, Age ?)

About the age of 11 or 12 I was completely won over by a mission visiting our small town. About six months after they had gone I found I had reverted completely to what I was before, and was deeply disappointed. Thereafter I was an agnostic. On July 1st, 1916 I was in the front rank to go 'over the top' in the Battle of the Somme. About 15 or 20 minutes later, having seen men killed or wounded all round me, my own apprehension by then being dulled, I became convinced there must be a God. Later I rationalized this feeling by deciding that these, my friends since 1914, were fit to go and I wasn't. Though I'm still a 'church-goer', I've never really accepted anything further, and now in my seventies I'm reverting once more to agnosticism.

(574, M, 75)

8(*e*) *Particular experiences, each contributing to growth of sense of awareness*

If the records in the last category revealed a sense of uncertainty and doubt, those in the present category show how a series of experiences contribute to a growing sense of spiritual awareness. In the first of the two examples I give we see how experiences of three quite different kinds may have the same emotional effect. Our second example in which the respondent 'was filled with a great surge of joy' that 'came instantly' is reminiscent of the examples in 7(*b*) (p. 52), but here it corroborated what the person had 'known and experienced at other rare "peak" moments' during her life.

I have become steadily more convinced that 'There's a Divinity that shapes our ends, rough hew them how we will', and experiences such as the following confirm and strengthen this view.

In my early twenties . . . in Wales, I went for a walk one evening alone. The path led up to a very narrow precipice walk along the hill's edge, and while I was there . . . the setting sun blazed out turning the whole world crimson and gold, there was a gust of wind, and I felt as if I had been swept into the very heart of all that glory and colour, taken over by something outside myself of which I was yet a part.

The same thing happened on my first visit to Chartres Cathedral. It was when I turned and saw the blue west windows hung like jewels on velvet. . . . Again I was part of some creative force outside myself, so that I could not move, and found myself shaking with the strength of my emotional response.

It does not necessarily take great scenic views or great art or architecture to induce such a state. About 14 years ago when life was difficult and I was in a state of near despair one evening, the quality of sunlight seemed to change, and this time, though the scenic beauty all round was magnificent, it was the colour and pattern of a common weed's tiny clustered flowers which I found I was really seeing for the first time, and in the contemplation of which I was again swung into that wider vision and participation.

(821, F, 63)

I was transported into what I can only term 'reality', and was filled with a great surge of joy. This was fundamental, and I was caught up into it and was a part of it. I felt a great sense of awe and reverence, permeated by the presence of a power which was completely real and in which I had my part to play. I knew that all was well and that all things were working together for good. The experience came instantly; I can't say how long it lasted. It corroborated what I have known and experienced at other rare 'peak' moments during my life.

(11, F, Age ?)

(ii) In relation to others

8(k) *Identification with ideal human figure, discipleship, hero-worship*

We see from the two examples how powerful the influence of a spiritual leader can be.

At the age of 10 I came into contact with an evangelical Christian who was then my primary school teacher. Mainly through his own force of personality he built up a large group of potential young Christians. In the years which followed a considerable proportion of these young people, myself among them, were virtually guided by him into Christianity.

(621, M, 22)

My only great wish was that in my next assignment I would be with a great Christian leader. The buoyant confident feeling in church told me that indeed this prayer was to be answered affirmatively. The result was that I work with one who has enabled me to grow, deepen and dedicate my life.

(66, F, 45)

8(*l*) *Development by personal encounter*

There is a great variety in the nature of these personal encounters as our three examples show. Regarding the first, one is perhaps tempted to adopt the cynical view that here we see the trick gambit of an ardent proselytizer; whether so or not we see the ultimate effect of the encounter. The next two examples, in complete contrast to one another, both illustrate the significance of human contacts in the development of spirituality.

I was alone one day at home when two men (Salvation Army) Officers came to visit my parents. They were new to us. On shaking hands one of them said to me, 'I hear you ought to become a Salvation Army Officer.' I was taken by surprise, because to my knowledge I had not discussed this matter with anyone. All I could say was, 'I did think about it at one time, but I don't think I want to go through with it now.' 'Well', said my Officer, 'God never makes a mistake, and if He has called you, you must obey.' For the next few weeks I was the most miserable girl alive. I was fighting my convictions. Anyway in the Watch Night service of that year I said to the Lord, 'If you want me, Lord, make me worthy, make me fit, and give me thy Holy Spirit.' And He did there and then. I will never forget the sense of freedom and power that came into my life.

(26, F, 91)

Between 10 and 13, I met my eldest uncle in London. This outwardly fierce man was nevertheless capable of being gentle. . . . two thousand years ago would have called a prophet. He used to develop moments of what could be called (wrongly) 'towering rage' . . . but I was not scared, merely in awe . . . I have seen and felt the divine force possessing and shining through him. It kindled a light in me, as also I know in my cousin. . . . . He has passed on a divine spark of life . . . knowing him was a religious experience, for in him one met a (humanly) unbearably high transmission of the Divine presence, the Shechina, the 'indwelling'.

(409, M, 33)

I have had a realization of something beyond mere earthly delight in the spontaneous caress of a child (not to be confused with sensual pleasure) or in the sudden recognition of an affinity with another person. Music and other arts can lift one into spiritual realms, but my point is that this entrance into the world of visions can be through simple, ordinary human contacts.

(63, F, 76)

8(*m*) *Participation in church, institutional, or corporate life*

There can be no doubt that the coming together for communal worship or prayer, or the meeting of kindred spirits to feel the divine presence, is for many people a powerful influence, as the following two typical examples show.

Of recent years religion has been a less personal experience but more a sense of a depth in and yet beyond myself. I became a Quaker about four years ago. Certainly in Meeting I have shared with others the Presence of God. A gathered Meeting is an awesome experience.

(100, F, 30)

In worshipping with others, this consciousness is increased by a communal sense of fusing together, as if many glowing embers were put together, so that their combined heat were to generate a living flame, leaping up towards the sun.

(238, F, 75)

8(*n*) *Development through contact with literature or the arts*

The number of people who have been influenced in the development of their spiritual life by literature and the arts, particularly the former, must indeed be large, perhaps larger than the proportion of those mentioning it in our accounts would indicate. It is likely, I think, that, whilst such influences may have had a lasting effect on many of our respondents, it is their present religious feelings that they tend to write about rather than their origin.

Entranced by Robert Bridges' anthology of poetry. Read poem after poem. Filled with sense of beauty. Suddenly a point of light appeared, distant, but intensely bright. 'It must be God' flashed into my mind. Felt I must know more about this phenomenon of light. I was no saint, therefore mystery remained unsolved. But I was left with strong conviction that God is Light and God is Beauty.

(45, F, 63)

Before I was 5, I was taken to a Sunday afternoon service at St. Mary's Cathedral. The stained glass windows, statues, the altar with its spotless linen, its candles and flowers, vied for my attention till my gaze became riveted on the huge crucifix above the rood screen, and my awe intensified when the priest, arrayed in shiny vestments, blessed us with the magnificent gold monstrance . . . When not at church I haunted museums and art galleries. On the ground floor of the Laing Art Gallery was a beutiful white marble sculpture of a reclining couple (Cupid and Psyche?). There was a rope all round but I could just touch the arch of the foot. 'God made man in his own image' comes unbidden after all these years, for in my childhood in poverty-stricken Tyneside, religion awakened my soul with its pomp and ceremony to an appreciation of beauty.

(886, F, 53)

8(*o*) *Experience essentially individualistic, involving isolation from or rejection by others*

Two examples so well indicate the nature of this category that comment is superfluous.

The first devastating flash of unusual insight occurred when I was quite a child. I remember that my mother had completely failed to comprehend something of vital importance to me. I must have been deeply hurt, then suddenly, with such power that I can still recall it, a sudden blaze of understanding took possession of my whole being; with it the conviction that I was alone, that I was a being apart, and must stand on my own. Swift, instantly upon this, was a great wave of exaltation. 'I am alone! Oh joy!' This was a lifting of the spirit which I shall never forget, so real as to be undeniable, although impossible to put into words.

(198, F, 60)

Long, slow growth punctuated by peak experiences seems best to describe my 'walk with God'. The need for, and use of, an indescribable leading outside myself and utterly unconnected with any other human being continues to characterize my life.

(52, F, Age ?)

8(r) In childhood*

I have had, especially during childhood, several experiences where I felt very strongly that a power in which I could be wholly confident was acting for and around me, even if at that time I was too little to give it a divine explanation. I already sensed the existence of God, without even thinking of him, and felt that he led us by the hand.

(845, F, Age ?)

As far back as I can remember I have never had a sense of separation from the spiritual force I now choose to call God and the natural world around me. From the age of about six to twelve in places of quiet and desolation this feeling of 'oneness' often passed to a state of 'listening'. I mean by 'listening' that I was suddenly alerted to something that was going to happen. What followed was a feeling of tremendous exaltation in which time stood still.

(786, F, Age ?)

8(s) In adolescence

Two years ago I was baptised at St. Anne's Baptist Church. This was not the culmination of a mental battle, nor the result of a sudden flash of insight. For a year I had been attending the Church, and had seen young people apparently without cares or worries, even though they, like me, were facing G. C. E. 'O' Levels. The only difference between them and me was that they were Christians, i.e. had accepted Jesus Christ as their personal Saviour. To me this sounded a hackneyed phrase, but it worked. To sum up, I tried praying, and did so for about two minutes. The result was an encompassing sense of peace, security and well-being. I will not pretend that I am a saint, I am continually doing wrong. However, when I pray, and really mean what I am saying, then I get this sense of peace. I am not what could be called a gullible person, more of a cynic in fact. Nor am I unintelligent. I got five 'O' Levels at fourteen.

(709, M, 16)

8(t) In middle age

It was when I was 48 years old, that I had my 'experience', and here I would like to emphasize that I was *not* seeking God (I thought I already had Him). I was *not* troubled or in need of a psychological or religious or any other sort of crutch or support, I had not had a traumatic experience which had thrown me off-balance (I have been given all these 'explanations')—I was fit, unconcerned, unworried and the familiar service was trundling along with its familiar lack of impact. An ancient saint, a retired missionary, was preaching on Faith and, as usual, he had my whole attention. At one point he said that faith by itself was all I'd got. He went on to illustrate.

*For explanation of absence of 8(p) and 8(q) see p. 69, line 3.

I sat there as if I'd been pole-axed. I was stunned and appalled. Suddenly I knew that for 48 years I'd been standing on the platform, I'd never even started the Christian life—more, I didn't even know what the Christian life was. Had anyone, five minutes before this, asked me 'What is Christianity?' I would confidently have said 'Christianity is the sum total of the teaching of Christ as given in the Bible.' Now I knew that definition was RUBBISH. Mark you, I didn't know what Christianity *was*, but I certainly knew what it wasn't. I don't know a single other word that was in that sermon: I went home with my mind reeling: I never said a word to my wife or the boys: I went straight up to my bedroom, shut the door, and knelt down before God and prayed saying, 'O God, forgive me for being such a FOOL all these years—but what *is* Christianity? Show me what it is, and whatever I have to do, whatever it costs, I'll go that way—but SHOW ME!' It was a prayer of total ignorance, of unconditional surrender, and I was never so sincere in my whole life.

I didn't know what had hit me: I only know that something tremendous had happened. Do you know what it was? I'd been converted.

(126, M, 63)

9. DYNAMIC PATTERNS IN EXPERIENCE

Extreme and clearly distinct examples of each of the categories in this section were not difficult to find. William James relied on striking or exceptional material of this kind to illuminate his *Varieties*. However a great number of accounts present intermediate characteristics; this is particularly noticeable when one comes to apply categories (*a*) and (*b*) below. For every one of those who will write 'it came unasked', or 'the initiative must come from the individual himself' there are several who have found it impossible to describe the encounter in such simple terms. Indeed, one of the most familiar paradoxes of Christian experience is here frequently given expression: that what appeared to be a purely human initiative seems on further reflection to be part of a far more complex and mysterious pattern. One has therefore to label the material according to these categories, as best one can.

Category (*d*) may seem unnecessary here: this form of experience seems to be covered already by 1(*d*) and 7(*i*). However it was felt that there was a place here for such accounts as seemed implicitly to negate or explicity to reject the notion of an initiative of any kind. It must also be added for good measure that some correspondents whose accounts come into this category (*d*) have also described experiences more appropriately labelled (*a*) or (*b*) thus compounding the contradictions already noted above.

We have divided this section into two sub-sections (i) for those experiences which may be deemed to be positive or constructive, and (ii) for those which are destructive.

(i) Positive or constructive patterns

9(a) Initiative felt to be beyond the self, coming 'out of the blue', grace

One night I suddenly had an experience as if I was buoyed up by waves of utterly sustaining power and love. The only words that came near to describing it were 'underneath are the everlasting arms', though this sounds like a picture, and my experience was not a picture but a feeling, and there were the arms. This I am sure has affected my life as it has made me know the love and sustaining power of God. *It came from outside and unasked.*

(356, F, 69)

About six to seven years ago, during a time of deep personal upheaval, a time when I really did not know which path to choose, I gradually came to discover that 'something' took hold of me, as it were, and I was more or less forced to act in a way not of my choosing but nevertheless one that time has shown to be the right way for me.

(458, F, 49)

9(*b*) *Initiative felt to be within the self, but response from beyond; answered prayers*

I have found prayer always helps; provided I am honest with God and ask for help in the right way—not to get out of a mess I don't like, but to be given help and strength to go through with it. My greatest insights about myself have come when I have prayed. I have been so impressed by the immense patience God seems to show. I may desert Him for years, but whenever I turn back, He always seems to be there, waiting. I think prayer is a question of leaving oneself open to any answer that my come—very often unexpected and not what one wanted, and yet it always leaves me with awe, reverence and gladness that I have made the effort. This seems to be a point: we have to make the initial effort. We are then met more than half way, but He never intrudes on us. He waits for us to approach Him.

(111, F, Age ?)

In our efforts to know the power we call God, it is only too evident to me that the desire and *the initiative MUST come from the individual himself.* Always prayer will be from the bottom of the heart, and always offered in the certainty that the answer or the power or the event will be forthcoming—when the time is ripe and not until. However, it has been my experience that *the answer will not be made available to us unless we have first prepared the way to the utmost of our ability at the time.*

(261, M, 53)

9(*c*) *Initiative and response both felt as within the self: the result seen as individuation (Jung), self-actualization (Maslow)*

Here is a category for a very small number of accounts which express religious feelings in somewhat specialized or psychological concepts. I give just one example.

Progressively, I found by experience that the little ego (conscious 'I') was only part of a more all-inclusive 'Self' with the increasing awareness that, if I would allow it, this 'Self' lived me, and lived me far more wisely than could my limited ego. At first appearing mainly as 'my' higher Self, progressively it was found to be collective in a supra-personal way—the higher one went in awareness, the more one realised that this Self was one with that of others, also with created things—with all. This is the nearest to an experience of God.

(354, F, 61)

9(d) Differentiation between initiative and response felt as illusory; merging of the self into the All; the unitive experience

The barriers began to fall and one veil after another parted in my mind. From a self-centred happiness I now wanted to share it with others, first those near me, then wider, until *everyone and everything was included*. I felt I could now help all these people, that there was nothing beyond my power—I felt omnipotent. The ecstasy deepened and intensified. I began shouting. *I knew* that all was well, that the basis of everything was goodness, that all religions and sciences were paths to this ultimate reality.

(983, M, 41)

(ii) Negative or destructive patterns

This second division of Section 9 contains some remarkable experiences of those who describe the feeling of being in the presence of an evil force. There was an average of 44.7 such examples per thousand records based upon the first 3000 received. It seems likely that the proportion of people who have such experiences may be much greater than our figures would suggest, for our appeal was for records of religious or spiritual experience rather than those of an evil nature, Glock and Stark (1965) in their Californian survey say that '32 per cent of Protestants were "sure" they had experienced a feeling of being tempted by the Devil, while 36 per cent of the Catholics were "sure".' In their taxonomy of religious experience, they draw up a classification of 'diabolic' experiences parallel to those they class as 'divine'. It must remain for future random surveys to give us more information on the proportion of the population who either believe in 'the Devil' or feel themselves in the presence of evil powers.

I can give here only one example from this single category 9(*m*), but would also refer back to another case given under 7(*q*), that of (667, M, 54) on p. 63.

9(m) Sense of external evil force as having initiative

As Archdeacon it was one of my jobs to direct young priests . . . It was our custom to say Mass every day and meditate for about half an hour afterwards. One of my curates used to meditate in his stall and I likewise in mine. There came a day when *I felt beset by an evil power like a grey cloud of evil*. After about ten minutes I could stand it no longer. I arose from my knees and went home. The second day it happened again. I got up and moved to the nave and prayed there without distraction. The third day I went back to my stall for meditation but was restless. Then my curate got up and went into the nave and knelt there, as if he was conscious of 'something' he didn't like. The next day he came to see me. He said: 'Have you been noticing anything in the Church after Mass lately?' I asked what he meant. He said: 'The Spirit of Evil. For several days I haven't been able to pray because *I felt this evil around me*.' I was very relieved to hear this, and told him of my own experience. The whole thing cleared up after a few days. Of course, in the West Indies there is a good deal of 'Obeah', Black Magic, and we were constantly having to deal with it. But on this occasion we could not relate it to any person or special happening.

(510, M, 70)

10. DREAM EXPERIENCES

We have a good number of accounts which describe experiences taking place either in dreams or other allied states of altered consciousness, such as a trance or day-dream. Not all of these are precise enough to enable us to distinguish clearly the different states involved. A few seem to come into the category of 'lucid dreams', as established by Van Eeden (1913) and thus defined by C. D. Broad (1962):

In a lucid dream, the dreamer is at the same time perfectly well aware that his physical body is asleep and quiescent, and quite differently located and oriented from the body which he is ostensibly animating in his dream. On awaking he remembers with equal distinctness both the actions of his dream-body and the simultaneous quiescence and passivity of his physical body.

Such dreams are evidently intermediate in character between the normal sleeping dream and the out-of-the-body experience, of which also we have had a number of accounts (see under 1(e), p. 35), some more precise than others. We must realize, however, that a dream may be described by the dreamer as 'lucid', when all that is meant is that it was exceptionally clear and vivid.

Clearly a proper study of this material will require a critical follow-up which should be made with many more examples. Of the importance of dreams to many of the individuals concerned as a channel of religious experience there seems to be no doubt. No analysis, however, of the different levels or states of consciousness involved is possible with the material as it stands. We must, of course, recognize that the contents of dreams cannot be regarded on the same level as those experiences that have been recorded from a fully awake condition; they may, however, give rise to new spiritual dimensions in normal conscious life, which may also be the case with 'dreams' that may occur during the state of 'unconsciousness' produced by a medical anaesthetic (see p. 95).

I will give only two examples from a very heterogeneous collection:

Three dreams were all dreamt within a week of each other. In their vividness they were quite unlike any other dreams I have ever had. They were dreamed in the late autumn of 1958, the year in which I lost my husband in the early summer . . . I was being swept along in a broad, swirling river towards the open sea. As I was being swept along I heard a quiet voice saying: 'Take hold of the rope', and beside me in the water I saw lying the end of a strong rope. 'Hold it firmly but easily', said the voice. I took hold of it in the way I had been told, and imperceptibly the raging waters became calm—or I quiet in their midst. I looked again at the rope and saw that it was no longer an end that I held; it stretched before me and behind me and I knew that I only needed to hold it in this way to be taken to the sea. I knew too that it had been there all the time. I was no longer afraid, and the waters that had before seemed so hostile sweeping me to the sea against my will, now seemed friendly. I awoke from this dream to feel that I had discovered the key to all life—the whole secret of being.

(128, F, 71)

I had a powerful lucid dream in 1965, in which I was 'dead' but only in the physical sense; in fact I was somewhere in dark space, feeling very alive indeed, and also feeling the invisible presence of 'God', whom I asked to take away everything that was inessential, but let me keep the essential. Upon which a huge storm arose, and as it buffeted 'me', I could feel that all kinds of superfluous, inessential components of my self were being blown away, as easily as dead leaves, and when the storm suddenly stopped, I felt essentially 'whole' and unharmed. It was a shattering and marvellous experience which greatly helped to remove some of my remaining fears and apprehensions.

(505, F, 46)

After this brief review of some of the examples of accounts illustrating the development and patterns of experience, we now pass on in the next chapter to consider those which show us something of their causes and effects.

6

TRIGGERS AND CONSEQUENCES

Many of our respondents tell us something of what it was that originally gave rise to their religious feelings, rather fewer tell us what have been the results of their experience in the later conduct of their lives. It is these elements in the accounts which we place in Sections 11 and 12—the last two main divisions of our classification.

11. ANTECEDENTS OR TRIGGERS OF EXPERIENCE

The divisions of this section are not exhaustive; there are few forms of experience, active or passive, which may not at some time or other give rise to feelings of a religious kind. We shall not try to list every kind of such circumstance recorded in our correspondence; the items which follow indicate the more common or striking types. Extreme examples may suggest to the dogmatic theologian that in the field of 'mystical' experience the 'sacred' is intrinsically different from the 'profane'; a wider study of the whole range of such experience makes it quite plain that such distinctions cannot be maintained. For this same reason drug-induced experiences are included in this section and not treated as a separate kind, although placed in a sub-section to themselves (ii) at the end.

(i) Antecedents other than the use of drugs

11(a) Natural beauty

The sense of wonder and joy engendered by the beauty or magnificence of the natural world has, of course, been a source of poetic inspiration since early in human history as many passages in the Psalms will testify and their message can be as meaningful today as when they were written so long ago. These feelings have often been the prelude to a religious experience as we have already seen under earlier categories such as 1(g) (p. 38), 7(o) (p. 61), and 7(v) (p. 66).

Whilst natural beauty may often have these religious effects, we must realize that not everyone who has ecstatic nature feelings will interpret them in recognizable religious terms. This is not the place to discuss at any length whether or not these experiences should in themselves be so regarded; a few words on current views, however, may not be inappropriate. Marghanita Laski in her study *Ecstasy* certainly takes the latter view. I have argued in *The Divine Flame* that, whilst not identical, there would appear to be a certain similarity between the feelings in the presence of natural beauty and those of an experience of the numinous.

This question has since been discussed in two important books by Michael Paffard. *Inglorious Wordsworths* (1973) is a study of transcendental experiences in childhood and adolescence based upon a large collection of accounts obtained by the questionnaire method. Here Paffard has an illuminating chapter discussing whether such experiences are to be regarded as religious or aesthetic; he explains why he has refused to categorize some of his respondents' answers as more genuinely transcendental than others and why he has 'been reluctant to call any of their experiences religious'. He goes on to say 'I am not hostile towards religion; indeed I hope my discussion . . . will be seen as tending not so much to secularize religious experience as to sanctify all deep transcendental experiences.' *The Unattended Moment,* (1976) is an anthology of such experiences taken from a range of autobiographies, but set within an essay of discussion; here Paffard draws attention to the feelings of some artists:

Sir William Rothenstein wrote in his recollections, *Men and Memories*, that 'one's very being seems to be absorbed into the fields, trees and the walls one is striving to paint' and believed the experience of painting out of doors gave him insight into the poetry of the great mystics, European and Eastern. 'At rare moments while painting,' he says, 'I have felt myself caught, as it were, in a kind of cosmic rhythm; but such experiences are usually all too brief.' Ben Nicholson is, perhaps, saying the same thing more laconically when he is quoted in a monograph on his work as remarking, 'As I see it, painting and religious experience are the same thing.'

Whilst I have thought it well, at this point, to touch briefly on this question of whether these feelings for nature are religious or not, we are here not actually concerned with an answer to this problem for we are only considering the extent to which natural beauty may give rise to experiences which the respondents themselves, in submitting them, have regarded as of a religious nature.

As a child in the country, I wandered by myself sometimes but was rather afraid when I became conscious of solitude and silence. I became increasingly aware of a Presence which I associated with nature around me. In my adolescence I gave It the name 'God', and aimed at being alone to commune with It.

Natural beauty and vastness has always aroused an attitude of worship in me, at times in spite of myself. The words of Psalm 8 have often been in my mind: 'When I consider the heavens, the work of they fingers, the moon and stars which thou hast ordained, what is man that thou are mindful of him. and the son of man that thou visitest him?' This attitude persists and is enhanced by the discoveries of the astronauts.

(603, F, 63)

11(*b*) Sacred places

The accounts which attribute spiritual feelings to the influence of sacred places are relatively few in our collection, with an average of only 26 per thousand in the first 3000 as compared with 123 per thousand in regard to natural beauty. They are experiences which embrace an important element in Otto's concept of the numinous; their nature can best be described in the words of some of our respondents themselves:

Another example of the numinous is the atmosphere at the Grotto of Lourdes. The strongest feeling of this state of mind was not when the place was thronged with pilgrims, though that was immensely impressive but early one misty morning when there were only a few people praying at the Grotto, and a visiting priest saying his early morning mass, in the open air, at the Altar before the spot where the Mother of God spoke to Bernadette. This was a moment for ever imprinted on my mind as being beatific, other worldly, one's whole being at peace. All the time I spent in Lourdes very happily, the feeling of being drawn to the Grotto was like the attraction of metal to a magnet. This feeling was remarked on by many other people who had visited Lourdes. It is a state which I have never experienced before, but which I think of as having been on holy ground.

(512, F, Age ?)

In 1943, at the age of 28, I was a sergeant in the British Army of the Middle East enjoying leave in Palestine. I made Jerusalem my centre. . . . Bitterly disappointed [after being hurried with tourists through the Church of the Holy Sepulchre] I made my solitary way across the Brook Kedron and ascended the other side towards Gethsemane, hardly knowing or caring where I went. I sat down in the Garden, which was completely deserted. Gradually peace returned to me, and I was suddenly conscious of a Presence. For how long I sat there I do not know, but this I know: Our Lord was surely present with me. I left the Garden of Gethsemane with a serene feeling of happiness . . .

(311, M, 54)

My third example is one sent by a university professor who tried to rationalize the process but has failed to find his explanation satisfactory. He is describing a visit to Fountains Abbey in Yorkshire, and in passing I might say how similar are his words on viewing the ruins to those used by another respondent (quoted under 2(*b*) on p. 40) in regard to Rievaulx Abbey who said 'I sensed a wonderful atmosphere of quiet peace.'

Whilst I was looking towards the ruins of the Abbey I felt a great sense of peace as though I saw myself in the flow of history and knew where I fitted in to it. Soon I was beginning to rationalise the feeling and see how I was being affected by the site and by the former magnificence of the buildings, and my historical imagination investing the area with activity and with people of past centuries. But even so I was not fully satisfied with my explanations to myself and I felt that the devotions of hundreds of religious people has somehow coalesced to give a corporate holiness to the place. It was this holiness, in the sense of wholeness, to which I briefly felt attuned as though I were really in touch with Life in all its continuity and purpose. I could not define that purpose nor see the end nor could I define my role in the working out of the purpose, but I was certain it was there and knew I had a part in it.

(853, M, 47)

11(c) Participation in religious worship

There are many accounts of the effects of corporate worship; I will give just one example.

There were about 6 or 8 ladies present, mainly middle-aged, myself—the only young person—and the man who was leading. We sang a hymn, then went to pray, and while he was praying I became aware of something right beside me—so close that I felt if I put out my hand I could almost have touched it. I knew instinctively that it was the Spirit of God. The little service went quietly on, and all the time the Spirit remained there beside me, until the final prayer, when it seemed to go just as quietly as it had come. Then the leader said 'I have been aware of the Spirit among us tonight, has anyone else felt it too?'—and everyone acknowledged that they too had been aware of it. This fact confirmed to me that I had not been imagining it, as it was felt simultaneously by a small number of people of varying age and background.

(125, F, Age ?)

11(d) Prayer and meditation

Naturally there are many examples describing the effects of prayer or meditation, but I need not discuss them here because they have been the subject of a special study both by Michael Walker and Timothy Beardsworth which I summarize in the next chapter (pp. 117 and 119). I will give just one example here.

I felt myself confronted with a situation which made me quite unable to cope with the various positions and problems I had to face. I realized, of course, that after such a long spell in hospital and not being a hundred per cent fit had a very great bearing on this, but even taking this into account I became so convinced of my utter inability to do the work required of me as a Methodist Minister, that I resolved to resign from the Ministry and to seek some other employment. After this had been in my mind for some ten days or so, one morning when I entered my office I had the experience of hearing a voice say to me 'What a fool you are, you seem to be leaving God out of everything.' The result was that I spent the next three hours in prayer without interruption. For me it was a time of complete healing and cleansing and assurance and never from that time have I had the slightest doubt of the sufficiency of God to deal with any little problem I might be concerned with either personally or in my work.

(231, M, 61)

11(e) Music

There can be no doubt about the influence of music in moving people to emotional experience of many different kinds: martial music carrying soldiers into war, the Marseillaise exciting the flames of social revolution, 'Land of Hope and Glory' evoking love of one's mother country or yet again operatic strains suggesting the feelings of romantic love. It is not surprising then that for a number of people profound religious feeling may be more powerfully generated by music than by the spoken word; nevertheless we have found only an average of 57 accounts per thousand in this category in the first 3000 records.

I was sitting one evening, listening to a Brahms Symphony. My eyes were closed, and I must have become completely relaxed, for I became aware of a feeling of 'expansion', and seemed to be beyond the boundary of my physical self. Then an intense feeling of 'light' and 'love' uplifted and enfolded me. It was so wonderful, and gave me such an emotional release, that tears streamed down my cheeks. For several days I seemed to bathe in its glow, and when it subsided, I was free from my fears.

(71, F, Age ?)

A friend persuaded me to go to Ely Cathedral to hear a performance of Bach's B Minor Mass. I had heard the work, indeed I knew Bach's choral works pretty well. I was sitting towards the back of the nave. The Cathedral seemed to be very cold. The music thrilled me . . . until we got to the great SANCTUS. I find this experience difficult to define. It was primarily a warning. I was frightened. I was trembling from head to foot, and wanted to cry. Actually I think I did. I heard no 'voice' except the music; I saw nothing; but the warning was very definite. I was not able to interpret this experience satisfactorily until I read—some months later—Rudolf Otto's 'Das Heilige'. Here I found it—the 'Numinous'. I was before the Judgement Seat. I was being 'weighed in the balance and found wanting'. This is an experience I have never forgotten.

(510, M, 70)

I was 17 then, and I was listening to a concert given by the Third Ear Band, whose music is based on the constant repetition and interaction of musical phrases set to a very constant rhythm . . . At first my eyes went out of focus. They slowly closed. I felt my whole consciousness swirl about inside my head in one violent convulsion, and when it stopped I was much more intent in my mind . . . I had a very deep understanding of the motions of the music, and a sudden sense of affinity of purpose between it and myself, though not an identification with it. My mind even withdrew further until I realized a complete division between my person—the mind—and what I now term my soul—the void . . . I had a representative image of my mind and this rapidly decreased in size until it was less than a pinpoint, leaving only the infinite void of my soul . . . I had a tremendously invigorating realization that my bounds as a human being were infinite . . . This experience has led me to realize the intrinsic wealth of everything in nature. I often feel that, say, a stone lying on a footpath is just as important to everything that is going on as I am.

(662, M, 18)

11(*f*) *Visual art*

Painters, etchers, and sculptors can all communicate deep spiritual feelings which may engender a sense of rapture in others. A work of art need not be concerned with a 'sacred' subject to bring this about, some quite simple natural scene may evoke great emotion in the onlooker, who may then find this difficult to put into words. Those who are moved by visual art need not necessarily be able to appreciate music to the full and vice versa. But both artists and musicians are *expressing the ineffable*. This tacit knowledge which comes to us through their skill and inspiration is on another level to that which comes to us through the spoken or written word. Artists and musicians have the remarkable gift of communicating *direct* to the spiritual level of those who are able to receive it. The mystic, on the other hand, has to try to translate his subjective vision into explicit words and complains that he cannot so express it and then the recipient has in turn to reconvert the message back into his own world of emotional feeling. Undoubtedly much is lost or distorted in this process of double translation.

What is it that the artist is doing? Those who lack the insight are often unable to appreciate why a landscape painting by a true artist is something quite different from the best possible colour photograph taken from the same position. The artist is not, of course, striving to give the most exact pictorial representation of the scene in front of him, but is attempting to convey what it is about that scene that moves him to paint it; he is, in a sense, making a caricature of it which emphasizes some features and plays down others in his attempt to express his deeper feelings, and no camera can do that. There is a modern fashion that runs down what is said to be 'representational art' as if it were simply trying to reproduce what is objectively there; if that were so, it would not be art at all.

Relevant to the second example I give below is a quotation from Aldous Huxley in his *The Doors of Perception*, p. 37, on the spiritual nature of visual art:

In China the rise of landscape painting to the rank of a major art form took place about a thousand, in Japan about six hundred and in Europe about three hundred years ago. The equation of Dharma-Body with hedge* was made by those Zen Masters, who wedded Taoist naturalism with Buddhist transcendentalism. It was, therefore, only in the Far East that landscape painters consciously regarded their art as religious. In the West religious painting was a matter of portraying sacred personages, of illustrating hallowed texts. Landscape painters regarded themselves as secularists. To-day we recognize in Seurat one of the supreme masters of what may be called mystical landscape painting.

I must not be misunderstood and thought to be implying that all art is conveying spiritual messages of beauty and benign feeling; it may be just as powerful as music can be in conveying the horrors of war or stirring the human spirit to revolt. This, however, is not the place to launch into an essay on the emotional powers of visual art; here I am only trying to show how it may be an important antecedent to spiritual feeling. I give two examples, one from each of two different types of experience.

*This phrase was explained by Huxley earlier in his book (p. 13) as follows: 'I remembered a passage I had read in one of Suzuki's essays. "What is the Dharma-Body of the Buddha?" (The Dharma-Body of the Buddha is another way of saying Mind, Suchness, the Void, the Godhead.) The question is asked in a Zen monastery by an earnest and bewildered novice. And with the prompt irrelevance of one of the Marx Brothers, the Master answers, 'The hedge at the bottom of the garden.'

One day for a change I went into Birmingham Art Gallery where there were many beautiful things to see. I loved the pictures, but when I entered the room which had many famous religious pictures, I felt that I wanted to worship. However, the picture which attracted me most just then was one of the smaller ones. (I can't say the name of the artist.) It was a picture of Jesus looking very tired sitting on a wall which surrounded a well, and the Samaritan woman with her water pot. In my mind I recalled the story with which I was familiar, and then there came a wonderful peace and joy into my heart. I thought *He* knew all about that woman, and He knows me in a way that no other person does. He promised to give that woman living water, which would be a well of water springing up into Eternal Life, so then standing there I asked Him to give me Eternal Life. From that moment I had the assurance that life would be eternal . . .

(176, F, 80)

At certain periods of my life I have found the visual arts have had a considerable effect upon me. Chinese painting which to me expresses some of my deepest feelings with regard to nature (with its ability to give the slightest hint of mist on the mountain, so that life is caught and held for a moment of time), makes it for me a truly spiritual work as against the static affirmative painting of the renaissance.

(651, M, 46)

11(*g*) *Literature, drama, films*

Literature, especially poetry, can, of course, like art and music, be the transmitter of emotions which may spark off a burning spiritual experience in the reader. Whilst art and music have this advantage over the spoken word in being able to communicate direct to the recipient's consciousness, poetry lies between the two in that there is 'music' in the words which may have a direct effect in carrying the feelings that the poet is intending to evoke in addition to the actual meaning of the words employed.

Drama, too, has had a long influence. Little of today's drama is specifically religious, yet there are many moments in the modern theatre that are capable of kindling religious feeling. Bernard Shaw, in spite of his so frequently paraded cynicism, was a profoundly religious man as can be seen in his *Saint Joan* and *Back to Methuselah*. In the 1970s some found *Godspell* a deeply spiritual experience; two highly intellectual sisters, well know to me, went together to see this play and one was so moved that tears ran down her cheeks whilst the other could not imagine what her sister saw in it.

Here is one example of literature sparking off a spiritual experience:

We were brought up to fear and obey God. All the emphasis was on obedience and the dire consequences of sin. Little was heard of Jesus Christ and his love for mankind. The more menacing passages of the Gospels were quoted often— the separation of the sheep and the goats, the torments of Dives etc. In my early teens I somehow came across Sir John Seeley's 'Ecce Homo' and in one single reading all the old fear and dread were banished, transformed into a sudden joy, Life got a new and rapturous zest because oneself and every person we met, however, unimportant, or dull or poor or boring or disagreeable had a divine spark within and were capable of becoming something worthwhile to God. Chapter XIV 'The enthusiasm of humanity' was particularly inspiring. This love of people has remained as fresh as ever to this day, and has been of inestimable value in medical work, as well as in social and domestic life.

(628, F, (a doctor), 78)

11(*h*) *Creative work*

Ben Nicholson wrote: 'As I see it, painting and religious experience are the same thing'. D. H. Lawrence in his essay on 'Making Pictures' in *Selected Essays* (1950), wrote:

It needs a certain purity of spirit to be an artist, of any sort, the motto which should be written over every School of Art is: 'Blessed are the pure in spirit, for theirs is the kingdom of heaven' . . . This is the beginning of all art, visual or literary or musical: be pure in spirit. It isn't the same as goodness. It is much more difficult and nearer the divine. The divine isn't only good, it is all things. . . . Art is a form of religion, minus the Ten Commandments business, which is sociological. Art is a form of supremely delicate awareness and atonement— meaning at-one-ness, the state of being at one with the object. But is the great atonement in delight?—for I can never look on art save as a form of delight.

Among the small proportion of the population who are creative artists there may be many who regard their work as a spiritual experience. There are sixty- two such examples in our first three thousand records of which we give three. These are people who have the same feelings as those expressed by Ben Nicholson and D. H. Lawrence, but it occurs, of course, not only with painters, but with writers, and particularly poets, as the last of our three examples shows.

Religion and music were a part of my inspiration, the other was the close contact with nature itself. These things were to be the basic block-building of a story which was to carry me into the unknown and involvement in a task of which the odds were so heavily against me. As time went on, with a great deal of self denial and self discipline I began to feel nearer to God with paint and brushes in my hand than at any other time. This was very apparent to me as I went on. It was as if God himself was my driving force and inspiration.

(2939, M, 37)

The practice of art helps me to realize the utter relatedness of all things and all beings. The act of the creative experience is for me one of a peak experience (in Maslow's terms) or perhaps religious if defined in the more traditional way. I feel that often I am the duct through which the creation of art flows. If I am receptive the flow is great. If I am conscious of what others will think, or conscious of self- criticism, . . . then the creative flow is lessened and sometimes is just junk.

There is a point in the creative experience that is reached when I am no longer the creator, but the means by which creation is accomplished. It is difficult to put into words. It is as if I were creating, but that also I was standing back and watching the creation take place . . . both at the same time.

This is a thrilling feeling. This is why I am an artist.

(85, F, 40)

Poetry is just not an airy flight into the clouds around ivory towers. To use the bluntest prose, it is a precision instrument. I had already experienced the heights of aesthetic, humanist and religious feeling in communion with poets: now I made the crucial experiment.

I found an intensity of religious experience in writing my verses which increased to the point that at times they wrote themselves. More, they illuminated what had been obscure, they attained horizons undreamt of, and they had a validity independent of the *emotional* appeal of a sunset or a Mozart concerto.

(1873, M, Age ?)

11(*i*) *Physical activity*

We have only a few records to place in this category and only in some of these, as in our first example, would physical activity appear to be the stimulating factor; in others, as in our second example, it is difficult to say whether in fact it was the physical work that set off the experience or whether it was only coincidental with an experience which might have occurred had the person not been taking such exercise.

To amuse myself I write a great deal, mainly poetry or fiction, and I play classical music. When I am engaged in such tasks I am often 'taken out of myself' and feel hypermanic about the activity I am engaged upon and its wider implications and interactions. Similar experiences can occur in many activities. I have often felt that way when partaking in some physical exercise—cross-country running, boating, playing squash, climbing a mountain, exploring a cave. Much of my research involves field-work and visits to archaeological sites, excavation, and so on, and when I am undertaking such work on my own I am often assailed by such feelings of 'being a part of something Other/Bigger/Wider'.

(1996, M, 28)

One day I was sweeping the stairs down in the house in which I was working, when suddenly I was overcome, overwhelmed, saturated, no word is adequate, with a sense of most sublime and living LOVE. It not only affected me, but seemed to bring everything around me to LIFE. The brush in my hand, my dustpan, the stairs, seemed to come alive with love. I seemed no longer me, with my petty troubles and trials, but part of this infinite power of love, so utterly and overwhelmingly wonderful that one knew at once what the saints had grasped. It could only have been a minute or two, yet for that brief particle of time it seemed eternity.

(1753, F, Age ?)

11(*j*) *Relaxation*

In contrast to physical activity, some of our respondents relate their spiritual experience to a peaceful relaxation; it would seem as if the cutting off of physical exertion had the effect—to borrow a metaphor from William James—of opening the subliminal doors to 'a wider world of being than that of our everyday conscious.' I give two examples:

When I was at boarding school, lying on the Sussex Downs while the others were on the beach, I experienced an inrush of joy which transformed my whole attitude to my life and the school. Whereas I had been timid I was now confident, this was, with one of two lapses, a lasting effect. When my son was little he painted me a Christmas card giving the spirit of this experience without my ever having told him about it. However he knew the same downs.

(612, F, 60)

When I was around 47 I was floating on my back in the swimming pool in the back yard all alone and completely relaxed. Suddenly it was like a channel or pipe line from me to someone or something. I felt so safe, secure and completely unafraid. I didn't think too much about it at the time but the next several years my life was uprooted and I had a trying time readjusting. I believe this incident helped me to get through. It was like a warning that things would change and I wasn't alone to face it. I prayed a lot and things did work out.

(134, F, 54)

11(k) Sexual relations

A very small number of accounts may be placed in this category. What I have just said above, in the second paragraph relating to relaxation, applies here equally well. The doubt as to whether the experience should be regarded as religious is indeed expressed by the agnostic writer of the first of the two examples I give; nevertheless she goes on to relate how it 'opened the door' to a later recognition of what she evidently regards as a religious concept.

Still agnostic. (You may consider this ecstatic rather than religious.) Experiencing deep emotion when making love (to the man who is now my husband). A strong feeling of darkness—darkness which seemed the very womb of Time. Convinced that over the aeons we had always loved each other. A strong impression of 'the Eternal Now', which opened the door to a later recognition of the truth of reincarnation.

(45, F, 63)

(Aged 21) I fell in love with a married woman with whom I worked, so vital, so sexy, always seeking love, sex, men (her husband turned a blind eye as he did not want to lose her finally to her other lovers). The desire for her grew and battled with my sense of honour—a terrible longing, but at the same time I had a compassion for her husband and also some element of fear of being exposed by another woman at work who rather fancied me. After about a week of this pain of longing and fighting to 'do the right thing' etc., at a bus stop, the longing was displaced by a Substance that pervaded everything as well as being a part of myself, a Divine Essence because in it I could see the source of all love, beauty, goodness, wisdom, sex-appeal that the ordinary world could offer. It was more 'real' than world-real things, more substantial than matter/substance. . . .

(3038, M, 44)

11(l) Happiness

The number of accounts in this category is artificially small because we have only included those which have actually used the word 'happiness' to describe what triggered off their spiritual experience; from what we saw in the previous chapter, among the cognitive and affective experiences, the number would be very much larger if we included all those relating to a sense of joy, well-being, and other synonyms for happiness.

As a child, between the ages of approximately seven and ten, I had from time to time an experience which in retrospect I find difficult to describe and the nature of which I was never able to convey adequately, though I did try to do so, to my mother, and to one or two close companions. It was, in effect, a flash of extreme happiness, as sense of complete well-being, which invaded my consciousness *from the outside.* I write, a 'flash' of happiness, because the ecstasy itself was momentary, though sometimes at least, (I am not sure if always), I felt its approach, and it left a glow of contented feeling during which I longed passionately to be *good.* I loved, consciously. The mood was not maintained, of course. I fell from grace continually, but at those times, I knew that everything was conceived in goodness, and that only loving enough mattered.

(501, F, 63)

I am aware of a sort of 'consciousness' outside my own. I sense it . . . when I am in a state of happiness and well-being, and I feel there is a 'presence' whose hand I should like to grasp in affection and gratitude.

(670, F, 54)

11(*m*) *Depression, despair*

States of depression or of mental illness may, it appears, form the background for development in the spiritual lives of those concerned. I say 'it appears' because it is difficult to see how such a state *in itself* could be the trigger for the reported change; on a closer look it would seem that something deeper was going on, something which came to the surface in the state of depression and altered the life of the person. In our first example the emotional weeping and the desperate attempt at prayer would seem most likely to have been the real cause; in the second case perhaps it was the physical relaxation in the bath which caused a relief from the oppressive grief and allowed thoughts from the sub-conscious to well up and bring about the change.

The number of people who have come to find a greater spiritual awareness through states of depression forms indeed a relatively large proportion. I give two examples:

At one time I reached utter despair and went and prayed God for mercy instinctively and without faith in reply. That night I stood with other patients in the grounds waiting to be let in to our ward. It was a very cold night with many stars. Suddenly someone stood beside me in a dusty brown robe and a voice said 'Mad or sane you are one of My sheep'. I never spoke to anyone of this but ever since it has been the pivot of my life. I realise that the form of the vision and the words I heard were the result of my education and cultural background but the voice though closer than my own heartbeat was entirely separate from me.

(446, F, 54)

My husband died on 6 September 1968 and for nearly a year afterwards I was extremely depressed and nothing, just nothing, could console me. One morning whilst sitting in my bath, too depressed to think of anything at all, there suddenly came into my mind a brilliant golden hue, the like of which I had never seen before, and at its base there was a small black spot about the size of a pinhead. For what must have been a few seconds I felt very frightened until at last I seemed to realise that it was my husband. I cried out to him and at once the beautiful golden hue slowly faded away and I have not seen it since. This is all that happened but it left me with a great peace of mind and a conviction that all is well. I also think that my faith has become much stronger as a result of this experience.

(2389, F, 64)

11(*n*) *Illness*

What may be said regarding this category is, I think, very much the same as what was said under the previous one. The state of illness would appear to present the opportunity for the spiritual change to take place, rather than to be in itself the cause.

I was abroad in the mountains alone in a Pension except that I had made friends with one of four missionaries staying there. I went down to visit my doctor who took me at once to a surgeon—they both suspected cancer and advised immediate operation. I was to go to the Nursing Home next day and because of the trains had to leave the Pension at midday. I only had time to put my affairs in order and had no time for fearful anticipation but I did tell my missionary friend. She asked if she might tell the others and said 'We shall all be praying for you.' After the rush I had had getting off I dreaded the long time of waiting alone in the Home for the operation. To my surprise on getting into bed I immediately found myself surrounded by an almost tangible warmth, light and blissful peace and lay and basked in this really heavenly state for some hours. I had no fear of the operation at any time. It was only afterwards that I realised it must have been the prayers of my friends supporting me.

(683, F, 73)

In addition to this example I would refer the reader back to another, No. 614, given under category 2(*d*) on p. 41, which can just as well be used to illustrate the present section.

11(*o*) *Childbirth*

It is perhaps the physical and emotional strain surrounding childbirth, rather than the act of childbirth itself, which triggers off a change of feeling. Nevertheless I have a few examples of spiritual experience which was felt to be the direct outcome of the stress of childbirth: I quote two of them:

During the difficult birth of my only son, I called on God to let me die. Suddenly, I was in a vast space, with someone I appeared to know, and love. There was just a presence, nothing was to be seen. However, in some way I was made to understand that death was not yet for me. I saw a long passage, the figures of my husband and mother, and I knew I was needed by them. I remember thinking

'Ah, this is what it is all about, at death we go forward in time, and this business of living on earth is just a game, like small children playing at house.' I remember being very reluctant to leave this 'being'. I was told six weeks later that I had 'nearly had it' that particular night.

(1660, F, 53)

This experience came to me during the birth of my first son. I had a difficult labour, but half-way through, I distinctly saw the figure of Christ near my bed-side. I was fully conscious at the time. It is unforgettable, even though this was over 30 years ago. This figure was seen as though through a light mist with one hand slightly raised, and faded after a short space of time.

(2940, F, 66)

11(p) *The prospect of death*

There can be no doubt that the realization that one is likely to die in a relatively short time must indeed have a marked effect upon one's immediate outlook. We all know the celebrated saying of Samuel Johnson: 'Depend upon it, Sir, when a man knows he is to be hanged in a fortnight it concentrates his mind wonderfully.' Most of the cases we have in our collection concern the reactions of those who have been told they have, or have imagined that they have, a fatal disease; we see how differently people may react and how various their spiritual experience may be. I give two examples:

When I was 22 I became ill. The Doctors could not find out what was the matter, and as weeks passed and I became worse instead of better, I became desperately worried, convinced I had cancer, and was going to die. I reached a climax of panic in Church one night, when I realised the horror and loneliness of what I was now sure I should have to go through . . . At this time our Fellowship leader set us to do a piece of bible study each, for which purpose he lent me William Barclay's commentary on the letters of the 7 churches, in Revelation. I happened to be reading this during a lengthy wait in the Doctor's surgery, and I was forcibly struck by the way in which the early Christians were sustained through terrible sufferings, privation and persecution. Christ was alive to them, and very powerful, enabling them to bear everything joyfully, and it suddenly came to me that this same Christ was alive and powerful now, and I need no longer bear everything alone. I realised it didn't matter what I suffered, because He would be with me, giving me strength and courage. I decided to put myself into God's hands, with regard to the illness. I therefore went in to the Doctor and told him I felt fine (totally untrue) and would like to return to work, and he signed me off with a sigh of relief. I reasoned that either I would get better, or I'd get much worse and be rushed to hospital, either way, it would be God's will for my life, and I would be happy. That same afternoon, sitting out in the sunshine, I had an overwhelming conviction of God's love for me, and I responded in the only way that seemed possible, by making God the most important person in my life, and living only for Him.

(2361, F, 26)

15 years ago I had all the signs and symptoms of cancer of the colon. I spent half a Friday at St. Mary's and the specialist said 'It is difficult to think of any other

possible diagnosis which fits the facts.' There was to be a final test on the Monday. I left St. Mary's and took a walk to Marble Arch and along Oxford Street. I was startled by the brilliance of the colours of the street. Several people looked at me and smiled (They saw the deep peace on my face). I spent a weekend of deepest happiness. All my worries disappeared.—'I should be dead in 6 months.' I truly for once took no anxious thought. On the Monday the test proved that I had nothing seriously wrong and by the end of the week my brow was furrowed again.

(569, M, 70)

11(*q*) *The death of others*

We have a fair number of records in which the respondents have had a spiritual experience, often extremely vivid, brought on by the death of someone very dear to them. I need only give one example.

I had received an emergency call to my husband's bedside; he was dying of cancer. 'The end is near,' the nurse said, and drew curtains round the bed. I sat beside the bed in utter desolation—the worst moments I have ever known. There was a moving shadow as the breathing stopped, and then I lifted my eyes. Above the bed there was a shadow, but as I turned my head there was a soft glow, like a light in fog, and moving 'ticker-tape' letters forming into the three words:— TRUST IN GOD. Then it faded, the nurse came, and it was all over. I walked home from the hospital, and it was as if balm had been poured on a gaping wound.

(4, F, Age ?)

11(*r*) *Crisis in personal relations*

Here again we see periods of deep emotional stress leading to spiritual experience; and again I will give only one example.

I had been happily married for some fifteen years, when things started to change. My husband started to get dissatisfied with his work and it affected our home, as well as our relations. My children were growing up and I had to find something to do with my time, so I started to attend the adult night school. The second year at school I fell deeply in love with the teacher. Never, had I felt such a closeness to a human. This teacher knew of my feelings, and declared his to me. I told him I couldn't have an affair with him, he grew angry with me, and told me he was coming for me. . . . I knew that if I would be unfaithful to my vows I would never be able to live, to me, it would be worse than death. I knew that I had to go back to that class room and face this man. . . . Arriving that night, I was so terribly frightened, but I did make it to my seat. I was so weak that I could hardly sit up. He told me to turn to a certain page in the typing book. . . . The page contained an excerpt from Ernest Hemingway's 'The Old man and the Sea'.
    'Man was not made for defeat, he can be destroyed but not defeated.'
    . . . All weakness left me, and I felt thunder in my veins. At that moment I had the power of the Universe at my finger tips. I looked up at him, he grew terribly white, and scared. He was a man of questionable character, and had many affairs in his life. He wanted to add me to his long list of conquests. But it wasn't to be. As I looked at him, I could feel a power sitting alongside of me, telling me when

to look at him. Four years have passed since then . . . I do act and say things that I shouldn't, for I know better. God has shown me himself beyond any doubt. It has enriched my life and turned it completely around. I am no longer afraid of anything.

(42, F, Age ?)

11(s) *Silence, solitude*

A single example will illustrate the nature of the category.

I spent one week by myself in the cottage when I was fifty years old. During that week I experienced insights and inner flights of consciousness that would have been impossible to undergo in any other circumstances. The aloneness, the changing weather, and the grandeur of hillside and hurrying cloud so impressed my mind that my thought took flight. The turmoil of my mind was subdued, and my life rested in tranquillity . . . I was alone in retreat for a brief spell, reunited with a nature of heartbreak and searing beauty. I climbed the hill towards the sea, mindful of my fifty years, conscious of my intellect confounded, and my self a broken reed. Yet aware, so poignantly aware, of a reality which bound me to truth and locked me in unity with all life. In the moment of revelation there is no past or future, and it seemed my life was welded into one whole present as I reached the top of the hill and leant forward against the salty sea wind.

(500, F, Age ?)

(ii) The effects of drugs as the triggers of experience

We have so far received surprisingly few accounts of experiences resulting from the taking of drugs. We may divide them into those which are anaesthetic in the medical sense and those which are psychedelic, i.e. resulting from drugs taken with the express purpose of producing experiential effects. The two categories are, of course, fundamentally different from one another: the examples of experiences obtained under medical anaesthesia are really of the nature of dreams, whereas those obtained with psychedelic drugs are due to altered states of consciousness which occur when the subject is fully awake.

11(w) *Drugs: anaesthetic*

Several of these anaesthetic experiences are closely akin to those classed as 'lucid dreams' which we have discussed above (p. 79); and just as they often seem to merge into 'out-of-the-body' experiences, so among these accounts of anaesthetic effects there are some which do indeed describe very similar feelings. I will not, however, include such examples here, but give one which the respondent calls an 'anaesthetic revelation', for it shows how such a dream may act as the antecedent of a continuing experience in later conscious life.

A number of years ago, as a result of a dental extraction under anaesthetic I was privileged to enjoy what I now know can be termed an 'anaesthetic revelation' (although at the time I was an agnostic and read nothing of mysticism nor had any conception of such direct experience). From that time I have never wavered in my certainty of God's existence; all fear of death vanished and the world lost much of its reality. While still enjoying life I was conscious of its quality of impermanence, like a dream from which one would awake. At the later date, after much thought, prayer and reading I gained a more complete perception of a divine presence within, this time while in full possession of my faculties.

(384, F, Age ?)

11(x) *Drugs: psychedelic*

To what extent, if any, may the deliberate taking of drugs lead to a truly mystical experience? This is indeed a controversial question, one to which two widely contrasting answers have been given.

To illustrate this opposition we may take the late Professor R. C. Zaehner on the one hand and Aldous Huxley on the other. The contrast is conveniently made for us by Zaehner who opens his book *Mysticism: Sacred and Profane* with an attack upon Huxley for the views he expressed in *The Doors of Perception*:

It is, of course, a well-known fact that certain drugs,—and among them one may include alcohol,—modify the normal human consciousness and produce what can literally be called ec-static states,—states in which the human ego has the impression that it escapes from itself and 'stands outside' itself. Indian hemp and hashish have long been used in the East to produce precisely such a result. In the West, however, it has never been taken for granted that such states are necessarily associated with religion, while in the East there have always been sober spirits who regarded such 'religion surrogates' with the gravest suspicion. Mr. Huxley appears to have no such scruples, for he implies unmistakably that what he experienced after taking mescalin was explicable in terms of 'contemplation at its height'. (Cf. *The Doors of Perception*, p. 31.) Herein lies the importance of Mr. Huxley's thesis; praeternatural experience, whether produced by drugs or not, is equated with specifically religious experience.

Zaehner goes on to make a sharp distinction between religious or *sacred* mysticism and what he calls 'nature mysticism' which he would exclude from the field of spiritual experience; he further links the psychedelic experiences with those of the nature mystics and, similarly denying their religious value, classes them together as *profane*. The contrast between what he believes to be these two very different kinds of mysticism is, of course, the subject of his book. But how valid are his views? In regard to nature mysticism Michael Paffard in his *Inglorious Wordsworths* (p. 39) has clearly shown that Zaehner's reading of Wordsworth is at fault. He has more to say (on p. 208) in regard to Zaehner's views:

He is at pains to counter Huxley's suggestion that mescalin-induced experience could have the same value and significance as the experiences of the acknowledged mystics. He gives an entertaining account of his own largely disagreeable experiences under the influence of mescalin and argues that the pseudo-transcendental states induced by using such drugs, which affect the nervous system and chemistry of the body, must be fundamentally different from the gratuitous grace of God-given transcendental experiences occurring without chemical stimulus. He does not appear to me to have seen how double-edged his argument is: that the sensory deprivation, fasting and more drastic mortifications of the flesh practised by many of his acknowledged mystics may affect the chemistry of the body in very much the same way as do mescalin and other hallucinants.

This indeed was the view expressed some years earlier by that brilliant experimentalist the late Dr Walter N. Pahnke (1967). Pahnke was not trying, as some people would seem quite erroneously to have imagined, to debunk the religious side of mysticism by showing that almost exactly the same effects could be produced by drugs; on the contrary, he was a theological graduate of the Havard Divinity School who then took a medical degree and specialized in psychiatry with the express purpose of investigating the physiological conditions which facilitated the occurrence of mystical states. Pahnke was a profoundly religious man, as I soon discovered when I spent a day with him at his laboratory at Baltimore in the autumn of 1968. It should not worry us if it is shown that altered states of consciousness may be produced by chemical means; the chemicals themselves do *not* produce the divine ecstasy, but affect the brain in such a way that a rarely accessible region of the sub-conscious mind becomes available to those who already have, perhaps unknown to them, a mystical streak within them. They discover new depths within themselves. Let me now quote two passages from a joint paper by Pahnke and Richards (1966). On page 193 they say:

On the basis of [these] research findings ... it now appears possible to select almost any normal, healthy person and, combining a sufficient dose of a psychedelic substance with a supportive set and setting, enable that person to experience various altered forms of consciousness. The mystical experience seems the most difficult to facilitate, perhaps because of the as yet undetermined roles of personality variables; but nonetheless, these phenomena are now sufficiently reproducible to allow mysticism to be studied scientifically under laboratory conditions. Thus at long last, research into mysticism need no longer be limited to the scholarly scrutiny of various devotional or metaphysical documents left behind by such historic personages as Shankara, Plotinus, Meister Eckhart, William Blake, and Teresa of Avila. Persons can be studied extensively both before and after the experience of mystical consciousness in controlled settings.

Pahnke may have been over-optimistic in his ideas of what such research may do, but there can be little doubt that the altered states of consciousness induced by the taking of drugs does indeed facilitate an experience that could not otherwise be achieved under normal conditions. At least they should make us hesitate before dismissing all such phenomena as of no spiritual value; clearly there is a new field of research opening up and it would be a mistake to prejudge the issues that are likely to follow from it. A passage from Pahnke and Richard's paper indicates their view on the relation between psychedelic experiences and those of the religious mystics:

Perhaps one of the reasons mysticism has come to be considered other-worldly in the sense of being an escape from social responsibilities lies not in the nature of mystical consciousness itself, but rather in the poor methods that have been used by men to gain such experience. The medieval monk in his darkened cell and the hermit in the deep recesses of his cave, for example, used not psychedelic substances, but the tools of sensory deprivation, sleep deprivation, meditative disciplines, and fasting to elicit biochemical changes and unlock the door to unconscious levels of mind. The Hindu yogi uses similar methods in addition to autohypnosis and breath control, the latter increasing the amount of carbon dioxide in the blood and triggering unconscious levels of mind.

Here are two examples from our collection: one from a boy of 16 and the other from an adult about to be ordained:

I have smoked cannabis fairly regularly, for with it I suddenly found a beautiful world, and have witnessed many instances whose splendour could only be attributed to a supreme power. The only time I have used any other drug was when I brought some Morning Glory seeds . . . I swallowed and digested 100 of them, over a period of time. I decided to write down the effects as they occurred; the report however did not turn out as expected. My mind, I believe, was taken over by a spiritual force. I cannot stress enough that I firmly believe this to have been a spiritual experience, for its force on my mind, and since that time, was so tremendous as to be indescribable. It is now two months since I had the experience, yet its impression has not diminished: I now *know* that a supreme Force or God does exist.   (2313, M, 16)

Age 29—Although not yet ordained, that year I worked as a junior with an ecumenical ministry. One of the activities I was involved in was a 'Spiritual Discovery Group' that numbered clergy of several denominations as well as two psychologists, professors, etc. At one point we experimented with L.S.D. It would take a volume to detail the full spiritual experiences and insights, but I shall outline a few:

During my first experience I suddenly became aware of the oneness of all that was. That God is a very present force that flows through everything in existence. I had discovered this before, but now it had become more than a belief—I was suddenly aware of it as much as I could ever be aware of anything.

The second experience gave me such an overwhelming re-occurrence of the first that it is absolutely impossible to put into words that reality of God which I was suddenly AWARE. But it was as if I had suddenly opened my awareness to the AWARENESS. All the pieces of my theological knowledge fell into place creating an intricate pattern of the whole. I lost much that I had learned as isolated detail and in its place I evolved into what I can only term as 'Conceptual knowledge of God's wonder', which, if it is meaningless to the reader, I am sorry, but words are impossible. Many of the aspects of this 'Conceptual knowledge' were unfamiliar to me, but have since shown up in the writings of others.

                                                                              (2005, M, Age ?)

12. THE CONSEQUENCES OF EXPERIENCE

It is not always easy to distinguish between an actual experience and the consequences. Where it has been of a sudden or dramatic kind it may be easy to note certain obvious differences it has made, to see definite changes in the attitude of behaviour of the person concerned. In other cases such developments may be felt to be part of the experience itself, consisting as it does in a gradual awareness of new potentiality for growth and understanding. Because almost every spiritual experience worthy of consideration must have some effects, it might be thought to be superfluous to have a special division for them. It is useful, however, to have these classificatory labels to serve as a rough guide to those who wish to research on this or that kind of consequence; and for our general discussion of man's spiritual nature, it is appropriate to conclude this chapter with just a few examples of each of the three sections we have made to cover them. They should not of course be regarded as mutually exclusive.

Material relating to these effects is particularly difficult to analyse, for, as we have noted in regard to some other items, there is a great disparity in the explicitness with which they are described; while one person will devote a couple of pages to the ways in which his or her life has been transformed, another will merely say 'I have never been the same person since.'

12(a) Sense of purpose or new meaning to life

The two examples given are but an indication of the wide variety of ways in which people may be affected by their different kinds of experience.

I was seventeen at the time and working for my entrance examination (Medical) to St. Andrews University. I was also about to become a confirmed member of the Scottish Episcopal Church like the other members of my family. Although I had not taken religion seriously, I was not unduly perturbed. The afternoon was dry but rather overcast, and I was in the open a short distance from the village. Suddenly the sky ahead of me became flame coloured, and this was followed by such a feeling of utter peace and benevolence as to be quite impossible to forget. I think I can truthfully say that it altered my whole outlook on life, an experience compared with which all other things appear cheap and second rate.

(21, M, 76)

When in Calcutta on leave, an Indian rushed up to me with a little Bible text book in his hand—short, vigorous texts, with short comment and a brief prayer. I took it away and began to read it frequently, and meditated (early morning and night). After some weeks, I suddenly realised that God had been speaking to me through these texts in a wonderfully intimate way. My dormant soul suddenly came alive again, and I began rapidly to enjoy life, make friends, develop a sense of humour and even gain new physical and mental energy. Every moment of life now had a sparkling meaning and purpose, and I knew God was really longing to get through to me and enter my whole life.

(209, M, Age ?)

12(b) Changes in religious belief

It is only natural that a profound spiritual experience is likely to lead the recipient either to question former beliefs and perhaps replace them by others, or to see old beliefs in a new light or suddenly to become confronted with what appears to them to be an entirely new way of looking at the world and its relation to what they had previously only dimly thought of as something unreal and remote—something which they had hitherto conventionally called God.

(In addition to the examples given below we could well include record 225 quoted above under 8(*c*) on p. 70).

In August last year I had what I think can only be described as a religious experience. I was recovering from a very distressing love affair and was staying with some friends and their children at a beach cottage. The wife had, some months previously in London introduced me to a book on Chinese philosophy, the 'I Ching', and although it quite impressed me at the time I did not give much more thought to it in my preoccupations. Quite by chance—how important and strange that factor is—someone else gave me a copy of the very same book, just as I was about to leave for my holiday. When I arrived I started to read it in detail and I began to be aware of a feeling that I was about to grasp something terribly important. I was terrified to speak about it in case the feeling left me before I had properly grasped what it was about. For the next few days I gave the book my undivided attention and gradually I became aware that I had an explanation for the previously inexplicable, that there was an order in the intangible world of emotions, relationships and 'happenings' which followd a similar kind of order to things in the physical world. I realised that the natural (the nurturing of each in reference to the other) could produce harmony of being, or 'serenity' if you like, and that God was overseer of this. This insight made Christianity comprehensible to me and I realised that contact with God had to be reinforced and strengthened as it was vital to achieving the desired harmony. The ritual of religion now had a meaning which is why I decided to go regularly to church (C. of E.)
(2269, F, 54)

When in 1945 I went to Oxford the opportunity to listen to good preachers attracted me to attend church at times, in a detached and rather nostalgic mood. It was while listening to a sermon in St. Mary's, that I became convinced of the reality of God. Emotion was at a minimum, and although the reasoning held my attention from the start (I still remember some opening sentences . . . 'God, if there be a God, cannot be less than what we call personal'); this sense of being convinced was not basically intellectual either. It was just that I knew the preacher was speaking the truth. God seemed to me as real as the pew on which I sat—or, to put it another way, it was like running one's head in the dark against a brick wall when one hadn't expected it.

The result was that I came out of church thinking that if I valued my personal integrity at all, I could do no other than identify myself with the Christian community, and so I joined S.C.M. This conviction, unlike previous uncertain and fleeting ones, has remained with me ever since, and among various intellectual or emotional occasions in my religious life, it has stood out, reinforced by I think two other occasions since, when God has given me what I can only describe as a somehow self-authenticating or 'objective' awareness of Him.
(463, F, 30)

In November of 1968 my eyes chanced to light upon 'Honest to God' on the library shelves . . . In due course I reached the passage, or one of them, which Robinson quotes from Tillich's 'The Shaking of the Foundations' about God being depth and so on, which ends up 'He who knows about depth knows about

God'. The whole passage immediately impressed me as throwing, for me, a new light upon the situation and as being perhaps possibly of application to myself. However, I thought no more at the time but read on and other matters soon claimed my attention. As, however, the afternoon and evening progressed, I became increasingly suffused, as it were, with the joyous realization that I *knew* that God existed, that I could, as I suppose in retrospect I had wanted to be able to do, say 'I believe in God'. From that evening I lived in a state of what I can only describe as exaltation for the next few weeks, overwhelmingly aware of the feeling of closeness to God, to a reality that was constantly present in the midst of other activities. . . . I am also aware of a desire to pass on the good news— culminating in fact in teaching a few periods of scripture in the school where I already teach. Prayer has become a reality, not just something you were told you ought to do, and many sentences from the Prayer Book have taken on a quite new meaning—the one that springs to mind is 'Whose service is perfect freedom'. This and others mean something real instead of being words with a meaning which you understand but don't convey a known truth.

(2387, F, 51)

In contrast to these examples I will now include one from a person who might at first sight be thought by some to have changed against religion; it is clear, however, that she has moved from one form which was meaningless to her to another which provided her with a deep sense of spiritual reality. The following brief passages taken from a long statement will be sufficient to indicate this change which she so vividly describes in her full account:

It was not until I was nearly 40 that I was aware of having finally shaken off all the dreadful Churchianity that pervaded everything in those times. . . . Compared with my minute concern and delight with Nature in the small and the great, religion was completely phoney . . . Nothing I was given to read at school or at home helped at all, my real educational reading only began when I left school and could choose to read comparative religion, philosophy and science (I mean real science, not school chemistry). My life has been spent in getting rid of false impressions and struggling to become human. . . . I have entirely thrown off and repudiated my early religious feelings and ideas, thank goodness, and only when I had finally done so did I feel that I could be an honest, guiltless, socially poised person. The life of deceit and double talk/think which I led as a child was miserable. If present day psychologists were right I ought to be a neurotic if not a psychotic by now, but I'm not. I still read comparative religion together with as advanced science as I can obtain. I have sudden ideas about the nature of things and this is the kind of experience I would call true revelation, i.e. not revealed supernaturally but by the normal processes of one's own mind chipping away at the thing and eventually getting through to greater understanding. If Prime Cause there be, I'm very sure it will be found to be a part of universal nature, not something 'outside'. This belief is so reassuring because it removes God or whatever you call IT, from those damp distant clouds and brings it right here and all around. We *are* of one substance with the Universe and it won't stop to let us get off whether alive or dead.

(493, F, 60)

12(*c*) *Change in attitude to others*

A change of attitude towards others was found to be a marked characteristic of what Starbuck called the 'process of unselfing' in his study of conversions amongst protestant evangelical Christian communities, which formed an important part of his pioneering work *The Psychology of Religion* (1899) to which I referred in Chapter 1. He found that as a result of conversion the changed relations of his subjects fell into three groups depending on the object of attachment: closer relations to persons, to nature, and to God (or Christ); in a table of percentages, relations to others (either desire to help others or expressed as love for others) figured as high as 70 per cent, whereas a closer relation to nature gave 33 per cent, and to God or Christ 48 per cent (the figures add up to more than 100 because some subjects expressed a change of relationship in regard to two or more groups). I give three examples from our own collection:

I have always had a feeling of the 'otherness' of life but until recently any feeling of God's presence was always sporadic depending on external factors such as surroundings, music, weather, etc. and internal well-being. The rituals of the church seemed meaningless very often. However over the past eighteen months I feel I have established a permanent relationship with God through total commitment to Jesus Christ whose presence I feel constantly close—(I have never had a vision or mystical experience). I believe this different relationship to be the result of taking God's promises completely on trust and trying to live on two levels—my own and his. This has resulted in the most wonderful feeling of freedom and a flow of love and compassion for others—a much more complete understanding of their needs and feelings. I also have loads more energy and a courage to stand up for my ideals and enter into difficult relationships with people I have hitherto avoided. Far from chaining me into a narrow religious outlook on life I can now understand what Christ means that he has come that we may have life more abundantly.

(470, F, 41)

At the time I had no great trouble or distress, but I was feeling very wearied by the 'changes and chances of this mortal life' and rather overburdened with my role of support and comforter to my family and friends. This, to me, is a failure on my part to keep in close enough contact with God. I tried to 'wait upon the Lord and renew my strength', but somehow I could not make contact. Then quite suddenly and certainly from an outside source, I had an experience of God as Love which transcends and transfigures anything I have ever understood before. It was, I think, a vision of Heaven. There was such a power of love, healing all one's hurts, surely surpassing all of life's pains, utter reassurance that above, below and surrounding us is an abiding strong, never-changing love. . . . Although the brightness of this vision has to some extent faded, I know now that the love of God is so permanently triumphant and all-embracing that anxiety has no place, and discouragement cannot be more than a temporary setback. God is completely and satisfyingly in everlasting control. . . . Obviously in the light of such vision, one's care and concern for others become more vital and loving. In the light of that overwhelming love, understanding and compassion must supersede any other attitude to people, because the most difficult and awkward will perhaps find the greatest unexpected joy. In the face of this what can one do but worship and adore? It adds new dimension to 'living in hope'.

(195, F, 52)

The crisis culminated in December. On the 18th of this month, at about 3.30 a.m. after a night of pressing anxiety and fear of the future, I suddenly experienced something quite new and unexpected; a feeling of light and joy came to me, a conviction that all was now turning towards something better, that I was aimed to be a tool in God's hands. At the same time I realized that my difficulties had been caused by my own self-centredness and egotism. In the morning I wrote some letters in order to clear up certain matters with other persons and I experienced a strong desire to be of more practical help to my wife. Since that day my life is different. This does not mean absence of problems but conviction that they are meant to promote my inner development. 'The worst may become the best'—these words have proved true; as a matter of fact, to me they seem to be the very core of Christianity. I regard all this as a gift to me—nothing was planned or expected—a gift that is meant to be shared with others who need help.

(316, M, 71)

In addition I would refer back to a record (2, F, 41) which is used on p. 56 in relation to a sense of certainty, 7(*f*), for it is also a good example of the present category.

This completes my first general exploration of varieties of spiritual experience, their development, their dynamic patterns, their antecedents and their consequences, based upon the study of three thousand accounts. It is, of course, only a preliminary study, for, as I have said more than once, it is our hope that it is but a beginning, and that this material and that to be collected in the future will form the basis for an increasing number of studies into this side of human nature. In the next chapter I give a summary account of some such work already done by some of my colleagues at the Unit.

While it *is* only a beginning, it does represent some eight years' work and is already sufficient, I believe, to enable one to draw certain conclusions concerning man's spirituality; some of them are naturally more tentative than others. Different people will no doubt draw different conclusions; in the final chapter I will attempt to draw my own.

7

STUDIES FROM THE RECORDS

In this chapter I shall list the various detailed research studies which have been, and are being, carried on by various people and which are all based on our records.

CHILDHOOD EXPERIENCE

As a small child one of my favourite festivals was Trinity Sunday. It was mysterious and right, something far bigger than the words used in church about it, which sounded to a small child nonsense. But Trinity wasn't nonsense, it was holy, holy, as we sang in the hymn, and even the very young child could join in the sort of oneness with all things bright and beautiful and worship this Something so great and lovely that it didn't matter at all that it was not understood. It just Was. Looking back, I think this was a child's way of experiencing the wonder of Life, or Being, or Existence, or God.

Of the thousands of people who responded to our request for accounts of their experience some fifteen per cent started with some reference to their childhood. They were not asked to do this but as one letter explained, 'It is only today, gathering up the threads as it were, that I realise that this childhood experience set the pattern for subsequent ones.' Edward Robinson, who succeeded me as director of the Unit, was particularly interested in seeing how often an early experience had had a deep affect on religious outlook in later years, so he wrote back to the people concerned with a series of questions designed to throw further light upon the nature of that experience and the spiritual development which followed.

In this chapter I will briefly discuss Robinson's findings and conclusions, largely in his own words, which I have taken from a couple of articles which he wrote. The first article was entitled 'How does a child experience religion?' and appeared in *The Times Educational Supplement* (15 December 1972). In this he says:

The forms in which children express their experiences at different ages may to some extent be predictable; but it is a mistake to confuse the capacity for experience with the ability to express it. Conceptual expression may be a relatively late achievement, it may also be of secondary importance:

'I remember—I was about ten or eleven at the time—how I thought something that mystics always think; if I could remember what I knew then, I'd know everything. This experience—I called it 'It'—has followed me throughout my life. It has had a tremendous influence on my life, and has helped me to synthesize my thoughts and give them conviction.'

'I called it "It"'; 'It just Was'; I cannot here do more than hint at the variety of ways in which our correspondents have described those early encounters with 'It': as an awareness of a personal presence, as a feeling of unity with all creation, as a sense of destiny transcending the limits of a single life. But how far can we trust these later conceptualized interpretations?

The writers themselves often recognize their inadequacy:

'I think from my childhood I have always had the feeling that the true reality is not to be found in the world as the average person sees it. There seems to be a constant force at work from the inside trying to push its way to the surface of consciousness. The mind is continually trying to create a symbol sufficiently comprehensive to contain it, but this always ends in failure.'

In fact such admissions of failure carry their own authenticity; and from so large and various a body of evidence a convincing picture emerges of the kind of living contact that a significant minority of people have maintained with their own childhood—though it may not be possible to describe such a link with a precision that will satisfy the psychologist:

'My childhood experiences were extremely vivid and significant and authentic. Those that I had as an adult were of the same kind in the sense that an apple follows apple blossom.'

Robinson then goes on to point out that some correspondents would have liked to have expressed their feelings of religious awe at the time but that they received little encouragement from parents or teachers. Perhaps in some ways this was just as well for in trying to be articulate they might have lost the intuitive insight of childhood. Order, clarity, and rationality might have been inimical to intangible mysteries.

'I feel that all my education was a block and a barrier to real religious experience. I was always wary of delving too deeply into mystery and crossing thresholds. In adolescence I had the good fortune to find one wise teacher who understood my experience. It was a great joy to find even for this short period of months one teacher who understood "mystery"'.

A true balance is only reached when we recognize that, to use the language of Gabriel Marcel, we must never attempt to reduce mysteries to problems, and that this means, in the face of some experiences, being content to say no more than 'It just Was'.

In his second article Robinson discussed how authentic these accounts of childhood experiences are likely to be. ('Experience and authority in religious education', in *Religious Education*, September 1976).

To some five hundred of those who had written I wrote back, asking some fairly detailed and rigorous questions. I was concerned to assess how far these people felt they really had genuine and reliable access to the original thoughts and feelings of childhood, over an interval of, in some cases, more than 50 years.

With the mass of evidence that this questionnaire brought in I can't possibly deal in detail here. I can only say that I find it most impressive.

What was it then about their childhood experiences that compelled these writers to feel them worth recording? I think *authority* is the word: from the very beginning these experiences mattered, they were *significant*. They made a claim which later development always bore out. Of course memory is selective. All that we have here, it may be said, is what later reflection has found to be significant. And years of interpretation, often a great many years, will have left little of the original feelings unaltered. In one of the questions I put this suggestion: the majority rejected it. They protested that, distant as they might be in time, the actual feelings and insights of childhood remained distinct to them. The words available to describe them, yes; these might have changed; but the *sense* of the experience itself remained clear, accessible and, as I say, authoritative. What can one say in face of such a claim? Those who were less positive, admitting that early memories were not so simply recoverable, often gave as the reason the fact of growth: the long process of understanding that had its origin in some particular far-off event could not now be seen as distinct from the moment that sparked it off. 'Unless a grain of wheat fall into the ground and die' . . . Of all those who replied, only 13 per cent maintained that the experiences of childhood were more significant in the long run than those of later years. Nostalgia plays little part in these records.'

'The authoritative quality of these early experiences', he says, 'were felt to have come out in many ways,' and he goes on to say that he will consider here four of them: in relation to the family; in relation to school; in connection with the growth of 'conscience' and moral feelings: and finally in the emergence of self-consciousness and the sense of identity. I shall confine myself to his questions regarding the influence of family and school, and briefly with the more philosophical problem of the sense of identity.

How far [Robinson asked] did they feel that they owed their early religious ideas or feelings to the influence of their family, and to what extent was their childhood image of God derived from what they saw in their parents? Most were as positive in their replies to the first of these questions as they were negative over the second. The contrast was quite clear. Influences there obviously were, though many were insistent that to be influenced was one thing and to be determined quite another. On the derivation of images of God from a father (or mother) figure there was a strongly negative majority. Freudians may see in this rejection only a confirmation of their own theories; but so large a body of contrary opinion expressed here needs to be taken seriously. The reasons given generally reflected much thought; and there was often protest at so trivial an idea. After all, if parents themselves pass on a conception of God that transcends humanity, why should children accept a lesser one?

> 'I do not think that my early idea of God was derived at all from what I saw in my parents. God was, so I was given to understand, the great Creator of all things, mysterious, wonderful, to be worshipped, obeyed and loved. He knew everything about everything. One could as well say that one got an idea of an elephant by looking at an ant.'

Another writes:

'I don't think I ever had an idea of God as an actual person, for example, as an old man, as some children do at one stage. I think that even when quite young I sensed a kind of abstractness which was quite real in the nature of God, to which I could respond quite deeply because of something within me, of which I was then unaware.'

So while the majority felt that their early experience had clearly been shaped and even directed by family influences, this was not at all the same thing as saying that the origin of such experiences was to be found there. Many correspondents are quite positive that this was not so. [He goes on to give examples.]

'The impact of schooling', he says, 'was generally felt to have been even less creative.' He had asked 'How far had they felt it to have been a help or a hindrance in the development of religious awareness?'

Some of the answers [he says] reflect gratitude and appreciation, but the feelings most often recorded were negative or indifferent. There is no need to quote any of these at length; they range from:

'I do not connect any religious awareness with my school life, which was a happy, normal affair.'

to:

'Religion at school was hell.'

Of more interest were the minority who indicated what was of value to them. What comes out very strongly in many accounts is the sense of loneliness, the remoteness of teachers from what was so important to the child.

'"God is a spirit" etc.—one of the most consoling thoughts given to me. There seemed to be a strange absence of people who could get on with this idea. No one understood my realization of something beyond the physical self.'

Another recalls:

'My problem was to find someone who understood, and would allow me to express, the rich life and perceptions within.'

And another:

'I never felt close enough to anybody to discuss anything at all.'

In contrast to these are the (relatively) few who found teachers with whom they were able to make contact at a level deeper than that of mere instruction: adults with whom they could share their highest aspirations, and who exercised a profound and lifelong influence. Brief quotation cannot do justice to some of the moving and affectionate portraits to be found here. It is a significant comment on an all too common situation that good has often to be done by stealth:

'I used to hide in free moments in the empty art history room, and only dis-covered the year that I graduated that the art history teacher had known all along (for ten years) that I hid in there and had put out books specially for me. She remains a real friend of mine.'

The essence of such a creative relationship is well summed up in one account which ends thus:

'One could absorb from those from whom love emanated, whereas fear shrivelled and made stupid.'

From this rich and fascinating picture of school life there emerges a general impression of the irrelevance of the whole educational process to something that was going on independently of it at a much deeper level; something again that was felt to have an autonomous reality of its own, and so an authority.

Robinson finishes his article thus:

All mentioned some significant experience of childhood, these people to whom I was writing; could they, I asked, recall from those early days any particular moments of self-consciousness, when they first felt themselves to be individuals with some degree of freedom and responsibility? And were such occasions associated with any feelings or ideas that they would call religious?

The response here as before is hard to analyse in general terms. I mentioned no particular ages, and some described experiences from adolescence. But over half of those who replied   went further back; and the intense particularity of some of these very early memories, and the profound emotions often associated with them, suggest that we may be mistaken in thinking of 'the crisis of identity' as a phenomenon typical only of adolescence. Deeply disturbing experiences of this kind are recorded from the very earliest age, and with them often a bitter resentment of the patronising attitudes of adults.

'I remember distinctly being aware of thinking how silly grown-ups were not to understand, and I was conscious of playing up to them and trying to conform to the image they had of me. I felt myself distinct from them, separated by their lack of insight that there was far more of me than what they saw in me, the undeveloped child part.'

Another says:

'In my childhood we daren't let our elders know how mature we were. As for religious feelings and ideas—they'd been there all along.'

With this lack of recognition goes a sense of impotence:

'This inner knowledge was exciting and absorbingly interesting, but it remained unsaid because, even if I could have expressed it, no-one would have understood. Once, when I tried, I was told I was morbid.'

A volume by Robinson based on his study of childhood experiences has been published by the Unit under the title *The Original Vision* (Robinson 1977).

THE GROWTH OF RELIGIOUS EXPERIENCE

Robinson followed up his work on childhood by a study of a more limited number of people selected for treatment in depth to show the growth of religious experience during their lives. The Unit has published these findings as *Living the Questions* (Robinson 1978).

THE INFLUENCE OF THE VISUAL ARTS

Robinson is at present making a detailed study of those records which relate to the influence of the visual arts in the development of religious feeling and has inaugurated a special questionnaire inquiry on the subject. It is too early yet to discuss the findings, but he says, 'It soon became evident that distinctions between "sacred" and "secular" art were rarely meaningful in terms of the response evoked. More serious was the fact that twentieth-century artists seldom got a mention as being of religious significance, though the few who did were generally among those who had broken away entirely not only from the religious but even from the representational traditions of the past.' In an attempt to find out why this should be so he is now engaged in an experimental project in schools and colleges to see what kind of response is evoked, in the educational world, by the work of certain modern painters and sculptors.

THE INFLUENCE OF MUSIC

Dr Jackson Hill a musicologist who visits us from Bucknell University, Pennsylvania, is researching into the relation of music to religious experience using both our records and a questionnaire method.

QUASI-SENSORY EXPERIENCE

Timothy Beardsworth has been concerned with each individual's exact description of his quasi-sensory experience regardless of whether what seemed to him to happen, 'really' happened or not. His study has been published by the Unit as *A Sense of Presence* (Beardsworth 1977).

FLASHES OF INSIGHT

Brian Carter has been studying those experiences in our records which were claimed by those concerned to give them a sudden apprehension or knowledge of the truth. These curious flashes of insight show certain patterns, which, he suggests, differentiate three separate groups of people, 'Members of the first group', Carter says 'may be distinguished as being essentially either Christians or theists whose particular experience provides them with affirmation of belief and/or supports hope or expectation.' I give the following two examples from this group:

[While meditating during a time of emotional stress] I had—for how long I do not know—an intense feeling of having slipped out of time and of *knowing* in a quite different way from intellectual knowledge. Knowing with all my being what is meant by the concept God is Love. I felt that I had experienced divine love in its reality and immediacy.

There was a sudden freeing within and a swift indescribable illumination of mind, so subjectively vivid that I fancied a change even in the light around me. A deep sigh beneath this experience, an involuntary gaze upwards, and then I became conscious of an exquisite sense of relief and peace. My gloomy doubts had been instantly swept away, leaving behind a new belief in the existence of God and in the complete truth of doctrine.

In Carter's second group are those who, he says, differ from those just considered in three respects: firstly they made it clear that they had little or no time for organized religion or any traditional theistic or Christian beliefs; secondly whereas 'all the writers in the first group mention that prior to the experience they were going through a time of depression, anxiety or doubt, no one in the second group reported such a state'; and thirdly whilst those in the first group could recall what they *knew* in the experience and in all cases it not only confirmed their theistic or Christian belief but 'acted as a correction to their previous troubled state of mind', those of the second group had 'much greater difficulty in describing the knowledge content of the experience, or could not do so at all.' As Carter says, 'It might at first sight be supposed that we have here two quite distinct patterns of experience, but this is for future work to decide when more examples have been examined.' I now give two examples from this second group:

I had the feeling of seeing the ivy in the very sharp focus and then the feeling of everything opening out (or a veil being lifted) and a wonderful feeling of freedom (lightness) and a comprehension of everything. It is hard to describe. I remember feeling exquisitely happy and of saying to myself: 'So that is what it is all about!' I cannot say what 'I saw'—it was like infinity and radiance at the same time.

A great inward light seemed to illuminate my thoughts, I experienced a magnificent sensation of arrival. I was filled with joy as though I had just discovered the secret of world peace. I suddenly *knew*. The odd thing was that I did not know what I knew. From then on I set out to define it.

Carter's third group is the smallest one; I now quote from his report:

Although not forming such a sharp contrast as between the previous two groups, may nevertheless suggest another pattern. They are all women, and their experiences take place in relationship to bereavement or fear for a child's life. The first is very short. A mother's 11-month old baby is undergoing a serious operation to save her life. During the operation the mother goes to church to pray, then 'suddenly, as if miraculously, the burden was lifted from my heart. I KNEW she was all right—I said to my husband: "Don't worry, all is well"—and it was.'

Here again we see the 'sudden apprehension of knowledge or truth'. I will give only one other example which comes from a writer, who has suffered the loss of an especially close friend; a short while after his death she was out walking with her husband and:

We were talking of our dead friend when suddenly I knew that his spirit lived, and was as close to me that moment as it had ever been in life. When I say 'I knew' words are inadequate to convey the experience. This was 'knowing' more vivid and real than anything I had ever experienced in the literal sense. It was as if for a moment one had known reality, and in comparison the world of the senses was a dream. I was filled with an unutterable joy, which I shall never be able to describe.

SUSTAINED EXPERIENCE

Michael Walker undertook to study those sustained experiences of a power which *appeared* to the person concerned to be beyond the self. He has looked for those accounts which mentioned 'an awareness, for a more or less prolonged period, of a Power or Presence in their lives, sustaining, encouraging, strengthening, guiding or compelling them', and he writes thus:

Analysis of the first 1000 accounts yielded some 176 to whom these words applied, or who gave strong indication that they might apply. This does not mean, of course, that many of the others may not have had a sustained experience but yet gave no hint of it; one might argue, however, that if correspondents were giving an account of religious experience, they would be likely to mention something as fundamental as this if it had any real significance for them. . . . We must also remember that many who have such a sustained sense of a transcendental reality may not have responded to our appeal because they have thought that by our use of the word experience we have meant some more isolated dramatic revelation.

To 145 of these correspondents a questionnaire was subsequently sent in an attempt to fill out the details of their experience and their understanding of it;* replies were received from 110. The discussion that follows will be illustrated by excerpts both from the original accounts of experience and from the answers to the questionnaire.

In the original accounts, clear mention of an experience of being sustained, strengthened or guided occurred about sixty times; while experience of encouragement was mentioned, in separate examples, about thirty times (though clearly there is no hard and fast distinction between these shades of experience).

Walker now demonstrates their variety by quoting extracts from a large number of examples, from which I shall make a selection. He divides them into groups and sub-divisions as follows:

1. *Being sustained*

(a) This is sometimes described as a deep and prolonged awareness or conviction: 'a sense of infinite resources—a mixture of "underneath are the everlasting arms"† and a constant forward-looking of the mind and will for action.'

'From earliest recollections I have always been aware of the Presence, the goodness and the Fatherhood of God. There has NEVER been any doubt, even amid sorrow and difficulties and loss of dear ones. This is not anything that I am proud of—it is just a fact! Without a belief in God (a personal God—not MIND or anything like that) I don't think that I could have gone on living. Life has been too difficult, but with God I can face it as cheerfully as possible.'

'During the course of the years there has been a good deal of personal stress, and dimly sensed at first, but clearly realised in retrospect, I know there has

---

*The remainder of the 176 were not approached either on grounds of age—none over 80 were included—or of lack of address, or because they were known not to have replied to a previous questionnaire.
†Deuteronomy 33:27, a quotation frequently used by correspondents.

been a mysterious sense of support underpinning my life, so delicate as to be indefinable. The reality is there but words cannot give it form.'

(b) Sometimes the sustenance took a very practical form:

'I found myself at the age of 49, with a wife and family still mainly dependent on me, without a job, savings, qualifications, home or even furniture. I had believed, on the basis of past experience, that if this my biggest trial came to pass, the providential power which had hitherto sustained me would continue to do so, since it was my conviction that the crisis had occurred in the direct course of following him to whom I was committed. And I was not disappointed: the assurance remained, even in the first few hours and days, when I had not the faintest idea of how in actual fact these material problems were going to be overcome. In the event, being freed from crippling anxiety within, I was able to try systematically to set about the tasks before me. Presently that assurance that somehow I would get through or be carried through began to be confirmed. . . '

(c) Several correspondents ascribed their endurance of prolonged strain and stress to communion with God: for instance, one correspondent, who in her teens lost both brother and fiancé in the First War, and was left to protect her mother and younger sister against a drunkard of a father, describes how she drew 'even nearer to God as the only source of the sustaining power I needed for the part I must play'. She goes on to say how, in the process, her experience of God's reality became deepened:

'It was then that I became aware of a new element in my relationship to God. I was conscious of a certain intimacy in my approaches to Him, that my prayers were now coming from a new depth . . . which made it no longer an exercise of faith to pray to Him but a certainty that I was speaking to a personal God with whom I had such close personal relationship that I could not be dogmatic about it.'

Another correspondent, whose first wife was crippled with arthritis for 45 years, and whose second wife was tragically murdered, writes:

'I have always felt myself sustained in my darkest hours by a loving and understanding power . . . That abiding presence of a Father and a Friend has, thank God, become an increasing reality to me as the years have passed by, but it necessitates an effort at continual loyalty, such as any friendship demands.'

2. *Being encouraged*

Encouragement, or something like it, is most often described in the context of some trial or crisis, and often arising from a particular event or action.

(a) For instance, from reading a verse from the Bible:

'looking ahead to a change which would be bound to make my life a pretty lonely and frightening one for a time, I went into a country church to pray, and the phrase 'I will not leave you desolate. I will come to you'—appearing on the page open on the lectern—came home to me with the *immediacy* which I have come to believe is another "religious" phenomenon.'

(b) Or from prayer:

'I have had deeply troubled times in my life including a broken marriage and have certainly been uplifted and protected by a power to whom I can call upon during times of stress.'

This may be compared with the following:

'the response to prayer has seemed dramatic, in that I have received an almost physical sense of comfort in times of great stress . . . There have been times when I have not been able to pray—this I cannot explain—but when I did so—even in the most tentative and imperfect way—the response was there, and this is a humbling thought . . . All I can say is that I know in my essential being that the power is there, and I have over many years had ample proof of it.'

(e) Or from transcendental meditation [I am selecting only a few of the sub-divisions]:

'This practice has confirmed my inner faith in the existence of a divine power, in which all creatures—everything—participate, and which at the same time encompasses the universe, and whose meaning is love. This faith gives joy, meaning and purpose to all life, and in addition helps me to feel in the depths of my being the surrender implied in the words "Thy Will, not mine, be done".'

(g) Or from a sense of 'Presence':

'without any conscious seeking on my part, the Presence I knew and loved came most unmistakably to me, the same Presence I had first known as a child in the wood, and at other times as I grew older . . . On this occasion, that Presence brought the assurance that however much I might have to give up in the search for truth, no one could take that from me.'

In all the examples so far cited the source of the encouragement (whatever the means) has been felt to be a transcendental power: but it is quite possible for exhilaration experiences—which may or may not have a lasting effect on the recipient's subsequent life—to be ascribed to no supernatural agency. Here is an account in which any supernatural connotation is strongly rejected:

'At the age of nine, at boarding school, I knelt one evening as usual to say my prayers, as I had always done, when suddenly, like a flash, came the question, as if asked from outside myself: 'is there anyone to pray to?' and the answer seemed to come: 'No!' There was no God. This was followed by a great sense of relief, thankfulness, pleasure. I need never pray again. Why pray to nothing and no one? I never did pray again. Even during the most tragic experiences, and one overwhelming tragedy when my husband died, I have never felt that I needed anything supernatural on which to lean, to whom to appeal, but just the reverse. . . . At the age of fourteen, standing alone in the stern of a steamer taking me to France, leaning over the taffrail, watching the wake and smoky wraiths from the funnel diminishing to the horizon, rising from the water, as if the waves spoke to me, I heard a voice saying: 'All men are brothers! Every land is home,' And I felt quite stunned with joy. Henceforth I had a sublime faith. The whole world would be home and every person in it my brother . . . With such a religion, no supernatural beings were necessary or needed. I feel no lack of one, rather joy. It is much easier to explain many problems—example, of evil—without god and devil etc. than with them. I wish I could impart to everyone else my happiness and relief in being freed from any super-natural-centred religion—and I have studied them all with the deepest attention and sympathy—The universe became for me much more sublime and wonderful when I ceased to believe in such a faith. Man must be his own salvation. He can be, if he so wills to be. So could he be his own destruction.'

3. *Being strengthened or empowered*

An awareness or feeling of being strengthed or empowered to achieve things felt to be impossible unaided is clearly closely related to the feeling of being sustained, which has been already discussed; the very phrase 'a power beyond the self' implies an energising agency; in many examples, as in the following, prayer is regarded as the channel for this power:

[Here among several examples he gives one which has already been quoted in Chapter 7 under category 11(*d*) (p. 84); to save space I will let this suffice for this division.]

4. *Being guided*

A conviction of guidance from outside the self is a very common one. [I am now omitting the various sub-divisions he makes and quoting a small selection of the examples he gives.]

'Sometimes I have found myself directed almost against my will into a decision I could not justify in my own mind, and yet that decision always proved to be the right one.'

[Next he quotes the example number 16 which I have already given in Chapter 5 under category 7(*d*) (p. 55) and then after saying that sometimes such guidance is by intuitional conviction he gives the next example.]

'On returning to England, I prayed for guidance in connection with my new job. I was offered one quite near my old one, and verbally accepted, but when I tried to sign the form I could not. Neither did I get any peace of mind until I wrote asking to be released from my verbal promise ... For months I had no prospect of a job but ultimately I saw my present one advertised, and 'knew', before I had applied, that it was the right one.'

Whilst most of these examples express the feeling of guidance from *outside* the self, this is not always so as in the following example:

'my work has not been of a kind that I would have chosen for myself or been remotely interested in without this experience of a call which I can only describe as a "mental voice" from within me firmly telling me what I should do with my life.'

'Perhaps most common of all', says Walker, 'is the conviction of an overall arrangement of events in the correspondent's life, whereby they have been guided along a path':

'The experience of the last six months have ... confirmed my deep conviction that God is directly and indirectly guiding my life ... As well as being absolutely convinced of Divine Guidance in the larger issues of my life, I feel this guidance strongly even in some of the smaller events ... the pattern of my life seems to me to be a mosaic, in which everything, including seeming disasters, eventually turn to good (e.g. a mental breakdown, frequent eye-trouble, the giving-up of my career after thirty years to come home to look after my parents ...) I have come to feel almost apprehensive about the way the rough places in my life have become smooth ... '

'My own experience has been of many and wonderful ways that have just "happened", many through being "led" as it were, to various places or actions at certain times; sometimes seeming to be "guided" by personal "intuition" and at other times seemingly motivated by an "outside force" as it were.'

And here is another example of feeling a guiding power within rather than outside the self:

'I am much more aware of an immanent power of the spirit, than of one "outside" myself; I am sure that it guides and shapes my life, and that what seem coincidences are often part of a plan.'

Walker asked the respondents some questions, I can give no more than an indication of their significance. He writes as follows:

The first of the questions asked . . . was the following: "I have referred to this Presence or Power in rather vague, impersonal terms in order to include different people's understanding of it; do you think of it in personal terms, and if so, can you say why you do?"

The majority (over three-quarters) of those who replied to the questionnaire thought of the Power as unequivocally personal. Others, while generally agreeing with this, added a caveat against anthropomorphic personalisation, or said that to them God was spirit, and therefore in some sense beyond personality because beyond limitation. Only nine thought of the Power as definitely impersonal.

I have used the phrase "thought of" here. Can one separate experience from thought at this point? Is there some experience of God as personal which is analogous to our experience of other people as personal (without at this point attempting to go into the philosophical and cognitive questions surrounding personality)? The answer is clearly "Yes". About twenty correspondents described a direct awareness or sense of a personal Presence. In some cases a particular visionary experience is described which though not (or rarely) repeated, yet left an enduring conviction of personal friendship:

'I was kneeling at prayer before getting into bed and praying for release from this symptom, when I was taken quite suddenly into eternity. I was not aware of the bedroom, my bed or anything to do with my earthly life, but I knew I was in a different realm of life. I could see the form of someone, not his face, and I knew it was Jesus and that He was alive, really alive for me . . . since that time, the sure knowledge of the aliveness of Jesus has never left me.'

' . . . there is a definite sense of a presence, which though not physical is strong enough to be felt and I feel able to communicate with it as if to another human being.'

'I am conscious of this Presence (a sort of inward peace and fellowship). I cannot explain it or share it with another person and I am completely dependent upon it . . . '

'I speak of this Presence and the Presence responds—sometimes in verbal form and sometimes in giving a sensation of confidence . . . it is Christ I know as a person and through him I come into communion with the Presence who is in some way more abstract, yet has personal qualities—compassion, power, wisdom, goodness.'

The examples so far cited have shown a gradual progression toward a more cognitive, less sensory conviction of personality. Indeed the majority of those who said they thought of God as personal were clearly influenced by Christian concepts. Some only gave Christian belief as their reason for conviction of personality. On the other hand, others stressed that Christian belief was only part of the story:

'All this shows how much the Bible has helped me to express the feelings I have had, but I would *not* say that the Bible has induced them, because you just can't induce them, they come upon you like rain in drought, or sun on a cold day.'

Turning now to those whose conviction is of an impersonal Power, one can ask again whether there is a direct quasi-sensory experience of such a Power. Here are some quotations:

'I . . . feel it is a spiritual presence—which is difficult to describe in finite terms. But it is real in the sense that electric power is real.'

'The feeling of that mysterious "Power outside myself" is very real in times of stress though I can't give one outstanding example of its help; it is built-in to life.'

'I . . . know that since I concluded some years ago that my mind could not accept a personal God . . . I seem to have become more aware of this all-pervading power which to me is strength, comfort, joy, goodness etc.'

Clearly here are examples which seem qualitatively similar to some of those described under personal. Indeed, though the examples are fewer, a similar series can be discerned ranging from those who speak of a quasi-sensory awareness to those referring to an impersonal power on credal grounds.

As might be expected there is some evidence that where the Power is thought of as impersonal, any relationship with it is somewhat tenuous:

'[The Presence] does not seem close or friendly—just there in a rather detached way . . . I am not good at self-surrender and only use it as a last resort . . . I attend at Quaker meetings and there I feel I must just sit still and wait. Bits of insight come to me and there is an overall feeling of peace . . . I have been given strength and luck to change into a teacher.'

'The feeling of that 'Power outside myself' . . . has enriched my life but I am too ordinary and selfish to have responded to its deeper implications . . . I don't use formal prayers but I find meditation on things like goodness helpful. Above all, when I walk quietly in the country, I usually seem, in some strange way, to have my 'spiritual' batteries recharged.'

The question of relationship with the Power beyond the self brings us to a consideration of the role and effectiveness of prayer in the experience of the correspondents. In the questionnaire they were asked: 'Have you found your experience deepened or helped by particular conditions or actions (e.g. experience of crisis, prayer, self-surrender etc.)? If prayer is an important part of your experience, perhaps you could say a little more as to the sort of prayer you use.'

The overwhelming majority of those who answered (97 out of 110) said that they prayed, and most saw prayer as an important concomitant of their experiences.

Types of prayer used and qualifying factors mentioned were as follows:

set forms of prayer	19
free but with words	69
wordless prayer	27
intercession	42
prayer used frequently	61
prayer only occasionally	1
for specific things	33
not for specific things	11
listening for direct thoughts from God	7
praise or adoration	5
corporate prayer	4
prayers written down	1
thanksgiving	11
in tongues	2

(The numbers here give only those who stated, or strongly implied, that they used a particular form or frequency of prayer—no doubt, if asked specifically, most would widen the list.)

Other actions mentioned by the correspondents as of value to them were: meditation, Bible reading (and sometimes other literature), public worship, fellowship, sacraments. All these were mentioned relatively infrequently.

The correspondents were also asked about their experience of the answers to prayer. [Walker was interested in getting some indication of the proportion of people who felt that they experienced a particular kind of answer as is seen in the next question he asked.] The question was framed thus: '"When I pray coincidences happen: when I do not, they don't", said William Temple.* Can you point to what seem to be clear answers to prayer (in beneficial arrangement of events, not just in improving your own frame of mind)? If so, a brief description of the sort of answers you have had would be valuable.'

One might expect a person's attitude to the personality or otherwise of God to affect their attitude to prayer and their experience of answered prayer; and, not surprisingly, over half of the replies combined a belief in a personal God and in prayer with the conviction that prayer had been answered. In some cases a large number of specific answers were cited.

Whilst all who expressed belief in a personal God said that they prayed; a few (six) denied that they had had prayer answers of the type suggested. Some said that they did not feel it right to ask for such answers; others that they couldn't put a finger on any examples, but that they still felt prayer important and answers real if unidentifiable. . . . Several (twelve) felt that coincidences occurred in their lives independently of specific prayer:

'I do not think Providence deserts us because we do not pray.'

'While admitting the great importance of prayer, in my case I have found help

---

*This quotation was used by one of the correspondents, who derived it from *Dimensions of Prayer* by D. V. Steere, London, 1965, p. 85.

more by listening to God speaking to me, than by my speaking to Him in prayer. In His Word He speaks and reveals Himself, His will and His purpose. My praying is concerned in the increasing wonder and worship which these things cause. My petitionary prayer is limited and in very few words. However I can say ' . . . we know that all things work together for good to them that love God . . . according to his purpose.' One sees this in the impersonal book of one's life-story.'

In some cases specific prayer was not answered, or the answer was unpleasant or obstructive, yet in most cases it is seen in retrospect to have been the better way . . . '

[Other correspondents stressed the importance of two-way communication in prayer.]

Of the minority who expressed belief in an impersonal power, some said that they did not pray:

'regular prayer . . . has never had much meaning for me. The difficulty in accepting the idea of a personal God made the practice of prayer seem futile . . . I do, however, have a strong sense of wonder and a very real sense of gratitude though my gratitude is not directed to any "thing".'

Others said that they did pray, and most of these said that they felt prayer had been answered. In all of these cases, though the correspondents said that they thought of an impersonal Power, the rest of their answers showed that this was to some extent a matter of definition, and though they did not think of themselves as having a personal relationship with the Power, yet its activeness was in no doubt:

'I think of 'it' as an impersonal, self-operative, loving Principle.'

Walker goes on to discuss the moral and ethical implications of their experience, having asked in his questionnaire 'Can you give more exact evidence that your experience has made you a better person than you were before, or as far as you can tell, than you would be without it? (This question was asked, he says, with an alternative, concerning heightened achievement, which has been already discussed, and which removed any implication that their experience *must* have made them better.)

'This is clearly a very difficult question to ask any to answer of themselves' says Walker. 'As many pointed out, an experience of God has a humbling effect, and makes one more aware of failure.'

'No—I am a worse person than I would have been without the experience, because I have no excuse for my many failures.'

Those whose experience stretched right back as long as they could remember naturally expressed difficulty in assessing what they would have been like without the experience. On the other hand, some who had experienced a conversion from a dissolute life were vividly aware of renewal and improvement:

'I know this for certain, that because of Christ I am today a better husband, a better father, a better son, a better brother, a better employee, even a better driver, and certainly a better, happier and healthier man, and I have to thank my Lord for His grace and mercy towards me who so recently seemed beyond all help and hope.'

In general, most of those who answered this question felt, at least tentatively, that they had been made better through their experience—either they were happier or more secure, or had been given a new awareness of right and wrong, or increased love for others, or had experienced help only in unselfish actions.

For reasons of space I must omit his further discussion on this question and proceed to the last one in his questionnaire:

'Would you say that your experience followed your acceptance of particular beliefs or that your beliefs arose out of experience?' Several of the correspondents [he writes] said they found this the hardest question to answer, which is an indication of the extreme complexity of the issue. Here is the distribution of their answers:

Belief felt to be primary	18
Belief primary but interacting with experience	27
Experience felt to be primary	21
Experience primary but interacting with belief	6
Interaction—neither belief nor experience primary	29
Denies any belief	1
No answer or very doubtful	4

No clear picture emerges from this, except perhaps that the majority felt that the process for them was one of interaction—of beliefs accepted and reinforced by experience, or of experience sustained and strengthened by belief. Those who had some striking 'out-of-the-blue' initial experience tended to regard experience as primary; those who looked back to a conversion experience where they heard and accepted particular truths naturally regarded belief as primary.

PRAYER

Timothy Beardsworth studied our records for experiences relating to prayer and its effects. Whilst his work to some extent overlaps that of Michael Walker, it is really complementary to it.

After pointing out (as did Walker) how many among our respondents 'have described a steadily continuing disposition to live as if under the guidance of some power beyond the self' and, having given examples from our records of such feelings, Beardsworth goes on to say:

This continuous relationship depends on prayer, and many of the writers describe how they go about it . . . This need not mean praying with words. 'Wordless faith' is a very basic phenomenon, as is shown by the infant's relation with his mother (or even a dog's with his master) . . . Several accounts describe praying without words:

'It (prayer) is a quality of thought not to be confused with a quantity of words.'

'A something is encountered with which a personal relationship is established, and this is based not upon thought but upon love, as a child reacts to a parent.'

(cf. The Cloud of Unknowing—'He may well be loved, but not thought. By love may he be gotten and holden; but by thought never.')

'Experience of God's presence is always a 'person-to-person' consciousness . . . I very frequently lift up my heart, often without forming phrases.'

'I am aware of a 'consciousness' outside my own. I sense it . . . in times of great stress or anxiety when I 'pray', sometimes wordlessly, for some way out in intolerable situations. There is always an improvement, or I realise what I must do to help myself.'

'I pray . . . fairly regularly, not in set words, often not in words at all, but bringing forward ideas—gratitude, guilt, and people whom I wish well and want to help. I derive comfort from handing over these ideas, and get the feeling that they are received.'

'When I knew my mother would not live many months, I relied on this power to give what help and support I could to my parents, who to some extent depended on me in particular. This I would say I was able to do in answer to prayer—though it was not the sort of daily prayer said on my knees, but an inner consciousness of a supporting strength.'

Not only are words unnecessary, but one need not even have a very clear idea of whom one is addressing (cf. Buber 'He may be addressed, but not described.')—

'In times of distress I have often found my own pleas or prayers answered, sometimes by an inexplicable feeling of peace which seems to arise simply from the fact of praying—although I do not know who or what I am praying to.'

'From time to time a sense of stillness . . . in my kitchen as I worked I was in a worshipping state without any clear image of a person to worship.'

Sometimes it is easy—

'I find the consciousness of Jesus's presence the most natural thing in the world, so that prayer, in the sense of talking with Jesus, is just like conversing with another person . . . '

'Being a lonely child, I talked to God as many children talk to imaginary companions, and the habit has remained with me all my life . . . '

'I just felt I must tell Him of my unhappy situation in matter-of-fact, everyday language, just as I would have spoken to a true friend.'

'To pray is easy—I relax into the Presence, as I call it, and tell my problems or make my requests and leave them there . . . Petty jealousies and hurt feelings disappear . . . '

'Prayer for me is a very normal, natural activity. I am aware of an outside influence operating in my experience independently of me. I cannot produce it or turn it on at will. I can draw near to it, however, through prayer. The effect can be like a shot of adrenalin—fresh energy for work and other activities. Also it affects my attitude to people and to situations, changing both mind and mood quite radically at times. I experience a new freedom from anxiety . . . '

Sometimes it takes great effort—

'First, I experience a state of tension, all my body seems to yearn . . . '

'This feeling I have to search for every time. I have never failed to reach it, and take it for granted that it will always be available, but I go through a process of great tenseness and apprehension first . . . '

As to the exact nature of the relationship—

'What can I say? Faith is implicit (= tacit, as opposed to explicit). Not to be explained. But a personal relationship. Like human personal relationship. You cannot explain love. The mother (and the father) love the infant. The baby responds. Children get fond of their friends. They feel 'at home' with parents, brothers and sisters, friends, relations. Then they fall in love. This is not to be measured or explained. . . . I know, in a way I cannot attempt to explain, that I know God in a personal way . . . and find not 'it', but a 'You'—personal . . . This relationship brings love, rock-like, compelling, leaving no choice . . . On a personal level I just cannot help myself. Any more than I can help loving my wife and family, or feeling 'at home' with people I know and trust . . . An experience that can be repeated—that *is* repeated daily, hourly—bringing reassurance, personal contact . . . is the experience of prayer.'

He now goes on to consider some of the *effects* of prayer, particularly in regard to personal relations, (in quoting examples from the records he gives them numbers of his own for reference in his subsequent discussion):

(1) 'Prayer seems a two-way action. I pray for love that I may give more love to my fellow-man; and there is no doubt that I receive it in abundance. But the mechanics of the thing remain a mystery.'

(2) 'I say 'please, YOU, help me to start. Where must I begin?' and somehow— it is as if someone took me by the hand, the way we do for blind people so that they can orientate themselves—I am set in motion . . . When there is a tricky conversation to start, a new contact, a difficult phone call to make, or when I see lovers or other partners trying to find each other, I say to myself: "Please, Angel Raphael or whoever you are, help me with your presence", and it is a fact that I can easily find the right words, that I manage to put people at ease . . . Of course, one may say that "prayers" of this kind do nothing else than summon some energy within ourselves. But why should we feel so helpless without it, or so grateful when we have it?'

(3) 'My greatest insights about myself have come when I have prayed. I have often been shown unpleasant things about myself, but always in a most helpful and loving way, sometimes with a distinct sense of humour.'

(4) 'While I prayed, I suddenly felt, or rather knew, that I had everything out of proportion . . . I saw myself clearly in another light and in relation to time and other people as though I were standing beside myself.'

(5) 'every evening I reviewed the day's events in God's sight.'

One common thread, [he says] seems to run through these examples: the person is able to reproduce (towards himself or others) whatever it is that he feels is 'given' to him by prayer. Now (1) explicitly mentions this 'two-way action'—as he is given Love, so he can give love to his fellow-man; similarly, as (2) is guided when in doubt, so he too can give guidance to others, to 'lovers or other partners trying to find themselves'. The same applies to understanding; the feeling of being looked at, perceptively but kindly, enables the person to see himself in the same light; so (3) discovers truths about himself, as seen through the eyes of a 'helpful and loving' other; (4) suddenly sees himself from without, 'as though I were standing beside myself'; (5) sees the day's events 'in God's sight', i.e. from God's point of view.

This 'identification' of oneself with a supporting, understanding Other is part of what psychologists mean by 'infantile dependence', . . . Here are two more examples, not especially connected with prayer:

(6) 'I really do care about people as people because I see them in the light of the relationship I enjoy with Jesus Christ. I rely on His forgiveness of my shortcomings. Because of this I believe I can understand and forgive others.'

(7) 'I firmly believe the encounter with Christ turns me into a more selfless person with Christ-like insights into human nature, enabling me to understand my own and others' weaknesses better.'

In line with this is Archbishop Temple's prayer—'Help me, O Lord, to see myself as Thou seest me'.

'It seems, [says Beardsworth] as if dependence on God can make a man feel freer in his personal relations, by sublimating his persisting infantile needs, so that he is no longer always seeking the other half of an 'attachment system'—clinging to A, rejecting B, too shy to speak to C, etc. This new freedom is mentioned by (2)—'. . . I can then easily find the right words,—I manage to put people at ease . . . '; and many other accounts confirm it—

(8) 'Through this beginning I have learned as a practical effect that the most exhilarating sense of freedom in living comes from personal recognition of complete dependence on that "someone" whose character for me is mirrored in Jesus of Nazareth . . . '

cf. a Church of England prayer 'God, whose service is perfect freedom . . . '

(9) 'You see everything differently, clearer, on a different plane. You can enjoy things and people without having to *possess* them . . . '

(10) 'This power has a great effect because . . . without it I feel at sixes and sevens with myself and the world, uncertain of what I should do, lonely and needing affection, and because of this clumsy in my relationships with other people . . . To be in touch with it is to be set free from the hell of one's own self-centredness . . . '

(11) 'I need to be loved and to love others. Where does God come in? Well, what if I get hurt—and I do—then even if love comes and goes in my life, I know that Love with a capital L never changes. Love is eternal.'

The last example brings us to the fear of rejection, of getting hurt, which goes with excessive dependence on people—cf. T. E. Lawrence (1935, p. 563): 'There was my craving to be liked—so strong and nervous that never could I open myself friendly to another. The terror of failure in an effort so important made me shrink from trying . . . ' Faith banishes this fear of being rejected, because, as we see in (11), it no longer matters.

cf. (12) 'Acted in faith and found it worked: holiday camp in North Wales—shy—hardly dared to speak to anyone I didn't know—then occurred to me, perhaps others shy too—'Thou shalt love thy neighbour as thyself'—invited a girl for a row on the lake—she asked her friends—found suddenly I had several friends—gave thanks to God . . . '

Besides the fear of being rejected, on the other side of the coin which is infantile dependence, we find the tendency to reject others. So Lawrence goes on—'besides, there was the standard; for intimacy seemed shameful unless the other could make the perfect reply'. The dependent person sees others only in terms of his own needs; whatever will not satisfy those needs he rejects. Independence brings tolerance in place of these fastidious, demanding standards—

(13) 'As a person I became very much happier, liberated from fear, and able to give and accept affection much more freely. I ceased being hypercritical, because I ceased being on the defensive . . . I remember looking at some trippers going round the Cathedral, and feeling a warm affection for them, whereas before I would have felt a contemptuous dislike.'

(14) 'Going back on the bus that evening, I felt and was an entirely different person. I astonished myself by smiling at people, by making room for them instead of hating them for sitting next to me.'

(15) 'Where I had been depressed, I now felt hopeful; where I had felt isolated and forlorn, I now felt as if I had access to a great reservoir of friendship and sympathy. I ceased to feel cynical and hateful towards the people around me and instead was able to feel tolerant and kindly.'

This new freedom means that instead of just reacting to others as possible satisfiers (or non-satisfiers) of his own infantile needs, a person can see them as 'other selves', as beings analogous to himself. We saw the beginning of this in (12) '. . . shy . . . then occurred to me, perhaps others shy too—"Thou shalt love thy neighbour as thyself" . . . ' etc.

cf. (16) 'The presence of God so surrounded and enveloped me that I lost every irrational fear . . . Released from the prison of my own ego, I became able to understand something of the inner selves of other people . . . '

(17) 'I have had an increasing sense of God's pervasive presence . . . Since one of the results is an increasing awareness of other people, I know the experience is not an illusion.'

(18) 'I feel the needs of others more and have much more compassion . . . I cannot explain away (as illusory) the change in my outlook towards my fellow human beings.'

With this understanding of others comes increase in self-knowledge—

(19) 'The ego shrinks because of the gradual advance in self-knowledge which seems to be a natural accompaniment of the awareness of the other. One sees oneself as one is warts and all!' (cf. (3) and (4) above.)

Beardsworth ends by saying that these effects seem more remarkable than those he encountered among the quasi-sensory experiences. He has now, as Gordon Milburn Research Fellow of Trinity College, returned to our collections for a renewed study of prayer.

8

QUANTITATIVE RESEARCH

We have been building up a body of knowledge of the various kinds of spiritual awareness; we have collated and classified them and have examined these accounts to show some of their effects as experienced by members of the public. Our work has not however revealed the actual proportions of people in different populations who have such experiences, nor of those who deny ever having had anything of a remotely similar nature. So far therefore our studies have been qualitative. Now I wish to move on to the use of the quantitative method, to measure the extent to which members of a population may have this or that kind of experience.

There can be seen to be, I hope, a parallel between these stages and those in the development of the study of living animals and plants. I say 'I hope' because this parallel was indeed intended in framing the programme of our research. The building of a truly quantitative science of living things was however made possible only by the foundations laid down by the observations of the field naturalists who first explored the natural world. Just as in biology, the coming of quantitative ecology has not meant that the observations of the naturalists are no longer necessary, so with us the development of such a sociological analysis does not mean that the descriptive study of spiritual awareness must now be considered as over; far from it, there is so much more to be done to give us a better understanding of this spiritual side of man.

I have already related (p. 22) how David Hay, lecturer in Biology in the Department of Education in the University of Nottingham, came to collaborate with us. He sent out a questionnaire to the students in his own department on the occurrence of religious experience amongst them. The sample was one hundred people (fifty male and fifty female) drawn by a randomization procedure from the course membership for the one-year post-graduate Certificate in Education (1972-3) Nottingham. The sample was small but because of the low numbers, he was able to see each person privately and so to encourage him to speak freely and at length about his experiences. Each person was invited to attend for an interview in his office and this invitation was accepted by all but two of the sample. The total was then made up to a hundred again by drawing two more names at random from the course list. At the time of the interview each person was asked the questions on the schedule below and the answers were written down.

Questions

1. Academic subject

2. Age

3. Sex

4. Married or single

5. Do you feel that you have ever been aware of or influenced by a presence or a power, whether you call it God or not, which is different from your everyday self?

6. Would you describe the (these) experience(s) for me?
   (i), (ii), (iii) etc.

   (a) How old were you at the time (or when this first occurred)?
   (b) How frequently has this experience occurred (units, tens, hundreds)?
   (c) Were or are there particular circumstances in which the experience is most likely to occur?
   (d) Did the power seem personal or impersonal?

7. (a) Do you consider your experience(s) to be religious?
   (b) Why?

8. (a) How did you feel as a result of the experience?
   (b) How long did the feeling last?
   (c) Have your experiences had any permanent effect on your life?

9. Have you any opinion as to whether the experiences you describe have (or had) some function in your life?

10. What was your religious upbringing?
    (Including whether parents are practising.)

11. Do you have a religion or faith now?
    (Including whether church is attended.)

12. Would you be willing to write out an account of your experiences, whether everyday or unusual, giving your age at the time of the experience and any other factors thought relevant?
    Any material given to me should be marked with your code number, but not signed, so that confidentiality can be maintained.

David Hay clearly had the power of winning the confidence of those taking part; more than one person at the end of the interview made the remark 'Well, I never thought I would tell you that' (Hay 1974).

In this chapter I shall summarize some of the answers which I think will interest the reader most, the rest can be found in Hay's own report (1979).

In a response to the question 'Do you feel that you have ever been aware of or influenced by a presence or power, whether you call it God or not, which is different from your everyday self?' 65 per cent answered 'Yes' and 29 per cent 'No', while six per cent were not sure; when a divison is made between those respondents whose academic subjects are classed as science and those classed as arts, there is hardly any difference in the proportion of their replies to the same question. The more common kinds of the experience recorded among the hundred participants are the following in order of decreasing frequency (with the relative numbers of occurrence shown in brackets): awareness of a power controlling or guiding me (23); awareness of the presence of God (22); awareness of a presence in nature (19), and answered prayers (14).

Particularly interesting are the answers given to the question: 'Were or are there particular circumstances in which the experience is most likely to occur?' The frequency with which the different kinds of conditions elicited religious experience in order of decreasing importance were as follows: alone or in silence 35; times of severe distress or decision 34; close to nature 26; with close or trusted friends 21; times of great happiness or peace 15; during prayer or devotions 13; in darkness or dim light 12; at a church service 12; before works of art or in old churches 10, in no special circumstances 8. Hay discusses the very positive nature of these experiences and analyses the relation of their spiritual awareness to religious belief or faith. This indeed is a beginning of a quantitative sociological study of the spiritual nature of man. In Appendix II I give a selection of extracts from the personal reports of Hay's students picked out to illustrate their various kinds of experience; these provide a valuable comparison with those collected by the Unit, for whereas the latter came haphazard in response to a general and extended public appeal, Hay's examples are all from one particular group of a hundred individuals chosen at random at the same time and place.

FURTHER QUANTITATIVE RESEARCH BY HAY AMD MORISY

David Hay and Ann Morisy have co-operated in two pieces of research which, although different in the ways they were carried out, were essentially complementary. One included questions in one of the regular nation-wide surveys conducted by National Opinion Polls Ltd., which yielded a total of 1865 people (853 male and 1012 female) who responded to the questions on religious experience; the other was a more intimate survey, on the lines of the original pilot study, made in depth by tactful interviews among randomly selected members of the general public in the Nottingham area. Whilst the analysis of the results of the latter is still in progress, those of the former have been sufficiently examined to show their outstanding features and enable them to be compared with various American surveys. This formed the subject of a paper they presented to a meeting of the American Society for the Scientific Study of Religion at Chicago (Hay and Morisy 1978). The following information is taken from this paper and an article in *The Tablet* (Hay 1977).

In the nation-wide survey Hay and Morisy concentrated their attention on the instances where people say they have, or have not, been 'aware of, or influenced by a presence or power, whether referred to as God or not, which is different from their 'everyday selves'; this is the question Hay used in his pilot study and is taken, with slight abridgement, from one I introduced in our Oxford work. In their 1978 paper they refer to it as 'Hardy's question', but in discussing some of their results I shall instead refer to it as the 'key question', for it is the one they use most often. The overall frequency of reports of being aware of or influenced

TABLE 1

Overall frequency of responses to the key question
(shown as percentages)

Sex	Negative ('Never in my life')	Total positive response	Numbers in sample
Male	69	31	(853)
Female	58	41	(1012)
Total	63.6	34.6	(1865)

by a presence or power (the key question) is as shown in Table 1. The percentage total positive response is 36.4 per cent, which is much lower than the very high proportion (65 per cent) found in Hay's pilot survey among his post-graduate students. Hay suggested a variety of reasons for this; it could for example be that more intending teachers have a sense of religious vocation than do most members of the general population. While this may well account for a little of this higher percentage, the results of the nation-wide survey, as the authors point out, indicate another explanation. Table 2 shows the response to the key question compared with the ages at which their formal education ceased. It is seen that except for

TABLE 2

Response to the key question
compared with terminal education age
(shown as percentages)

Terminal education age	Negative ('Never in my life')	Total positive response	Number* in sample
13–14	63	37	(706)
15	71	29	(531)
16	64	37	(275)
17–19	56	44	(188)
20 +	44	56	(113)

*48 of sample still at school so not included in analysis

the response of those who left school at 13-14 years, (where the figure 37 is an artefact, as will be explained in a moment) there is a steady increase in the positive response as the extent of education increases; the positive response of 56 per cent of these whose education extended to 20 years or over is indeed approaching the figure found in Hay's survey confined to students having an average age of 22 years. The explanation they give for the artefact just referred to is the change in the law relating to school-leaving age, which in 1947 was increased to 15 years; this means that those in the survey whose terminal education age is given as 13-14 years must all be 44 years or older and because the survey also shows that, as we shall see in a moment, the making of a positive response increases with age, it is therefore likely that the positive response of these early school-leavers will be somewhat higher than expected.

Now let us look at this indication of increase in positive response to the key question according to age as revealed by the nation-wide survey and shown in our Table 3. It is apparent that this trend is nearly continuously upwards with age; somewhat under a third (29 per cent) of the 16-24 year-olds responded positively compared with nearly a half (47 per cent) of those 65 years and over.

TABLE 3
Response to the key question compared with age
(shown as percentages)

Age	Negative response ('Never in my life')	Total positive response	Number in sample
16-24	71	29	(335)
25-34	64	35	(368)
35-44	67	33	(286)
45-54	65	36	(310)
55-64	58	43	(248)
65 +	54	47	(318)

What is the real significance of this? Hay has a simple answer (*The Tablet* 1977): this 'is consistent with a phenomenon which turns up with more or less equal frequency from adolescence onwards, so that the longer a person has lived, the more likely he is to report it.'

In their paper Hay and Morisy go on to consider two suggestions that have been made in the past by some psychologists and anthropologists: that religious experience is more often reported among those who are more oppressed by an unjust society in that it might have a palliative function, or that it is associated with a low level of psychological well-being. If the first proposition were true one would expect to find a higher proportion of those who give a positive response to the key question among the lower social classes than among the upper strata; in fact the results of their survey, as shown in Table 4, are quite contrary to this.

TABLE 4
Response to the key question compared with social class
(shown as percentages)

Social Class	Negative response ('Never in my life')	Total positive response	Number in sample
Upper middle	54	47	(65)
Middle	50	49	(209)
Lower middle	59	41	(408)
Skilled working	68	31	(698)
Unskilled + Subsistence	67	32	(485)

Nor does the nation-wide survey give support to the hypothesis that religious experience is associated with a low level of psychological well-being or neurosis, for in it they included the Bradburn Balanced Affect Scale (Bradburn 1969) as a short measure of psychological well-being. The range of possible scores on the scale is from minus 5, indicating a very low level of psychological well-being, to plus 5, indicating a very high level. Approximately equal sized high and low scoring groups were formed by splitting the sample at the +1/+2 scoring boundary. As can be seen in Table 5 people reporting religious experience are significantly

TABLE 5
Response to the key question
compared with psychological well-being
(shown as percentages)

Score on Bradburn Scale	Negative response ('Never in my life')	Total positive response	Number in sample
High (> + 1):	47% (494)	54% (336)	(830)
Low (< + 2):	53% (550)	46% (288)	(838)
Total numbers:	(1044)	(624)	(1668)*

*Only those completing all items on Bradburn Scale were included in the analysis.

more likely to report a high level of psychological well-being than those who do not. (The measure of significance as given by the χ^2 test is 6.4768, a value for *p* of 0.02.)

There are many other interesting results from their nation-wide survey to be found in their paper. Hay and Morisy are certainly carrying the study of religious experience into the realm of measurement. I have little doubt that this is only the beginning of a wide expansion of such sociological studies. In this sense the spiritual side of man can indeed be studied by the scientific method. Such quantitative analyses must, however, go hand in hand with a continuing attempt to gain an ever deeper understanding of the essence of those remarkable elements in his nature which can never be the subject of scientific inquiry: they are akin to those of art, poetry, love and affection which can be studied only through a careful comparison of qualitative accounts of human experience.

In dealing with the spiritual nature of man I have not in this book been concerned with his religious rituals and practices; before passing to the concluding chapter, however, I feel I should not fail to remind the reader that at times these activities have led man to commit the most appalling atrocities. I am not blind to this evil side; it is an aspect which I think is likely to be linked through evolution to our past animal behaviour. I have discussed it in my earlier book *The Divine Flame* where I quoted the ending of one of Marett's Gifford Lectures (1932, p. 90); I do so again as follows:

Thanks to the grosser forms of the sacrificial rite, the middle religions—not those of savages so much as those of the half-civilized peoples—reek of blood like a shambles. It was the sacrifice of Iphigeneia that called forth the protest of Lucretius in immortal verse: *tantum religio potuit suadere malorum*. Yet if the facts are so, let us face them fairly. If religion is liable to unloose the beast in us even while seeking to free the man, we must learn how this deviation occurs, so that religion may be kept to the true direction. As psychologists, then, we must not be content to speak together in whispers about the lust or the cruelty that found their way into the religious complex together with the noblest of the human tendencies.

9

WHAT *IS* SPIRITUALITY?

I had at first thought of calling this chapter 'The Nature of Spirituality'; put like that, however, it would have seemed a grotesquely over-ambitious proposal— almost like suggesting that we had solved the very nature of the universe itself. It is one thing to talk about 'the spiritual nature of man' meaning that side of his make-up which, if not always leading him to have what he might call religious feelings, may at least give him a love of the non-material things of life such as natural beauty, art, music, or moral values; it is quite another matter to talk of the very nature of spirituality itself. Who would be so foolish as to imagine or pretend that he could make such a definitive pronouncement?

So I have decided to end this book with a statement of what I conceive to be some of the essential features of man's spiritual nature—particularly in regard to his religious feelings—as revealed by the foregoing study. Others may draw other conclusions; the reader, however, will expect me at least to say what I consider our work is showing and even hope that I shall be bold enough to suggest how I think it may affect our way of looking at our world. I can only stress that the views I here express are those of one who has lived with the incoming records— the accumulating evidence—for some eight years.

It seems to me that the main characteristics of man's religious and spiritual experiences are shown in his feelings for a transcendental reality which frequently manifest themselves in early childhood; a feeling that 'Something Other' than the self can actually be sensed; a desire to personalize this presence into a deity and to have a private I-Thou relationship with it, communicating through prayer. I shall now discuss each of these characteristics in turn.

TRANSCENDENTAL REALITY

First and foremost I would say that those three very different elements of superstition, wishful thinking, and contradictory theological theories which have made so many intellectuals shy away from a serious study of religious phenomena have, taking the records as a whole, been little in evidence in the accounts of spiritual awareness sent to us. If these three elements have characterized much of institutional religion in the past, our records of personal spirituality have, I believe, shown us something quite different; for the great majority there is a strong feeling of a transcendental reality which has in most cases little, if any, connection with any one of these elements. And further, whilst corporate worship may have a deep meaning for some, institutional religion plays little part in most of these accounts.

It has been suggested by some authors that there are two main kinds of religious experience, the *numinous*—the awareness of the holy as defined by Otto (1923)—and the *mystical*, the feeling of the merging of the self with a divine reality; it is, however, I believe, this feeling of a transcendental reality that is far more important than these other two elements, for not only does it form a part of both of them but is the essential element in so many other kinds of spiritual experience. The point has been well expressed by Davis in his book *Body as Spirit* (1976) where on p. 23, he is discussing Ninian Smart's views. He writes as follows:

His estimation that the phenomenological difference between worship and con-templation—that is, between numinous experience and mystical identification—is more important than the phenomenological similarity of each having a trans-cendent focus. I disagree with that assessment. For me, the fact that both experiences relate to the transcendent, however differently conceived, is a more basic feature than any of their differences. It marks off both types of experience from other levels of human experience, whether intellectual, practical, aesthetic, or moral.

Yes, it is surely this transcendental element that is fundamental: the feeling that there is a spiritual reality that *appears* to be beyond the conscious self with which the individual can have communion in one way or another—and whether spoken of as God or not—is indeed the most characteristic feature of the vast number of records we have received. We see this vividly in all the examples of childhood experience recalled by the adults who have written to us.

EARLY CHILDHOOD MANIFESTATIONS

Robinson has suggested that some 15 per cent of all the correspondents, who now number over four thousand people, looked back at their early experiences and regarded them as of vital importance. All Robinson's evidence suggests that this feeling of our relation to the transcendental is something fundamental in the human psyche showing itself in the early stages of life. He ends his book, *The Original Vision* (1977), with the following paragraph:

The great majority of those whose experience led me to make this study are men and women in whom the original vision of childhood has never wholly faded.

But are they typical? And what of the rest of us who have no such memories? If the child within me dies a little more each day, how, asks Marcel, am I to be faithful to myself? And when I cannot do this, 'I am no longer there, I do not exist any more'. In Brancusi's words, when we cease to be children, we are already dead. But if childhood in the wider, timeless sense is in some mysterious fashion connected, or even to be identified with, that kind of awareness that is truly to be called religious, it could be that by learning once more to respond to the demands made upon us by the something-more-than situation we may discover that there is still a spark of life in the child within each one of us.

A SENSE OF PRESENCE

It is the 'Something More' felt in childhood which expresses so well the element of the transcendental that is at the heart of nearly all religious feelings. We saw it clearly in the work of Beardsworth on those more dramatic quasi-sensory experiences, where this sense of presence is yet another expression of the same reality but suggesting, as indeed is so often the case, that it may have a strong personal element. The final passage from Beardsworth's study, *A Sense of Presence* (1977), makes the point well:

In sum, what impresses us most about these accounts? First, one is struck by the dependent, personal (I–You) basis of the experiences. If one chooses to talk of hallucinations, then these are not the experiencing of hallucinatory sensations (particular colours, sounds, etc.) but of hallucinatory meetings; 'person', not 'sensation', is the basic element; more often than not there is an inter-sensory overlap—e.g. something, or rather someone, is not only 'seen', but 'heard' or 'touched' as well, or else they are felt to be 'there' just as surely without any sensory evidence at all.

Next, strong emotion tends to colour not only the experience itself and its effect, but also the situation leading up to it. Very often the experience brings a sudden dramatic reversal of feeling—e.g. from the depths of despair to unbounded joy.

Then there is the point that, while some contributors locate the 'voice', 'light', 'presence' or whatever in the outside world, others say it is 'within', while still others say it is both at once,—' . . . a Presence which in a strange way was both about me and within me'. This seems to be symptomatic of a general indistinctness between 'inner' and 'outer', 'self' and 'other', active and passive (i.e. whether I am doing it or it is being done to me) that may occur in moments of high excitement. Thus with 'voices', one contributor felt he was being addressed by the voice of another that nevertheless 'seemed to come from inside myself'. The 'meeting', then, is no ordinary sort of meeting. The 'You' may be (to quote from the Upanishads) 'both without us and within us'; 'closer is he than breathing, nearer than hands and feet'. An English philosopher, F. H. Bradley, writes 'the reality of God means his actual presence within individual souls, and apart from this presence both he and they are no more than abstractions'. Buber puts it more simply: 'In the beginning is relation . . . There is no "I" taken by myself, but only the "I" of the primary word "I–You" '. If 'You' is said, the 'I' of 'I–You' is said with it.

The feeling of Something Other than the self—whether felt as a sense of presence or not—is indeed characteristic of the great majority of those other experiences of a cognitive or affective kind which form the great array of variations reviewed in Chapter 4; they embrace all those feelings of joy, peace, security, awe, reverence, and wonder, as also of exaltation and ecstasy, of hope and fulfilment. These feelings are particularly evident in the examples selected for study by Walker; he is especially interested in those who 'state their conviction that all or much of their lives has been influenced by a Power felt to be beyond the self ... sustaining, encouraging, strengthening, guiding or compelling them'. I have said that these feelings of a power beyond the self are characteristic of the great majority, but there are a few exceptions as in the example given by Walker on p. 115 where the writer says 'I am much more aware of an immanent power of the spirit, than of one "outside" myself; I am sure that it guides and shapes my life, and that what seem coincidences are often part of a plan.'

PERSONALIZATION

I believe our approach to what we call God must be one as to a person. It was clearly not until man had developed speech of a sufficiently coherent quality to enable him to talk about his various feelings that he began to discuss the curious experience he had of there being something intuitive in his life that at times he became aware of, something not felt by his physical senses, but by some deep inner conviction. I think that we have already seen some evidence that suggests that this is not idle speculation, for is it not likely that primitive man had experiences similar to those found by Robinson among the young children of our own society before it was crushed out of them by over-sophisticated education?

This strange feeling for 'something other' over long periods of time developed into primitive religion in various parts of the world. In each case they gave it a special name, for instance the Polynesians called it *mana*, the North American Indians *waken*. It was Marett, the social anthropologist, who first emphasized the importance of this universality, as I have already briefly indicated in the quotation given on p. 6. Let me add a further short excerpt from one of Marett's later works (1935):

A play of images sufficiently forcible to arouse by diffused suggestion a conviction that the tribal luck is taking a turn in the required direction is the sum of his theology; and yet the fact remains that a symbolism so gross and mixed can help the primitive man to feel more confident of himself—to enjoy the inward assurance that he is in touch with sources and powers of grace that can make him rise superior to the circumstances and chances of this mortal life.

However crude man's early efforts were in approaching this mysterious power which seemed to be beyond the self, they were, as Marett says, sufficient to make him feel that he received help, strength, and encouragement. 'Religion' said Malinowski (1936), 'makes man do the biggest things he is capable of.'

Certainly religion has been a most important element in the evolution of man in his social phase and in the development of civilization.

I think it likely that because religion has been so important in man's social evolution, there has developed with it some passionate feelings giving rise to religious conflict, in comparison with which there is nothing more powerful except the jealousies of sex (that other very important element in the process of evolution). There is, I believe, another parallel with sex: the element of love. The bonds of affectionate feeling—or love—have been developed certainly twice in the evolution of the higher animals: between mating pairs and reciprocally between parents and offspring. When those feelings of a beneficient power from beyond the conscious self came to be recognized by man it was not unnatural for that power to be thought of in a personal way. This process of personalization was consolidated. I believe, by building the child–parent relationship into it. Whilst we owe something to Freud, I do not think it is entirely as he supposed, nor do I believe that his super-ego, the internal father figure, is the real explanation. There is undoubtedly a devotional love relation to this personified power beyond the conscious self, more akin to a child–mother relationship; to explain this however, I must make a digression into the studies in animal behaviour.

In the long evolution of animals two opposite types of social behaviour have been developed in a wide range of different animal groups such as fish, birds, and mammals; these are the acts of aggression and of submission. Again and again we see the former exhibited, usually by the males of the species, in fighting with rivals for the possession of territory or mates, or their position in some social hierarchical system; equally common are the acts of submission whereby one of a pair of fighting individuals, who is losing the battle and realizes he cannot win, suddenly makes a sign which at once prohibits the other from continuing the fight further, so that loss of life within the species has been prevented. Commonly among animals we see such acts of submission performed in relation to more powerful members of the same species; it is not unnatural therefore for such acts to be developed in man in relation to this imagined person—the personified power—felt to be beyond the conscious self. Thus we may have acts of obeisance as well as devotional love developed in man's dealings with his God and he has the urge to go down on his knees before this great mystery. This is not I believe to be thought of as superstitious act, but a part of human behaviour having its roots deep in man's biological history. There is, however, something else linking the devotional love of God with the animal world which we must briefly discuss in relation to this problem before we finally draw our conclusions. In saying all this I hope I shall not be thought to be in any way denigrating the idea of the divine; this is not at all what I intend.

The Dutch anatomist Bolk (1926) put forward the view, now widely accepted that man in relation to his ape-like ancestors is permanently in a more juvenile condition, in a state known to biogolists as neoteny or paedomophosis; he is what Desmond Morris called 'an infantile ape'.

Among some of the important juvenile characters of man is the retarded closure of the sutures between the bones of the skull, allowing a great development of the brain during a long period of growth after birth, so giving a long period of education, of learning by experience. There is also, in addition to various physical characters such as the flatness of the face helping in stereoscopic vision, the long extension into adult life of the pleasure in play. These are all changes brought about by natural selection; I mention them especially in order to compare them with the changes that man himself brought about by his own selection of various characters in the dog; by selective breeding man altered the dog in an extraordinary way.

In addition to producing different breeds which exhibit juvenile physical features, such as drooping ears, shortened muzzle, and domed skull, man was able to alter the dog's behaviour. The dog remained juvenile and transferred its loyalty and obedience from its own kind to man. To quote the words of that great pioneer in the study of animal behaviour, Konrad Lorenz (1952):

One of these juvenile characters which has become permanent in the domestic dog, expresses itself in the peculiar form of its attachment. The ardent affection which wild canine youngsters show for their mother and which in these disappears completely after they have reached maturity, is preserved as a permanent mental trait of all highly domesticated dogs. What originally was love for the mother is transformed into love for the human master.

Thus we now have an animal which is not only loyal and obedient to his new master but has towards him a devotional love relationship. Here I believe we see within the biological system something very like man's feelings towards this great mystery that he feels beyond himself, the mystery he personifies.

However man may have seen in the past the mystery he personifies, it would be a mistake today to believe that his devotional love relationship is to a deity situated 'out there' in space. In *Honest to God* (1963) Bishop John Robinson said that the image of God must go and he was reporting what so many profoundly religious people had been thinking for a long time. The idea that God is within the mental part of the living world, instead of out there in physical space, should not shock, for it is not new.

Jung talked of God as a part of the subconscious (1963, p. 910); Durkheim of the consciousness of the consciousnesses (1915, p. 444). I believe that the nature of God is essentially one of personal qualities and that man's relationship to this presence must be a devotional, personal I-Thou feeling, but I do not feel it incumbent on me to visualize him sitting on a cloud, as it were.

Neither Jung, nor Durkheim, Freud, nor indeed any one else has yet solved the mystery that so many feel to be a reality and call by the name of God. This presence is know to us only through experience, either our own or from that of others. What we need is more data, more and more accounts, more and more observation. I would like to think that the studies at our Unit are helping, however modestly, to build up acceptable knowledge. For is not this mystery as worthy a quest as that for the ultimate nature of matter?

THE PHENOMENON OF PRAYER

The element of spirituality which is at the heart of all religion is the phenomenon of prayer. It is the channel of the 'I-Thou' relationships, Again and again correspondents write of their communion with this power, but rarely do they mention the use of such set prayers—however poetically beautiful may be their language—which form part of the liturgy of institutional religion. Few would deny the power of such language to effect many in a religious way, just as they may be affected by church music; the prayers made in solitude have, however, another function and are very different. They may sometimes be made without words, but more often they are spoken or thought in the extempore language of the heart, in a devotional love relationship. We have already seen many examples of such prayer and their effects discussed by Beardsworth in Chapter 9. In Chapter 5 we saw that prayer or meditation was mentioned as an anticipatory factor leading to religious experience (category 11(d) by 407 respondents in the first 3000 records, or 13.6 per cent, and those from the same total who recorded a sense of prayer answered in events (category 7(u)) were 415 or 13.8 per cent. But the category which had the greatest frequency of all was that among the dynamic patterns of experience 9(b) which we labelled '*Initiative felt to be within the self, but response from beyond*'; there were no fewer than 968 examples in the first 3000 records (an average of 322.7 per thousand or 32 per cent).

'One common thread' says Beardsworth, 'seems to run through these examples: the person is able to reproduce (towards himself or others) whatever it is that he feels is "given" to him by prayer.'

To express my personal views about prayer let me give two short quotations from my book *The Divine Flame* (1966):

If it is to be real and to work, it must be as deep and sincere as human love. Without such sincerity, or emotion, faith if you like, it makes *no* response at all; with the right approach, however, lives can be transformed, seemingly impossible tasks achieved, and the drabness of the world turned to joy (p. 175).

As the making of physical fire was one of the great milestones in the rise of man, so also I believe was his discovery of prayer as a means of kindling and fanning a flame he found within him; a flame which, like a spiritual engine, has brought him to higher and higher things. Let him not throw it away (p. 244).

I certainly believe that the phenomenon of prayer, as demonstrated in the experience of man, reveals a fundamental fact about the nature of the universe and tells us more about the mystery we call God.

It seems to me that the effects of prayer, the answers if you wish to use such terms, are of at least two kinds; there may well be more, as some people would certainly believe, but let me deal with the two which seem to me to be the most striking: the general and the particular.

The effect of general prayer is the sense of receiving help, strength and encouragement, power, and a great zest to do much that one feels is worth doing for the good of the world and one's fellows. It is well illustrated by Bartlett's comment which I have already quoted on page 54; where he points out that he has neither the right nor the knowledge to reject the testimony of those he has known and respected who have accomplished many acts outside the range of unassisted humanity and have said that it was God working through them.

The effect of particular prayer is the sense of receiving answers to all kinds of different and difficult personal problems put before God. It seems to me much more difficult to imagine how this can possibly come about, yet I believe there is overwhelming evidence that it is a common occurrence. There certainly appears to be 'a divinity that shapes our ends, rough-hew them how we will'. I will now attempt to offer an explanation, one with a psychological basis, but I hope none the worse for that.

The answers to our particular individual problems sought in prayer do not always come at once and the solution that eventually dawns upon us, is, as often as not, not at all what we expected. We have all experienced going to sleep thinking of some difficult problem and awakening in the morning with a solution—an answer that comes from our own subconscious. Would it not be more in keeping with what we know of nature for each of us to have our own built-in solution-provider, but one which is unlocked as it were by the power we tap in prayer? The suggestion I am here making owes much to the views of the social psychologists, Claire and W. M. S. Russell, expressed in their contribution to the book *Theories of the Mind* (1962), although they are not concerned with prayer at all. After discussing Freud's view that we may repress what seem to us to be irrational motives only to find that they may return unawares to affect our behaviour, the Russells present us with this striking illustration:

Shakespeare, as usual, provides a splendid example. When Hamlet is about to leave for England with Rosencrantz and Guildenstern, he is in no doubt about their reliability and his own prospects. 'There's letters seal'd; and my two school-fellows, Whom I will trust as I will adders fang'd,' etc. (Act III, scene iv). In the same soliloquy he even outlines a strategy—that of hoisting the engineer with his own petar. By the time he is on ship-board, he has repressed all this, and goes to his cabin to sleep. But the repressed intelligent observation is still at work. In his heart (as he tells Horatio in Act V) 'there was a kind of fighting that would not let me sleep . . . our indiscretion sometimes serves us well, when our deep plots do pall; and that should learn us there's a divinity that shapes our ends, rough-hew them how we will'. Restless with insomnia, he has a vague impulse to look at the letter. He opens it, finds the order for his assassination, and proceeds to carry out the strategy he had formed in Denmark—without remembering this at all. To him it seems like a new and strange inspiration: 'ere I could make a prologue to my brains, they had begun the play,—I sat me down, devised a new commission, wrote it fair' and so on. Anyone who has noticed him— or herself having this sort of experience will recognize the perfect accuracy of the poet's description. The 'divinity' is, of course our own intelligence. This sort of behaviour is specially common in a particular class of the personality type we have called 'idealistic', to which Hamlet conforms in all other ways. The chief feature is a readiness to repress (either instantaneously or after first voicing them) accurate observations about the *hostile* intentions of others.

It seems to be likely that the solutions to our individual problems are always within us if only we could reach them, and that the act of prayer brings them to the surface. In *The Divine Flame* (p. 236) I expressed this idea as follows:

Instead of supposing that one great personal-like Deity is thinking out simultaneously the detailed answers to the millions of different problems of all the individuals of the world, is it not more reasonable to suppose that some action is set in motion by prayer which draws the particular solution for each one of us from our own minds? In saying this I must again make clear that I am not implying that I believe this destroys our conception of the Divine. All the evidence of religious experience, I believe, shows us that man makes contact with this Power which appears partly transcendent, and felt as the numinous beyond the self, and partly immanent within him. I also think it likely, however, that it may well be this uplifting power which does in fact activate the subconscious solution-providing mechanism in a way which would not otherwise be possible. In a similar way it may be the same power which assists in the healing of a sick person.

Such a view I find is not without some theological support; Bishop John Robinson, in his book *Exploration into God* (1967) (p. 115) writes as follows:

The God who 'answers' prayers or 'makes' people well again is inevitably seen as disposing the events of nature and history or the lives of individuals in a way which envisages him as standing above the processes, manipulating them from the outside. What we need is a conception of prayer that organically relates the processes themselves to the depths of the divine creativity and love.

AN EXPERIMENTAL FAITH

Without I hope appearing to be too evangelical, for this book is not the place for that, I wish now to suggest that the spirituality of man might be increased in the future by what I call an experimental faith. Here I want to use the words *experiment* and *experimental* in a particular way, in fact in their original meaning before they became associated in the modern mind with the methods of science. The first meaning given to the word 'experimental' in the *Concise Oxford Dictionary* is 'Based on experience, not on authority or conjecture'; this being so, would it not be better, some would say, to speak of an experiential faith so as to avoid confusion with the scientific meaning? My answer is 'No', because the faith I am thinking of would be one based not only on general experience but on one which in part is like that described in the first meaning given in the same dictionary to the word 'experiment', i.e. a 'test, trial or procedure adopted on the chance of its succeeding'. 'What a poor kind of faith' the faithful may well say, and I would agree if that were all there is to it; that however is not all that I mean. To become a real faith the word 'chance' in the definition must become converted into 'certainty' by the very experiment having succeeded. I do not mean a faith based upon prayer which is undertaken, as it were, just on the off chance that it may succeed. I mean a prayer undertaken by an agnostic or an atheist who, having studied the records of experience, is now prepared, with profound sincerity, to attempt the quest for a period of, say, at least six months; it might perhaps be a prayer beginning something like this. 'God, if there is a God, help me to find you, and having found you, help me to have the strength and courage to do what I feel to be Thy will.' Childish, isn't it? Yes, for that, I believe, is the biological essence of the matter.

The spiritual side of man is not the product of intellectuality. The development of the mind, now so strongly influenced by the achievements of the physical sciences, has tended to dismiss, as childish wishful thinking, this deeper property of life. It is child-like just because it is even more fundamental to life than is this recent amazing innovation—mind; it indeed was the very nature of the teachings of Jesus as they have come down to us: 'Whosoever shall not receive the kingdom of God as a little child, he shall not enter therein.' (Mark 10:15).

When speaking of God as Father, Jesus invariably used the childish word *Abba*. John Taylor, now Bishop of Winchester, in his book *The Go-Between God* (1972), brings out so well the child-like relationship which Jesus had to the presence of God. He writes (on his p. 93) thus:

That ... trustful dedication points to the dominant I–Thou relationship in this Spirit-possessed life, namely his incomparable awareness of God. More than all the others who absorbed his whole attention, this was the Other in whom he was immersed. God was the never-forgotten presence, yet Jesus' relation to God was never dutiful; it was ardent and glad and totally relaxed. It expressed the absolute acceptance of his creaturehood and an untroubled dependence, without a shadow of subservience. It was the fully responsible partnership of one who, in Bonhoeffer's phrase, 'Made his whole life a response to the question and call of God'. This astonishing relationship was perfectly expressed in the baby-word '*Abba*', 'Daddy', in which we catch the actual sound of Jesus' most characteristic and intimate utterance.

To return to what I was saying about an experimental faith. I like to think that our studies at the Religious Experience Research Unit are not only helping, however modestly, to build up an academic knowledge towards a better understanding of the spiritual nature of man, but that they are, as I have suggested, also providing the evidence which, as it accumulates further in the future, may induce others to make the act of faith which is expressed in the words of Jesus as reported in the Gospels (Mark 7:7 and Luke 11:9): 'Ask and it shall be given you; seek and ye shall find.' While the idea of receiving Divine help reaches its height and glory in the Gospels, it did not, of course, arise there; long before that the psalmist was singing:

I will lift up mine eyes unto the hills, from whence cometh my help. My help cometh from the Lord (Psalm 121).

'The thing is immemorial and universal' as Aldous Huxley says in the Introduction to his *The Perennieal Philosophy* (1947); 'Rudiments of . . . [it] may be found among the traditionary lore of primitive peoples in every region of the world, and in its fully developed form it has a place in every one of the higher religions.'

HISTORICAL PARALLELS

I have recalled enough examples from earlier pages to illustrate what I believe to be the main characteristics of man's religious feelings, notably transcendental reality, early childhood manifestations, a sense of presence, personalization and the phenomenon of prayer. How similar are these conclusions to those of that great pioneer and master, William James? In the concluding chapter of his *Varieties* he writes:

Summing up in the broadest possible way the characteristics of the religious life, as we have found them, it includes the following beliefs:-
1. That the visible world is part of a more spiritual universe from which it draws its chief significance;
2. That union or harmonious relation with that higher universe is our true end;
3. That prayer or inner communion with the spirit thereof—be that spirit 'God' or 'law'—is a process wherein work is really done, and spiritual energy flows in and produces effects, psychological or material, within the phenomenal world.
Religion includes also the following psychological characteristics:-
4. A new zest which adds itself like a gift to life, and takes the form either of lyrical enchantment or of appeal to earnestness and heroism.
5. An assurance of safety and a temper of peace, and, in relation to others, a preponderance of loving affections.

I think the reader will recognize that James's summary of what he regards as the main characteristics of a man's religious life, based, as is ours, upon records of experience, is indeed similar to our own. Are my conclusions coloured by having first read those of James? In the whole of this book, as well as in the fore-going brief discussion, I have been drawing particularly upon the findings of my colleagues. I believe that there can be little doubt that the results of our research do confirm the views first put forward by James three-quarters of a century ago. In my first chapter I emphasized the brilliant innovation of this pioneering work of James and Starbuck, and said how we were humbly following in their footsteps; it is now most gratifying to find that our work fits so well on to the foundations they laid. Does this mean that our task is accomplished, that there is no more for us to do? Far from it.

Perhaps to the point of tedium I have several times stressed the importance of making more studies of the many different aspects of our growing collections of material; if the foregoing points do in fact represent the main characteristics of man's spiritual life on the religious side, they need to be filled out in all kinds of ways and extended in many directions. The studies must be applied to other cultures—to other faiths. James himself, in discussing his own work and that of Starbuck, pointed out (in his preface to Starbuck's book) that their material was almost entirely from Protestant Christianity and predominately of an evangelical kind and said that 'for comparative purposes similar collections ought yet to be made from Catholic, Jewish, Mohammedan, Buddhist and Hindoo sources.' It is vital, I believe, that we should establish whether these characteristics which we have been discussing are indeed applicable to mankind as a whole. Aldous Huxley in his *The Perennial Philosophy* seems to suggest that they are; so also do the findings of those social anthropologists who work among the more primitive peoples of the world.

Whilst I have said that others may come to other conclusions I do not think they can deny the existence of the elements of experience we have so far discussed; what they may well debate are the conclusions that may be drawn regarding their significance for man's philosophy of life, for they tend to undermine some cherished modern dogmas. If our work, together with that of Hay and a number of others who are carrying out surveys among random samples of the population continue to show that there is a pronounced proportion of people who have these feelings, and further that their lives are markedly influenced by them, then I believe we must revise the widely accepted outlook held by so many intellectuals of today.

There is today almost no scientific theory which was held when, say, the Industrial Revolution began about 1760. Most often today's theories flatly contradict those of 1760; many contradict those of 1900. In cosmology, in quantum mechanics, in genetics, in the social sciences, who now holds the beliefs that seemed firm sixty years ago?

This was written by Bronowski in his *Science and Human Values* in 1964, and, of course, more changes will come in our scientific outlook. Man has had so many of his illusions shattered and swept away over the centuries that I doubt if a change in our concept of the nature and the location of God will be more shocking than finding that the earth was round and not at the centre of the universe, or that man was not separately created. We are due for another change. The spiritual nature of man is, I believe, being shown to be a reality. We now need a new biological philosophy which will recognize both this and the need to study consciousness as a fundamental attribute of life. I hope this book will encourage the quest. How much faster would be the progress if only a tithe of the resources devoted to physical and chemical research could be available to provide so many more to take part in the exploration. I have the faith to believe that it will come before it is too late.

APPENDIX I

Tabular material giving additional information regarding the data discussed in Chapter 2.

Table I

The frequency of occurrence of records of experience containing examples of each of the various classificatory subdivisions found in the collections of each of the first three thousand accounts received shown separately and then given as the *average per thousand* for the whole of the first 3000 records. The numbers shown in each column total much more than 1000 because many of the accounts contain elements of several different categories.

Classificatory subdivisions	First thousand	Second thousand	Third thousand	Average per thousand
1(a)	115	179	250	181.3
(b)	9	38	88	45
(c)	50	89	125	88
(d)	63	59	56	59.3
(e)	37	68	74	59.7
(f)	7	4	5	5.3
(g)	24	30	19	24.3
2(a)	62	69	90	73.7
(b)	41	65	104	70
(c)	27	25	41	31
(d)	11	30	28	23
3(a)	7	14	25	15.3
(b)	14	21	52	29
(c)	42	58	61	53.7

Classificatory subdivisions	First thousand	Second thousand	Third thousand	Average per thousand
(d)	12	22	21	18.3
(e)	5	2	9	5.3
4	5	12	16	11
5(a)	35	52	23	36.7
(b)	67	69	72	69.3
(c)	5	20	21	15.3
(d)	49	92	98	79.7
(e)	17	22	63	34
6(a)	38	11	32	27
(b)	30	30	43	34.3
(c)	4	2	5	3.7
(d)	12	1	6	6.3
7(a)	228	250	281	253
(b)	202	230	204	212
(c)	61	68	66	65
(d)	160	177	136	157.7
(e)	80	57	61	66
(f)	236	182	166	194.7
(g)	49	52	41	47.3
(h)	14	2	60	25.3
(i)	94	51	55	66.7
(j)	41	43	29	37.7
(k)	53	36	81	56.7
(l)	25	9	9	14.3
(m)	44	31	45	40
(n)	16	15	7	12.7
(o)	24	14	8	15.3
(p)	34	41	34	36.3
(q)	37	35	53	41.7
(r)	25	21	25	23.7
(s)	9	16	9	11.3
(t)	89	117	135	113.7
(u)	107	150	158	138.3
(v)	238	189	180	202.3
8(a)	2	1	1	1.3
(b)	116	110	48	91.3
(c)	191	175	160	175.3
(d)	9	11	21	13.7

Classificatory subdivisions	First thousand	Second thousand	Third thousand	Average per thousand
(*e*)	134	139	164	*145.7*
(*k*)	3	2	13	*6*
(*l*)	100	113	126	*113*
(*m*)	26	35	28	*29.7*
(*n*)	159	117	77	*117.7*
(*o*)	24	24	33	*27*
(*r*)	144	124	85	*117.7*
(*s*)	141	127	103	*123.7*
(*t*)	87	76	48	*70.3*
(*u*)	10	5	8	*7.7*
9(*a*)	115	151	106	*124*
(*b*)	232	368	368	*322.7*
(*c*)	1	8	5	*4.7*
(*d*)	15	38	14	*22.3*
(*m*)	69	33	32	*44.7*
10	69	92	102	*87.7*
11(*a*)	170	124	74	*122.7*
(*b*)	33	23	22	*26*
(*c*)	122	112	119	*117.7*
(*d*)	153	130	124	*135.7*
(*e*)	93	58	19	*56.7*
(*f*)	43	23	8	*24.7*
(*g*)	100	76	70	*82*
(*h*)	18	24	20	*20.7*
(*i*)	10	14	5	*9.7*
(*j*)	18	10	22	*16.7*
(*k*)	5	4	3	*4*
(*l*)	4	1	17	*7.3*
(*m*)	179	183	189	*183.7*
(*n*)	55	84	101	*80*
(*o*)	7	9	10	*8.7*
(*p*)	7	8	31	*15.3*
(*q*)	26	32	26	*28*
(*r*)	33	44	35	*37.3*
(*s*)	24	8	14	*15.3*
(*w*)	12	8	12	*10.7*
(*x*)	6	5	9	*6.7*
12(*a*)	249	177	128	*184.7*

Classificatory subdivisions	First thousand	Second thousand	Third thousand	Average per thousand
(b)	50	35	31	*38.7*
(c)	109	60	62	*77*

Table II

Age and sex distribution of the first three thousand respondents*
(*The highest number in each column is shown in heavy type*)

Age range in years	First thousand Male	First thousand Female	Second thousand Male	Second thousand Female	Third thousand Male	Third thousand Female	Total
Under 20	12	4	8	11	9	10	54
20–29	26	30	18	29	17	28	150
30–39	25	53	22	37	25	29	191
40–49	32	104	27	67	37	80	347
50–59	49	**119**	32	**126**	40	128	**494**
60–69	**52**	95	**45**	117	**63**	**139**	391
70–79	39	65	37	95	39	103	378
80–89	17	27	13	33	22	52	164
Over 90	2	2	3	3	2	6	18

*Unfortunately nearly a third of the respondents failed to give their age as requested so that the two columns for each thousand received do not in fact total a thousand; the last column gives a total of only 2187.

APPENDIX II

This is a selection of extracts from the descriptions of experience elicted from post-graduate university students by David Hay in his pilot survey of 1972 which is discussed in Chapter 8 and now described in full in the *Journal for the Scientific Study of Religion* (1979). The information in the brackets at the beginning of each quotation refers to the coded identification number, the sex, and the academic subject of each person. Thus, the first extract below comes from a male physics graduate given the code number 14.

AWARENESS OF A POWER CONTROLLING AND GUIDING ME

(14 : M; Physics) I don't believe in God and I don't not believe in God, but I feel there's something in my mind which I don't control but which controls me. I don't make decisions myself, this, whatever it is, makes the decisions for me.

(65 : F; German) I believe there is something there, and it is very important to me that it is there, but this has no relation with official Christianity . . . something I feel inside me, which I feel seems to be guiding me, yes.

(75 : F; Geography) I suppose it's a feeling that you're not in charge of what you do.

And an example of a specific incident:

(26 : M; History) It was just about dark and I was looking out of the library window over ———— . I was aware of everything going on around me, and I felt that everybody had rejected me—and I felt very alone. But at the same time I was aware of something that was giving me strength and keeping me going . . . Protecting me.

Then there is an interesting description of the beginning of what 'might be' an experience in this category, and its forceful rejection. It is instructive to compare this extract with the first one in the next category. The fact that they are comparable, plus the mention of 'prayer' in this one, points to the fact that the boundaries between classes of experience are blurred and in one or two cases the coding is rather arbitrary:

(47 : M; History) At times of selfishness, I stumble into other worldliness, when I feel the need to lean on some emotional peg, (I suppose some people would call it prayer). But when I catch myself, I stop it, by saying 'There is no power that can help me' . . . The aspect of subservience disgusts me.

AWARENESS OF THE PRESENCE OF GOD

(53 : M; English and Drama) It's something that is there all the time. One's awareness of it is limited by one's willingness to submit to it. Very often it demands an unconditional giving which is not as easy as shutting ourselves off. This experience is the true end of man.

(23 : M; English) I've been interested in God and what it meant since my teens, and during the study of Victorian poetry, particularly Tennyson and Browning and their searchings for God, I thought about their problems which seemed relevant to me. I began praying, not really sure that there was a God. At one particular time there was (after a great deal of thought) a great relaxation came upon my mind and everything fitted together. It only lasted for a moment, perhaps 4–5 seconds . . . I really felt God was communicating with me.

(24 : M; English) At this time, if I'm lucky (during yoga exercises) I seem to latch on to something akin to a pure emotional state. A sense of happiness. There is definitely some sort of power there which seems to greet me, to embrace.

Now an example illustrating how one person sees the effect of a particular knowledge system on her experience:

(87 : F; Biology) Around the age of 14 I had a definite feeling that there was something there, but at the age of 16 or 17 this feeling stopped. At that time acquiring new knowledge, especially scientific knowledge, seemed to make such a thing untenable, and in a short time I stopped having this kind of feeling.

And another which seems to overlap with the next category:

(38 : M; Geography) Quite often, but not always, when I am in trouble I go for a walk on the moors. Like last week, I was walking along, when looking over the valley, I got this strange feeling. I suddenly went cold and then hot again. My mind turned to thoughts about what life is all about and I felt I was not alone. [Later refers to this presence as 'God'.]

AWARENESS OF A PRESENCE IN NATURE

(5 : M; History) Frequently I have a very simple awareness of a presence which is engendered in everything around me.

(112 : F; English) The last time I went up to Malham, going through the gorge there, and then when we went up round the limestone pavement, it was so peaceful. I was with a friend, but we didn't say anything. It just seemed as if we were very insignificant and felt very humble.

(29 : M; Classics) Quite a lot of us were in a van going to a gig somewhere. It was coming on to dusk. We came over a hill and we could see stretched out a flat

piece of land with orchards and a low mist which obscured the horizon. It just gave the trees in the groves a distinctly mystical, magical look. It seemed like the setting for something mysterious. It seemed out of time . . . It would seem to be information or a revelation for me.

(42 : M; German) I'd say it was an intoxication with the sights, sounds and forces of nature. A feeling of power coming through my body from internal and external sources . . . I can't distinguish what is divine and what is temporal. It's nothing to do with the Christian God.

The final experience described in this category had an interesting sequel. My informant was so impressed by the immediacy of what he calls elsewhere 'this immensely powerful benign force', that he ceased bothering to go to church, which now seemed to him, at best, second-hand:

(15 : M; Agriculture) About 5 years ago, sitting on a mountain top in the middle of Dartmoor, I was waiting for some people, and had been there for several hours. I felt that I wasn't alone, but I felt very content although I had to wait all these hours. It came quite suddenly and went on for at least an hour until the others arrived.

ANSWERED PRAYER

Once more, in these examples, the legitimacy of sharp subdivisions between categories comes into question since there seems to be a link up with awareness of the presence of God:

(81 : F; English) When I pray . . . I am not praying in a vacuum; there is a response and I feel that at the time of praying, otherwise I think I'd eventually give up.

(45 : M; Biochemistry) During a period of great distress, I went to pray alone in the chapel. My motives were to find help beyond that of a human being. I found that help came more readily than from any other person.

(5 : M; History) In hospital having had tonsils out at the age of 16. The wound haemorrhaged and there was a lot of panic as the small hospital was not used to dealing with this kind of emergency. During this time I felt no fear. I had prayed when the bleeding started, and the next day, looking back, I felt there had been a presence during the crisis.

My next informant has some feelings of agnosticism about her experience:

(72 : F; French and German) It was a car accident and my brother was badly injured. I couldn't get in touch with the hospital. I prayed for him, crying and everything, until I went off to sleep exhausted. I was aware of something there— perhaps because I needed it. I don't know whether it's due to praying or not, but things have turned out right.

And lastly in this section, a thoughtful account from someone whose present religious position is one of very firm agnosticism:

(62 : F; History) When I was 13, and my father became ill, I began to feel as though I needed something else in life, and seemed to find the answer in prayer ... for about two years this whole experience seemed very real to me, and my belief in this 'something' which I called God at the time, was very strong. It was a very personal feeling, just between me and 'God' and I never made any attempt to tell others of my beliefs. But I think it did give me comfort, even if what I was ultimately asking for was not granted. I think it probably meant more to me then than it does now, my memory being coloured by my present attitudes [of agnosticism].

EXPERIENCE OF A UNITY WITH NATURE

These may correspond to what R. C. Zaehner (1957) calls 'panenhenic experiences'. As I understand him, the distinction is that whilst the pantheist sees God in all things, in the panenhenic experience all things are seen as One:

(11 : M; German) I'd been walking in the woods alone and it was on coming out of the woods and looking towards the fields over a gate that I had a sort of visual image of everything being brighter and larger than life and at the same time I had this feeling of understanding and being a part of it. I've never forgotten it. I didn't think I would tell you about it.

(27 : M; Philosophy) It's like losing your particular sense of identity and it's just like, say, looking at a tree. You see certain things happening to the tree and you have words to describe it. There's nothing between us, the tree and me.

(102 : F; English) I can remember walking out in a field on our farm, by myself, and it was a fine blustery day, and it (the wind) was cutting out other sounds. I can just remember this feeling of being part of a whole sort of universal sensation, really, it was—in which I was completely involved. So the experience was first felt by me but spanned way out beyond anything I could encompass.

The examples above seem to fall into the category of what Stace (1960) calls 'extravertive mysticism'. Both the next two accounts refer to experiences during transcendental meditation, but contrast with each other in that whilst the first still sounds 'extravertive', the second appears to be moving into the 'introvertive' state in which all sensuous images disappear from consciousness:

(44 : M; German) I've been doing some TM recently and I find occasionally as my thoughts become more and more refined, there's a feeling of being part of a whole. It's a very physical awareness of myself as an organism which relates to a greater organism.

(6 : M; Geography) I should say I've had a going into one's self, but at the same time seeming to split off from my own personality. This was on certain occasions when I've been doing Transcendental Meditation. It was almost like falling into an abyss. You lost all sense of body or time.

ESP, OUT-OF-THE-BODY, VISIONS, ETC.

First, an experience which seems to suggest extra-sensory perception:

(48 : M; Drama and English) It was a Friday. I had lectures from about 10.00 a.m.– 3.00 p.m. Three hall-mates had gone to London the day before. I didn't know when they were coming back. I attended the first two lectures and then at 12 I had a very strong desire to go back to Hall, ran out of the university building. A bus turned up instantly (I was in quite a worried state actually) and I went back to Hall. Just as I entered the corridor, the telephone rang. Another bloke answered it and told me that my friends had been involved in a car crash the previous evening.

Next, an out-of-the-body experience:

(35 : M; History) It happened in Church. It was ——— parish church. I had never been in it before, although I had known it since boyhood. I had gone to visit the grave of an old man I knew. I went into the church, sat down and was thinking about the old man and that I would be like him one day. At the same time I was thinking about my break up with my girl friend. I found I was asking God for guidance. It came upon me that I was high in the air above the church, looking down on it and the countryside round the church. Paradoxically, I could see through the roof of the church and see my body sitting there with its head in its hands. The experience lasted a few seconds but it was intensely vivid. In a flash I found myself back in my body.

And a visionary experience:

(63 : F; Theology) A week after I met ——— , we were sitting looking at each other's eyes in a bedroom and there began to be a beam passing between our eyes and also a third eye in the middle of our foreheads. This lasted for about two hours and we didn't say a word to each other. Towards the end of the two hours, and also it came and went in waves, and we began to know that we had known each other in a previous life. Because we had known each other, we *knew* each other.

And now an example of the power of a traditional religious act to trigger off rich (if at times inaccurate) mental imagery:

(32 : M; History) Sort of had an ecstatic moment when I was receiving Holy Communion, sometimes, when I was a teenager. Imagery from the Bible would flash through my mind, for example, of a man on a white horse carrying a two-edged sword, and the passage in Revelation of a woman giving birth to the earth [sic]. I feel my sins are forgiven.

AWARENESS OF AN EVIL POWER

Dabbling in occult matters is a fairly widespread minority interest amongst students, and the majority of descriptions in this category were associated with this; in particular, experimenting with Ouija boards:

(45 : M; Biochemistry) I've experienced evil. We were asking questions and testing

in a seance with a Ouija board. It was a purely experimental situation, where the answers that were given had, to us, a logical explanation. On one occasion, answers were not given, so we asked why. The answer spelt out CHRYSTOS and the glass ended opposite a person wearing a crucifix. At this pointed I opted out.

(36 : M; Chemistry) We were in a room of an old house, using a Ouija board to try and pick the winner of the Grand National. Virtually for a laugh, after not getting any sense out of it, we attempted to induce some reaction using the 'circle-of-hands' technique. For a while we took it in turns to call upon spirits to show themselves, when suddenly one of the people in the ring broke the circle, lifting his hands about six inches off the table, turning very pale at the same time. At first we told him to stop messing around, to which he replied in a strained voice that he couldn't help it. Then two people tried to push down on either hand, but we couldn't force them to go back on the table. At that moment the family dog entered the room, and as if sensing something there, shot out. The commotion caused by the dog drew our attention way from —— , and his hands flopped onto the table.

Next, madness experienced as the presence of evil forces:

(29 : M; Classics) I had the experience of being the prey of powerful forces which could destroy me and cast me out. Madness led me to see significance (signs ?) of their power in things I experienced and read.

Lastly, a spontaneously occurring experience in the countryside, at night:

(15 : M; Agriculture) I was out one night in Sussex, near —— , and when I came to a ruined building, I felt the presence of something evil, which made me feel extremely uncomfortable and frightened . . . On no other occasion in my life have I had such an overpowering feeling of the presence of evil which invoked such fear in myself.

CONVERSION

Only four of these. I am aware that the extracts chosen to represent the various categories are very heavily weighted on the arts side. The reason was not that their experiences were any more striking than those of the scientists, but that the language used to convey them translates their force better, in cold print. That none of the four conversion experiences comes from an arts graduate therefore stands out, though of course it probably has no particular significance:

(7 : M; Physics) At university I began to feel the 'gay life' had nothing to offer, life seemed meaningless and all came to a climax about a month before 1st year exams. I was feeling pretty anxious. One night in my room, as I was going to bed, things were at bursting point. I said 'I give you my life, whoever you are'. I definitely felt somebody was there and something had been done. I felt relief but not much else, emotionally. It was like a re-direction and this was a gradual thing.

Next, a rather formal and traditional description:

(17 : M; Chemistry) Over approximately 2 years both through the reading of the Bible and through the faithful preaching of the same, I came under a conviction of my own sin and was brought to faith in the Lord Jesus Christ. It's a God-given thing—not at all the work of man.

And the experience of an opportunity offered, but rejected:

(46 : M; Mathematics) I woke up one night when I was 17 or 18 with this sudden urge for prayer which I'd never experienced before. It gave me a very uneasy feeling because it was a strange experience to me that I'd never had before. It's never happened since . . . I consider (it) the opportunity that is talked about when I could have become a true Christian and been baptised or not . . . I never really told anybody about it at the time. In a way it stopped me going to church— because when I didn't take it up, and become a proper member of the church, I felt it was hypocritical to go any more.

Finally, an experience both ecstatic and gentle:

(73 : F; Maths and Physics) In adolescence after receiving instruction for confirmation, one day in Church I prayed for Christ to come into my life. A sense of relief, the peace of God, something fantastic.

BIBLIOGRAPHY

Argyle, M. (1958). *Religious Behaviour*. Routledge and Kegan Paul, London.
—— and Beit-Hallahmi, B. (1975). *The Social Psychology of Religion*. Routledge and Kegan Paul, London.
Back, K. W. and Bourque, L. B. (1970). Can feelings be enumerated? *Behavioural Science* 15, 487–96.
Bartlett, Sir F. (1950). *Religion as Experience, Belief, Action*. Oxford University Press.
Beardsworth, T. (1977). *A Sense of Presence*. Religious Experience Research Unit, Manchester College, Oxford.
Bolk, L. (1926). *Das Problem der Menschwerdung*. Jena.
Bradburn, N. (1969). *The Structure of Psychological Wellbeing*. Aldine Publishing Co., Chicago.
Broad, C. D. (1962). *Lectures on Psychical Research*. Routledge and Kegan Paul, London.
Bronowski, J. (1964). *Science and Human Values*, p. 740. Penguin, Harmondsworth.
Case, E. (1976). *The Odour of Sanctity*. Privately printed (see footnote p. 43).
Cohen, J. M. and Phipps, J.-F. (1979). *The Common Experience*. Rider, London.
Crick, F. H. C. (1957). Nucleic Acids. *Scientific American*, September issue, p. 9.
Crookall, R. (1966). *The Study and Practice of Astral Projection*. University Books Inc., New York.
—— (1970). *Out-of-the-body Experiences*. University Books, Inc., New York.
Davis, C. (1976). *Body as Spirit: The Nature of Religious Feeling*. Hodder and Stoughton, London.
Dawkins, R. (1976). *The Selfish Gene*. Oxford University Press.
Dixon, B. (1975). *New Scientist*, 10 July. London.
Durkheim, E. (1915). *Elementary Forms of Religious Life* (trans. J. Swain). Allen and Unwin, London.
Evans-Pritchard, E. E. (1956). *Nuer Religion*. Clarendon Press, Oxford.
Freud, S. (1928). *The Future of an Illusion* (trans. W. D. Robinson-Scott). Hogarth Press, London.
Glock, C. Y. and Stark, R. (1965). *Religion and Society in Tension*. Rand McNally, Chicago.
Greeley, A. M. and McCready, W. C. (1974). *The Mystical, the Twice-born and the Happy: An investigation of the Sociology of Religious Experience.*(Mimeographed copy of an unpublished paper.)
Green, C. (1968). *Out-of-the-body Experiences*. Institute of Psychophysical Research, Oxford.
Gurney, E., Myers, F. W. H., and Podmore, F. (1918). *Phantasms of the Living* (abridged edn.). Kegan Paul, Trench, Trubner & Co., London.
Hanson, R. P. C. (1977). *The Times*. 21 May, London.

Hardy, A. C. (1942). *Natural History Old and New*, an inaugural address, University of Aberdeen, [reprinted from the *Fishing News*] Aberdeen.

—— (1951). *Science and the Quest for God*. Lindsey Press, London.

—— **Sir A.** (1965). *The Living Stream*. Collins, London.

—— (1966). *The Divine Flame*. Collins, London. (Re-issued, 1978, RERU, Manchester College, Oxford.)

—— (1969). The Religious Experience Research Unit—A Report on Its Beginning. *Faith and Freedom*, **23**, Part 1, Manchester College, Oxford.

—— (1970*a*). Exploring the world of the spirit. *The Times*, 28 March, London.

—— (1970*b*) A Scientist Looks at Religion. *Proceedings of the Royal Institution of Great Britain* **43** No. 201, London.

—— (1970-5) RERU Annual Progress Reports. *Faith and Freedom*, **24-9**, Manchester College, Oxford.

—— (1971). Leaflet entitled 'Research into Religious Experience: How you can take part.' Reprinted from *Faith and Freedom*, **24**, No. 3, Manchester College, Oxford.

—— (1975). *The Biology of God*. Jonathan Cape, London.

Hardy, A., Harvie, R., and Koestler, A. (1973). *The Challenge of Chance*. Hutchinson, London.

Hay, D. (1974). More Rumours of Angels. *The Month*, **235**, No. 1283, p. 796.

—— (1977). Religious Experience, *The Tablet*, **231**, No. 7150, p. 694.

—— (1979). Reports of Religious Experience by a group of post-graduate students: a pilot survey. *Journal for the Scientific Study of Religion*. (In press.)

—— **and Morisy, A.** (1978). Reports of Ecstatic Paranormal or Religious Experience in Great Britain and United States—a comparison of trends. *Journal for the scientific Study of Religion*, **17**, 255-68.

Hinshelwood, Sir C. (1959). *Proceedings of the Royal Society*, Series A, **253**, 439-49.

Huxley, A. (1946). *The Perennial Philosophy*. Chatto and Windus, London.

—— (1954). *The Doors of Perception*. Chatto and Windus, London.

Huxley, Sir J. (1962). *Education and the Humanist Revolution*, Fawley Foundation Lecture, University of Southampton.

James, W. (1902). *The Varieties of Religious Experience*. Longmans, New York.

Jefferies, R. (1883). *The Story of My Heart*. Longmans. Green & Co., London.

Jung, C. G. (1963). *Memories, Dreams, Reflections*. Collins and Routledge and Kegan Paul, London.

Kerin, D. (1914). *The Living Touch*. G. Bell and Sons, London.

—— (1960). *Fulfilling*, (3rd edn., revised). Courier Publishing Co., Tunbridge Wells, Kent, England.

Langdon-Davies, J. (1930). *Man and His Universe*. Harper and Brothers, London.

Laski, M. (1961). *Ecstasy*. Cresset Press, London.

Lawrence, D. J. (1950). *Selected Essays*. Penguin Books, Harmondsworth.

Lawrence, T. E. (1935). *Seven Pillars of Wisdom*. Jonathan Cape, London.

Leuba, J. H. (1896). Studies in the Psychology of Religion. *American Journal of Psychology*, **7**, 309-85.

—— (1901). The Contents of Religious Consciousness. *The Monist*, **11**, 571.

—— (1912). *The Psychological Study of Religion*. Macmillan, New York.

—— (1929). *The Psychology of Religious Mysticism*, (Revised edn.). Kegan Paul, London.

Lewis, C. S. (1955). *Surprised by Joy*. Geoffrey Bles, London.

Lienhardt, G. (1961). *Divinity and Experience: The Religion of the Dinka*. Clarendon Press, Oxford.

Lorenz, K. Z. (1952). *King Solomon's Ring*. Methuen, London.

Malinowski, B. (1936). *The Foundations of Faith and Morals*. Oxford University Press, London.

Marcuse, F. L. (1959). *Hypnosis—Fact and Fiction*. Penguin Books, Harmondsworth.

Marett, R. R. (1920). *Psychology and Folk-Lore*. Methuen, London.

—— (1932). *Faith, Hope and Charity in Primitive Religion*. Clarendon Press, Oxford.

—— (1935). *Head, Heart and Hands in Human Evolution*. Hutchinson's Scientific Books, London.

Maslow, A. (1964). *Religions, Values and Peak Experiences*. Viking Press, New York.

Medawar, Sir P. (1957). *The Uniqueness of the Individual*. Methuen, London.

—— (1960). *The Future of Man*. Methuen, London.

Morris, D. (1967). *The Naked Ape*. Jonathan Cape, London.

Otto, R. (1923). *The Idea of the Holy* (trans. J. W. Harvey). Oxford University Press.

Paffard, M. (1973). *Inglorious Wordsworths*. Hodder and Stoughton, London.

—— (1976). *The Unattended Moment*. SCM Press, London.

Pahnke, W. N. (1967). LSD and Mystical Experience. In *LSD, Man and Society* (ed. Leaf and Debold). Wesleyan University Press, Middletown, Connecticut.

Pahnke, W. N. and Richards, W. A. (1966). Implications of LSD and Experimental Mysticism. *Journal of Religion and Health*, **5**, 175–208.

Polanyi, M. (1958). *Personal Knowledge*. Routledge and Kegan Paul, London.

—— (1959). *The Study of Man*. Routledge and Kegan Paul, London.

Poulain, A. (1901). *Des Grâces D'Oraison*. Paris; (translated as *The Graces of Interior Prayer* by L. L. Yorke Smith, Routledge and Kegan Paul, London, 1910, and enlarged later edition 1950).

Robinson, E. A. (1972). How does a child experience religion? *The Times Educational Supplement*, 15 December.

—— (1976-8). RERU Annual Progress Reports, *Faith and Freedom*, **30-2**, Manchester College, Oxford.

—— (1976). Experience and Authority in Religious Education. *Religious Education*, **74**, 451–63.

—— (1977). *The Original Vision*. Religious Experience Research Unit, Manchester College, Oxford.

—— (ed.) (1978). *This Time-Bound Ladder: Ten Dialogues on Religious Experience*. Religious Experience Research Unit, Manchester College, Oxford.

—— (1978). *Living the Questions*. Religious Experience Research Unit, Manchester College, Oxford.

Robinson, J. A. T. (1963). *Honest to God*. SCM Press, London.

—— (1967). *Exploration into God*, SCM Press, London.

Russell, C. and Russell, W. M. S. (1962). Raw Materials for a Definition of Mind. In *Theories of the Mind* (ed. J. Scher). Macmillan, New York, and London.

Samuel, Lord (1949). Presidential Address, 1948, *Proceedings of the Royal Institute of Philosophy*.

Shaw, G. B. (1924). *Saint Joan*. Constable, London.

Sherrington, Sir C. (1940). *Man on his Nature*. Cambridge University Press, Cambridge.

Simpson, G. G. (1950). *The Meaning of Evolution*. Oxford University Press.

Stace, W. T. (1960). *Mysticism and Philosophy*. J. B. Lippincott Co., Philadelphia.

Starbuck, E. D. (1899). *The Psychology of Religion*. Scribners Sons, New York.

Steere, D. V. (1965). *Dimensions of Prayer*. Darton, Longman, and Todd, London.

Stocks, Baroness M. (1964). The Religion of a Heretic, *World Faiths* (Journal of World Congress of Faiths) No. 60, p. 2.

Sunden, H. (1959–66). *Religionen och rollerna*. Ett psykologiskt studium av fromheten, (lst edn (1959), 4th edn (1966)). Stockholm.

—— (1972). *Människan och religionen* (4th edn). Stockholm. (German edition: *Gott erfahren*. Das Rollenangebot der Religionen. Gütterslch 1975.)

Taylor, J. V. (1972). *The Go-between God*. SCM Press, London.

Temple, W. (1934). *Nature, Man and God*. Macmillan, London.

Tyrell, G. N. M. (1953). *Apparitions* (Revised edn). Gerald Duckworth, London.

Unger, J. (1976). *On Religious Experience: A Psychological Study* (Trans. D. C. Minugh). Almquist and Wiksell International, Stockholm.

Underhill, E. (1911). *Mysticism*. Methuen, London.

Van Eeden (1913). A Study of Dreams. *Proceedings of the Society for Psychical Research*, **26**. London.

Weatherhead, L. D. (1965). *The Christian Agnostic*. Hodder and Stoughton, London.

Webb, C. C. J. (1945). *Religious Experience*. Oxford University Press.

Whiteman, M. (1961). *The Mystical Life*. Faber, London.

Zaehner, R. C. (1957). *Mysticism Sacred and Profane*. Oxford University Press.

INDEX

References to the bibliography are given in bold type

Don't Watch
the Market

Set Up
Banking Alerts

MONEY HACK$

275+
Ways to Decrease Spending,
Increase Savings, and Make
Your Money Work for You!

Shop Clockwise at
the Grocery Store

Fill Your Gas Tank
on Monday

Never Let Your
Rewards Expire

Start a Seasonal
Side Hustle

Go On a
Money Date

Make a
Wish List

Pay Taxes Now to
Save Later

Save Money on
Financial Planning

LISA ROWAN

Adams Media
New York   London   Toronto   Sydney   New Delhi

Adams Media
An Imprint of Simon & Schuster, Inc.
57 Littlefield Street
Avon, Massachusetts 02322

First Adams Media trade paperback edition September 2020

ADAMS MEDIA and colophon are trademarks of Simon & Schuster.

For information about special discounts for bulk purchases, please contact Simon & Schuster Special Sales at 1-866-506-1949 or business@simonandschuster.com.

The Simon & Schuster Speakers Bureau can bring authors to your live event. For more information or to book an event contact the Simon & Schuster Speakers Bureau at 1-866-248-3049 or visit our website at www.simonspeakers.com.

Interior design by Julia Jacintho
Interior images © 123RF/elena polina, pakete, lembergvector, natashapankina, Kittisak Taramas

Manufactured in the United States of America

10 9 8 7 6 5 4 3 2 1

Library of Congress Cataloging-in-Publication Data
Names: Rowan, Lisa, author.
Title: Money hacks / Lisa Rowan.
Description: Avon, Massachusetts: Adams Media, 2020. | Series: Hacks | Includes index.
Identifiers: LCCN 2020015849 | ISBN 9781507214077 (pb) | ISBN 9781507214084 (ebook)
Subjects: LCSH: Finance, Personal. | Budgets, Personal.
Classification: LCC HG179 .R69295 2020 | DDC 332.024--dc23
LC record available at https://lccn.loc.gov/2020015849

ISBN 978-1-5072-1407-7
ISBN 978-1-5072-1408-4 (ebook)

Contents

CHAPTER 3
Get Debt-Free 95

CHAPTER 4
Make More Money..............137

CHAPTER 5
Plan for the Future 173

CHAPTER 6
Protect Your Money 209

Introduction

Hacking your way to financial independence is one of the best ways to get your life on track.

If you follow the hacks in this book, you'll start to see results right away. In some cases, those results may be small at first, but a penny saved is a penny earned, and if you add up enough pennies... well, you can see where this is going. You'll find that as your financial independence grows, other things in your life fall into place!

The 275+ hacks in *Money Hacks* will help you get started today with improving your money management. You'll find information on everything from the basics of personal finance to more complicated questions such as investment and retirement planning. You'll find simple but effective hacks that will save money and offer better ways to make it work for you.

Money Hacks will teach you how to:

- Make small changes that help you save money...without even noticing
- Stop overspending, even on things you think you need (like groceries)
- Choose the best repayment plan to finally tackle those student loans
- Make the most of your credit card by learning about rewards
- And more!

Whether you're making your first budget, wondering how you'll ever pay off your debt, or thinking about how to afford that one big thing you daydream about, *Money Hacks* has your back. And when you hit roadblocks along the way and need a boost of motivation, you can revisit any page for a quick refresher to help you get back on track.

CHAPTER ONE
Curb Mindless Spending

HACK 1

Avoid the Spending Trap!

How many times have you anxiously waited for your next payday, confused about where all your money went? Odds are, you're not fully aware of your spending and what triggers it. And those small purchases add up quickly to eat away at your budget.

Take a look at your debit and credit transactions for the past month or so to identify your spending patterns:

- Do you pick up breakfast sandwiches on your way to work?
- Are your bar tabs all from happy hours that went later than planned?
- Can you never get out of a big-box store for less than $50?
- Do you keep picking up the bill for lunch with friends?

Once you know when, where, and why you're spending more than you're comfortable with on a regular basis, you can strategize how to pull back. Think about breakfast the night before to avoid the morning rush. Send your friend a Venmo request for their share of the bill while you're still sitting at the diner. Set an alarm on your phone so you don't order "just one more drink" after happy hour has ended. Head to the store after work—when you have less time to browse.

It's hard to avoid spending traps when you have no idea what they are. Once you get intimate with your spending habits, you can restructure your time and activities—not necessarily to cut out those expenses completely, but to pull them back to a more comfortable place.

HACK 2

Make a Financial Bucket List

It's possible to make a budget that doesn't feel restrictive and severe. You just have to put your money in the right bucket.

Rather than make an extensive budget spreadsheet with lines for each and every way you've ever spent money, break your budget into just three buckets:

- Essentials bucket (50 percent)
- Savings bucket (20 percent)
- Everything Else bucket (30 percent)

Your budget will look like this:

FIRST, PLAN THE ESSENTIALS

Fifty percent of your budget should go to "needs." This includes everything from your rent, to the parking garage at work, to your groceries and prescriptions. If it's an expense that rolls around every month and is necessary for daily survival, it goes into this bucket.

NEXT, SAVE A LITTLE

Any money you put in your savings accounts—whether it's short-term savings or contributions to a retirement account—goes into this bucket. If you're paying off debt of any kind (credit cards, student loans, medical bills), put those monthly payments in the Savings bucket too. It should add up to about 20 percent of your take-home pay.

AND NOW FOR EVERYTHING ELSE

If it's not essential, it's not helping you save, and it's not help-ing you get out of debt, then it goes into the Everything Else bucket. Some things that might fit here:

- Your gym membership
- Holiday gifts
- Concert tickets
- Magazine subscriptions

Having a hard time filling up that Savings bucket? See what ex-penses from Everything Else you can reduce or cut out completely.

HACK 3

Don't Quit Cold Turkey—Cut Back

The idea of cutting out a budget category probably makes you nervous. But being mindful about your spending doesn't have to be an all-or-nothing game. Instead of forcing yourself to go entirely without, reduce spending on that category by just 10 percent each month. You won't see sudden, drastic change in your budget, but the shift will be a lot easier to stomach.

Say you spent $148 at coffee shops last month. The idea of never buying coffee is enough to make you want to hide from your budget forever, but what if you challenged yourself to spend just 10 percent less on coffee this month? That's $14.80 less, for a total of $133.20. Then, next month, see if you can bring that expense down by 10 percent again to $119.88. By introducing incremental shifts instead of huge, radical changes, you're more likely to stick with your new, moderately reduced habits.

HACK 4

Never Miss a Payment

While you may get reminders by email when your bills are due, don't rely on them as the sole reminder of whom you owe money to and when. Whether you use a paper planner or the calendar on your phone, put the due date for every single bill—and the amount—on your calendar each and every month.

Don't let yourself get lazy after a few months, thinking you've got all those due dates memorized. Having your bills noted on your calendar each and every month is a reminder of how much you're spending on recurring costs month in and month out. If there's an area that needs attention, it'll be on your mind the minute you open your calendar.

HACK 5
Make a Wish List

The tricky thing about avoiding impulse buys is that it's not the *stuff* that's the problem—it's our brains. When we're feeling sad, stressed, or even bored, our brain searches for happiness. And from childhood, we learn that getting something new (a toy, candy, or some other reward) makes us happy—at least, for a little while.

But that immediate sense of happiness doesn't last. If you buy something on a whim without thinking through whether you really want to spend your money on it, you can end up with buyer's remorse (and often a headache-inducing return process, if you can even return the item). Instead of giving in to the urge to get something fun and new, resist impulse buying by instituting a cooling-off period whenever you want to make a purchase you haven't already planned.

There are a few ways you can do this. One option is to make a wish list of all the items you want. Maybe it's a new pair of boots, the new book by your favorite author, or those earrings you saw in a boutique window. Then wait a week. Revisit your list and see if you feel as excited about the items on it as you did when you first wrote them down. Don't check the price to see if the item went on sale—just revisit your gut reaction. If you still want the item, go ahead and get it if your budget allows. But if your interest has waned, it's a sign it just isn't worth your money.

HACK 6
Do the 10/10 Rule

Don't think you can last a week with that object from your wish list on your mind? Work up to it with the 10/10 rule from writer Kristin Wong. When you want to buy something, wait for ten minutes. Then, if you're still thinking about the item and it costs less than $10, go ahead and get it. But if you're still not sure after ten minutes and it costs more than $10, put it back. This rule gives your brain time to cool down from the initial excitement of potentially buying something, but you won't agonize about it for too long. It helps curb impulse buys especially well when you have limited time to shop.

HACK 7
Simplify Your Coffee

Fancy coffee drinks can put a pep in your step...but can also drain your wallet. If cutting caffeine is out of the question, it's time to be strategic about your order.

One option is to find a cheaper drink that tastes just as good. If you enjoy frosty blended drinks, maybe an iced coffee with a shot of your favorite flavor would hit the spot. If you like frothy milk, replace your latte with a café au lait. If you're not sure what to try, ask your favorite barista if there's a "simpler" version of your favorite drink.

Or strip down your order to the basics and customize on your own. Order your coffee extra-hot and wait until you get into the office to add a splash of almond milk!

Maybe this trick only saves you 50 cents—maybe a dollar. But over time, that amount can add to your savings without leaving you feeling sluggish.

Hack Your Spending with the Envelope Method

Controlling your spending doesn't stop at making a budget and allocating your money to various categories. Next, you have to stick to the plan you create. One way to do that is to go old-school and spend more cash money instead of swiping all the time.

The envelope method, a favorite of personal finance expert Dave Ramsey, involves putting exactly the amount of cash you have budgeted for each category in a physical envelope. Your envelope categories might include:

- Groceries
- Toiletries and cosmetics
- Gas
- Pet food and care

That's just to name a few. Make envelopes for each category that appears in your budget. When the envelope for that category is empty, you're done spending in that category for the rest of the month. You can pluck cash from another envelope if you really need to make a purchase in that now-empty category, but you'll have to make a sacrifice somewhere in the end.

The envelope method isn't a great fit for recurring expenses you pay online or by mail, like housing costs and utilities. But for anything that varies—and any category that has potential for you to save money on the fly—the envelope method is a good option.

And don't worry, you don't have to carry a bunch of envelopes full of cash with you everywhere. Know you're going out to dinner and a movie? Take your "restaurants" and "entertainment" envelopes and you'll be all set for your night out.

HACK 9
Aim for Zero

Want to feel even more in control of your money each month? Try using a zero-based budget. With this method, every single dollar you bring home each month gets allocated to a particular category. The goal is to make your expenses for the month match your income to the penny.

That doesn't mean you should spend every penny you make. It means that every penny is accounted for and assigned to a budget category. You'll still determine how much money you want to go toward savings, credit card payments, student loan payments, eating out, and gifts. This method ensures that you aren't underspending in areas that are priorities to you (like transferring money to savings or giving to charity), while also giving you strict limits for those discretionary categories you're not as good at predicting each month (like groceries or entertainment).

If you find your total for the month comes to something below zero instead of zero exactly, you'll have to decide which categories to adjust in order to hit that magic number. Working out the math can take time, and it might seem daunting, but if you want a strong foundation for your finances, it's worth trying.

Be prepared to reallocate funds as needed throughout the month to maintain that perfect zero. It's also a good idea to leave any leftover funds in a "miscellaneous" category for your first few tries to provide a safety net, just in case.

HACK 10
Carry Big Bills

When you open your wallet and see a couple of crumpled dollar bills, you probably don't feel very rich. With enough of those dollars, you can visit the vending machine at work or grab a drive-thru dinner on the way home.

But how would you feel if you opened your wallet to find a crisp $20? Would you still feel compelled to spend it? Or would you want to hold on to it as long as possible?

Researchers have found that you're less likely to spend a single large bill (like a $20 or $50) than the same amount in smaller bills. Once you break a larger bill into smaller currency, the likelihood that you'll spend it increases. The next time you visit the ATM or request cash back, opt for $20s instead of smaller bills. You'll probably find that you hold on to them a little longer.

HACK 11
Declutter Your Phone

Here's how most shopping apps wind up on your phone—you're browsing in a store, when you notice a sign that says you can get a discount on today's purchase if you download the app and show it at the register. The app is free, it takes two minutes, and it's a way better proposition than signing up for a store credit card. But before you know it, you have five or ten store apps on your phone, and you can't figure out how to get them to stop sending you notifications about sales you shouldn't miss.

Want to cut the clutter from your phone and get fewer distractions trying to separate you from your money? Simply delete the apps. If you change your mind down the road, you can always re-download the app.

Unfollow Your Favorite Brands

Some experts claim we see more than five thousand advertisements every day. That may seem extreme, but there's no doubt that you see at least a few dozen when you're scrolling through your favorite social media feed.

It's easier than ever to keep up with your favorite brands, but that convenience also creates the temptation to make unnecessary purchases. And social media sites use your interests and activity to show you ads they think you'll like, which increases that temptation.

Next time you feel yourself getting sucked into an endless scroll of picture-perfect ads, unfollow the businesses you've liked. You won't be able to avoid ads completely, but you'll be able to dodge those constant reminders of new items, "can't-miss" sales, or limited-time offers that can derail your budget. It may feel extreme at first, but decluttering your social feeds is far less restrictive than trying to reduce your scroll time overall, and it'll help you avoid the temptation to spend.

HACK 13

Keep Temptation Out of Your Inbox

What do you look at first when you pick up your phone or open your laptop in the morning? It's probably your email inbox, which, by the time you wake up each day, is packed with promotional emails from businesses. Some of them are brands you enjoy and shop frequently, while for others, you may wonder how you even got on their mailing list in the first place.

Each company that emailed you wants the same thing: your money. And who can resist the pull of a 20 percent–off coupon, a clearance sale, or a buy-one, get-one-free offer?

You can. If you have a hard time resisting the temptation of all those promotional offers cluttering up your inbox, it's time to unsubscribe. Many web-based email services make it easy to unsubscribe with a single click right when you open up that sale email. Or, if you need some help battling back the clutter, you can sign up for a free service like Unroll.me.

What about those times when you're shopping for something specific and you don't want to miss your chance to use a coupon code? Set up a new email account just for promotional emails, and only check it when you have a specific store or website in mind. Set up an email with an obvious name like stephanieshopping@emails.com to remind you of its purpose—and that it should be used sparingly.

HACK 14

Don't Fall for the
Free Shipping Trap

Free shipping on orders over $25. Over $35. Over $75! Some stores seem to make it impossible to get your online order shipped for free. And, of course, your cart somehow always tends to come in just a penny or two short of the minimum. So, you go hunting around for something inexpensive to buy to push you over the threshold to free shipping.

Unless you truly need another pair of socks, remove those extra items from your cart and stick to what you originally planned to buy before you looked at your total. Then check the price for shipping—yes, regular old full-price shipping. In most cases, you'll find that the cost to have your order shipped is less than the cheapest thing you'll find on the entire website.

Plus, looking at your cart with shipping fees added gives you one last opportunity to make sure you really want to make that online purchase. Are you willing to pay $5 to have that sweater arrive in a week or less? Are you willing to pay $9 for your new gadget to be delivered via priority shipping? If not, you might just be bored and shopping for the thrill of it. In that case, can you delete the whole cart and save your money? If you're confident the cost of shipping is worth it for the item you've chosen, then it's probably a well-planned purchase.

HACK 15

Streamline Your Subscriptions

When you subscribe to a magazine, streaming service, or makeup trial kit, you probably notice the cost per month. What's $5 or $10 here or there? So, you start adding more streaming services, or a newspaper subscription, or another app, or you sign up for one of those companies that sends you a new pair of yoga pants every month.

But the cost of subscribing is more than just the monthly fee—you're paying twelve times a year for that product or service. Do you really need that much of what you're paying for?

Review your transactions from the past month to see what digital and physical subscriptions you're buying. While you're at it, check whether the monthly price is what you expect. Many subscriptions start you off at a lower introductory price, then increase it once you're hooked. Or perhaps you signed up for a free trial, then forgot to cancel the service once your trial ended.

Auditing your subscriptions doesn't mean depriving yourself of the content or products you enjoy. It simply requires you to take stock of where your money is going. Once you know, you can consider the cost per year for those subscriptions. You may discover a few you're not enjoying as much as you hoped. If that's the case, it's time to cancel and put that money back into your budget, where you can spend it on something that matters to you.

HACK 16
Ditch the Shopping Cart!

This tip works best for people who get around on foot or by public transit, but even if you drive a lot, you can try it too. The next time you run into the store for "just a few things," challenge yourself to purchase only what you can carry. In theory, that means you only purchase the things you set out to buy in the first place: toilet paper, dog food, a frozen pizza for dinner.

But the minute you pick up a basket—or worse, start pushing a cart—the more likely you are to find excuses to buy items that aren't on your list. It's hard to pass up a discount or walk past the item that jogs your memory of something you need.

But if you can't carry it, it doesn't come home with you—at least, not with this tactic. That means buying the appropriate size of what you need, rather than the extra-large package. It means telling the cashier you "just need one" when she tells you about a buy-one, get-one-half-off deal.

If you can't easily get the items home in your own two hands (or that tote bag you always take with you), they don't leave the store. If you've ever waddled home under the weight of overstuffed shopping bags and vowed you'd never do that again, you'll find your load is a bit lighter in no time.

HACK 17
Write It Down

Want to keep a better eye on your money? Get a reality check by keeping a handwritten money ledger for an entire month. It doesn't have to be fancy—you can keep your money log in a small notebook, inside your planner or agenda, or on a legal pad you keep at your desk.

The only thing you have to do is write down the amount you spent, where you spent it, and when. If you purchase a variety of items in one place—say you pick up groceries, an item of clothing, and some home improvement tools from a big-box store on Saturday—break down your receipt by category to get even clearer on where your money is going. Be sure to update your log each day, if not immediately after you make each purchase. At the end of the month, add up what you've spent in each category and think about how each one makes you feel. Does your spending seem lopsided? Do those purchases make you feel happy, sad, or neutral?

On its surface, keeping a handwritten log doesn't prevent you from spending money. What it *does* help you do is reflect on what you've spent and how you've spent it. It can help you recognize patterns in your spending or categories where you may be spending too much. Then, you can use your ledger to help you make your budget or re-evaluate it to match your priorities.

HACK 18

Save 100 Percent

Window shopping is a fun way to pass the time, until a sign tempts you with an ad for 40 or 50 percent off. "I should take a look inside," you might say. "I could save 40 percent."

Do you know what's better than saving 40 percent? Saving 100 percent. That's how much you'll save if you never walk into the shop in the first place. You probably don't need anything there anyway (check your list of wants if you're unsure).

Imagine your local gourmet food shop is going out of business. Cheese is 50 percent off, and bottles of wine are 40 percent off. Those ingredients would make a delicious low-cost picnic for you and a few friends. But if you're not already planning that picnic, you're just spending money to stock up. The cheese might even go bad before you have a chance to enjoy it.

Saving 100 percent is the ultimate money-saving hack: You can't spend any money if you don't go inside. You'll keep 100 percent of your money in your pocket, maximizing your savings without spending a dime.

HACK 19

Reconsider Whether Membership Is Worth It

It's not just Amazon Prime. So many retailers offer faster shipping and other perks for shoppers who pay for a membership. They can offer great savings if you're a frequent shopper. But you might find that the perks aren't enough to make your investment truly worth the cost.

Take a look at your membership accounts at e-commerce sites like *Amazon*, *Sephora*, or *Barnes & Noble*, as well as traditional shopping memberships like Costco or Sam's Club. Are you really shopping there enough to make it worth the cost of paying up front for shipping?

One way to evaluate whether you need a membership for free shipping is to look at the total cost of each order you've made in the past few months. Do your orders typically exceed a spending threshold that provides free shipping anyway? Unless you're spending small amounts of money on frequent orders, you can probably eliminate your need for the membership with a bit of planning before clicking "place order."

HACK 20

Stop Those Free Trials

Who wants to pay for something before you're really sure you want it? It's so convenient to try a new product or service by taking advantage of a free trial.

But did you read the fine print on that free offer? Usually, a company will require you to save your credit card information so it can start charging you after your free trial ends. Some trials last a week, while some last two weeks, a month, or more. These different lengths make it hard for you to track what's due when, and make it more likely that the free trial will wind up costing you money. Bankrate found that 59 percent of people who signed up for a free trial were later charged against their will!

Avoid being in that 59 percent by thinking twice before signing up for a free trial. If you truly want to try a product or service before paying, take note of the day your free trial will end and what the balance will be if you don't cancel. Then put a note on your calendar for three to five days prior to that expiration date to make sure you don't miss your chance to cancel in time.

If you want another layer of protection, use a prepaid card or a one-time-use virtual credit card number when you sign up for your free trial. Some services won't allow you to use a prepaid debit card to sign up for a free trial, but many will.

Make a List

No matter how well you budget for those month-after-month expenses, the irregular ones can trip you up. Maybe your car insurance is due twice each year, your alumni association fees are due in May, your magazines all renew in July, and the domain for your personal website renews each October. Sure, you can mark those due dates on your calendar, but how can you plan ahead for them instead of stealing from other categories during the month when the bill arrives?

It's all a matter of division. Make a list—consider an online spreadsheet so you can keep it updated—of every single yearly, biannual, or quarterly bill you'll pay this year. Add them all up, then divide the result by 12. That's how much money you need to put aside each month so you're prepared when these irregular but scheduled expenses roll around. You might call this line in your budget "subscriptions and dues," referring to your list when you want further details.

When it's time to switch things up—maybe you decide to quit one professional association that's not serving you and, instead, join a different one—you can do the math on your separate worksheet, then make a change to a single line of your monthly budget.

Just don't forget to put that monthly allotment somewhere you can access when you need it—and somewhere that won't tempt you in between bills. If you have a savings account linked to your checking for stashing short-term savings, that would be an ideal spot for it.

Check Your Bank Account

How much money is in your checking account right now? If you don't know the answer, it's time to set aside a few minutes each day to check on your money.

Many banking and finance apps make this easier than ever: You can set a notification to pop up at the same time each day with your balance. Start every morning with a reminder of your balance, and you're more likely to keep that amount in mind as you go about your day. If money is tight, you get a reminder not to overdraw your account; if your balance is flush, you can feel comfortable for the day or maybe challenge yourself to save a bit extra today. A little awareness each day—especially when you don't even need to manually log in to your bank account to check your balance—can go a long way in providing financial peace of mind.

Never Start a Tab

"Do you want to start a tab?" It's the most innocent question you'll hear at a bar or maybe even at your local café. Why *wouldn't* you want to just pay one bill at the end of your visit? Because it's too easy to ignore how much money you're spending until it's too late.

If you pay round by round, you'll see and feel the money leaving your hands (or at least, imagine it leaving your card), leave a tip, and think a bit harder about whether you really want another drink. By making it harder to order a drink knowing you have to take the extra step of paying right away, you're less likely to complete the process a second or third time.

HACK 24

Think Big with "Bonus" Money

How you manage your money depends in part on how often you get paid. You'll budget differently if you get paid once per month versus twice per month, and so on.

But if you get paid every other week, pay attention to the calendar: You get twenty-six paychecks a year. Typically, you'll get two paychecks per month for a total of twenty-four. But twice a year, you'll get a third paycheck at the very tail end of the month. When it happens depends on your pay schedule and the calendar, so look ahead to count out the months when you can plan to receive an "extra" paycheck.

What you do with that "extra" money is up to you. The thing that matters more than having this "bonus" check is that you decide ahead of time how you'll use it.

- If you've had some unexpected expenses, now's the time to pay them off.
- If your expenses for the next month are already covered, you might throw that money into an extra debt payment (more on that in Chapter 3).
- If you're planning ahead, you might choose to stash that third paycheck into savings for when unexpected expenses crop up.
- If the rest of your budget looks good, you could use the extra cash to boost your retirement account.

However you choose to allocate that third paycheck, make sure you have a plan for that money so you can avoid the temptation of spending all of it on one fun weekend.

HACK 25

Frame a Positive Narrative

So often we explain our choices around how we manage our finances as negatives. "I can't afford that right now," we say when friends ask us to join them for a night out. Or we scold ourselves: "I really need to cut back on my grocery spending" or "Ugh, I really shouldn't have agreed to get this coffee."

All that sort of language is going to do is make you feel even worse about the choices you're making (or should be making). Instead of framing your financial decisions in the negative, state them in a positive way. That doesn't mean you have to be a Pollyanna, or fake positivity. Simply give yourself credit for the actions you're taking.

A few examples to help you get started:

- "I can't afford that right now" becomes "I'm prioritizing other parts of my budget this month, so I'll have to skip this time and join you for the next night out."
- "I need to cut back on my grocery spending" becomes "I'm challenging myself to reduce my grocery spending. This week I'm going to try a new recipe that uses a lot of ingredients I already have."
- "I can't believe I spent $5 for this latte" becomes "Hmm, maybe this isn't where I truly want to spend my money. I'll enjoy this treat today and experiment with other ways to reward myself next time I want to get out of the office."

HACK 26

Stop Trying to Be Perfect

Do you know the phrase "The best is the enemy of the good"? If you're constantly striving for perfection, you can work yourself into a frenzy and end up not accomplishing anything. To combat your desire to be perfect, focus on being just good enough. Author Ramit Sethi argues that you only need to get your finances 85 percent "right" in order to be generally successful with money. He calls it the 85 percent solution.

Think about your finances as they stand right now. Perhaps you've sketched out a budget, you set up automatic transfers to your emergency savings, and you have a good credit score. But you're not saving for retirement. You're probably 60 percent of the way there, to make a rough estimation. Set up a Roth IRA (more on that in Chapter 5), set up automatic contributions, and choose a target date fund, and you'll easily hit 85 percent.

Doing those administrative tasks may not be as satisfying as finding hundreds of dollars in your budget per month to invest or choosing a complex set of investing options, but by taking those few steps to set up your retirement savings plan, you've already done most of the work.

Take a spin through your finances and list out all your accomplishments, from choosing a budgeting style to autopaying your bills. Give yourself credit for all the positive actions you've already completed. You're probably a lot closer to 85 percent "right" than you realize.

Sweat the Big Stuff

Want to make the biggest changes to your budget to see the most dramatic results? Use the 80/20 rule, also known as the Pareto principle. That rule says that 80 percent of the effects are driven by 20 percent of the causes. For your money, that means that 20 percent of the money you spend (items you buy, bills you pay) eats up 80 percent of your budget. Instead of examining your budget line by line and wondering where you're going wrong, start by focusing on the areas where your spending has the biggest overall impact. This may feel obvious in some areas, like housing or food. But if you can break down some of the costs within those key categories, you may spy a few spending decisions that have thrown the balance into a tizzy.

Say you go to the drugstore and buy two nail polish colors, a bottle of shampoo, and a bottle of conditioner. But on your way to the checkout counter, you think about that weird noise your hair dryer made the last time you used it. You pick up the cheapest one they've got, but it's still way more expensive than anything else in your basket. If you analyze that receipt, you'd probably find that 80 percent of the total was due to the hair dryer.

Check your own spending by seeking out the most expensive items on your receipts and the most expensive portions of your monthly bills. Can you cut back on those highest costs to create a more noticeable reduction in spending?

HACK 28

Savor a Splurge All Month

There's no need to cut your favorite café or store completely out of your budget. Instead of depriving yourself completely, purchase a gift card at the top of the month. When you run out of money on the gift card, your shopping comes to an end.

When friends or family members ask what you want for your birthday, request a gift card to the café or store where you have a self-imposed spending cap. If you already stop at Starbucks a few times a week, they—and you!—know you'll enjoy every cent of that gift card, no matter the amount.

HACK 29

Recalculate Prices As Hours of Work

Say you take a spin around Target. How long would you have to work to pay for the entire cart? The next time you find yourself with a full cart or basket, take the items out one by one and ask yourself how long you'd have to work to pay for each one. If that new book costs $25 and you make $18 per hour, is it worth one hour and twenty-four minutes to "earn" it? If you lose 25 percent of your pay to taxes, you'd probably have to work more like one hour and forty-eight minutes to earn the book.

Thinking of prices in terms of your time isn't always effective—for instance, if you start doing it at the grocery store, you'll be there all night. Try it at big-box or specialty stores where the items you're eyeing aren't considered essentials.

Opt Out of Overdraft Protection

Modern banks are all about convenience, claiming to make it easier than ever to manage your money. But one of those common convenient features is overdraft protection.

It sounds great, but it's usually not free. The fee, which can easily hit $30, is incurred each time you swipe your debit card and the bank moves money from your savings to cover your purchase. You could easily go an entire day, completing errands as you go, without realizing you're racking up fee after fee.

But instead of relying on this expensive "protection," opt out of overdraft protection completely. Then, put the pressure on yourself to keep an eye on your balance each day.

Live in the Future

On the first of the month, don't sit down to make your budget for just this month. Budget two or three months ahead to help you catch birthdays, irregular expenses, or even irregular income. By staying a few months ahead, you can anticipate what your financial situation will look like and whether you need to make any meaningful changes. Being prepared never hurts, especially when it comes to your finances.

Just don't forget to review and update your plans each time you check in on your budget. You'll need to make adjustments as that month grows closer, and that doesn't mean you've failed at budgeting in advance. Even the most experienced financial wizards still have to adjust their own budgets from time to time.

HACK 32
Spend on the Buddy System

Sometimes when you go over budget in a certain spending category, the only consequence is that you're disappointed to have less spending money overall. But what if you tied your discretionary spending categories to one another, giving them each a buddy?

For example, you might give yourself a budget of $100 per month for indoor cycling classes and a budget of $100 for the Friday happy hours you always attend with your work friends. Tie them to one another, and every time you're tempted to blow your budget for one of them, you'll have to face the consequences of spending less in the other. If a friend invites you to attend an extra workout class, are you willing to give up one Friday night happy hour in order to pay for it? If the answer is yes, then honor the commitment and shift your spending to accommodate your adjusted budget.

This buddy system concept comes from behavioral economist Dan Ariely, who says that setting "anti-goals" helps you understand what you're giving up each time you spend money.

AN IMPORTANT CAVEAT
Don't tie two vastly different goals together, like your workout classes and your retirement fund. Stick to your discretionary spending areas so there's something more tangible (and enjoyable) to consider than a line on a portfolio growth chart.

Save Money on Settling Up

Peer-to-peer payment apps like Venmo, Zelle, and Cash App make it a snap to exchange money from your mobile phone for free—no more waiting for your friends to pay you back for dinner from two weeks ago.

But these apps have to make money somehow, and it's usually by charging a fee if you connect a credit card to your account and use your card to send money. It's typical to see payment apps charge a fee of about 3 percent for the convenience of using a credit card to send funds. And while that might not seem like a lot, it adds up quickly.

Imagine you owe your roommate $30 for groceries and you use a credit card to send her the money via a mobile app. A 3 percent fee means you're really paying $30.90 total. Do that three times a month (your roommate loves grocery shopping, it turns out), and you've paid an extra $2.70 that doesn't even go to your roommate and could have been used on an extra jumbo-sized bag of pretzels for your weekly movie nights.

Instead, stick to your checking account when you need to send money transfers with mobile apps, and plan ahead so you're not scrambling to take out money via instant withdrawal.

HACK 34
Make the Holidays Stress-Free

Years ago, banks offered Christmas funds, special savings accounts you contributed to all year. When the holidays rolled around, you didn't have to worry about how to budget for gifts—you could withdraw your Christmas fund without having to compromise your finances elsewhere.

Whether you visit the bank in person or do most of your banking online, there's nothing stopping you from creating a Christmas fund of your own. Don't worry about shopping all year long and stashing away gifts. Simply divide the amount you typically spend on holiday gifts by 12 and move that amount to savings each month. If you travel during the holidays or host a gathering, include those costs in your holiday budget.

The "Christmas fund" method is good for other holidays too. If you plan all year for your family reunion or don't want to miss the annual girls' trip to the beach, prioritize saving for these events and you'll be better prepared when it's time to pay the tab.

HACK 35

Swear Off Spending

Can you imagine going a whole month without spending a single dollar? A no-spend challenge can provoke you to revamp your financial mindset by spending zero dollars beyond your necessary recurring expenses like housing, transportation, and groceries.

It's become the standard to do a no-spend challenge that lasts an entire month, but if you're just getting started, try doing a no-spend weekend or a no-spend week. Then work yourself up to a month. It takes determination and willpower to make it happen, but first, you need to do some preparation.

HOW TO PREPARE FOR A NO-SPEND CHALLENGE

You'll want to make plans in advance for any spending you'd normally do in that month. Think about things like purchasing gifts for upcoming birthdays, making home repairs, or buying tickets to social events. Next, find alternatives for your usual leisure activities that come with a cost, like swapping an evening at your favorite jazz club for an open-mic night.

Some people who do month-long no-spend challenges do it without purchasing groceries. Instead, they prep and freeze meals in advance, or clean out their pantries to use items that have lingered there.

ACCEPT IMPERFECTION

Can't make it through your whole no-spend challenge? Don't give up! Take notes about what happened so you can learn from the experience. Even if you can't go an *entire* month without spending money, you're sure to save a lot more than you've grown accustomed to while getting a reality check about your spending habits.

HACK 36
Live the Cash-Only Life

It's so easy to swipe your way through your monthly expenses. One traditional method to reset your finances is to leave your plastic at home and stick to cash.

Can you really swear off cards in a world where so much spending happens via automatic recurring payments? Don't worry about the payments you have set up for your rent, utilities, or insurance. Focus your all-cash month (or cash diet) on your face-to-face transactions:

• Buying groceries
• Fueling up
• Going to yoga

Switching to cash is important because it increases what's called the "pain of payment." When you swipe a card, it doesn't feel like you're paying for anything. You're just shoving a piece of plastic into a machine and receiving an item or service in exchange for that motion.

Using real, tangible cash makes you feel the impact of your spending as soon as you do it. Imagine the dread you've felt logging into your credit card account to see how much you spent recently. If you used cold, hard cash, you've already spent that money—it's not on a growing tab for you to deal with later.

By paying with physical cash and feeling that "pain" now instead of later, you can be more proactive in making good financial choices as you go, rather than facing them down the road. Try paying with cash for an entire month, and you may be surprised at how your finances transform during just a few weeks. Pair this method with the envelope system for an extra challenge.

Make It Harder to Shop Online

Nothing kills the buzz of shopping online or via mobile app like having to get off the couch and dig your credit card out of your wallet. It's tempting to save your payment information on that website so you can shop more quickly next time and check out with a single click.

But that convenience could be costing you money. A Bankrate survey found that 64 percent of people save their credit card number online or in mobile apps. And retailers know that if you save your payment info for next time, there's much more likely to *be* a "next time" that you'll visit their website and make a purchase.

Saving your payment info takes the pain-free experience of paying with plastic to a whole new level. Not only are you using a card, but you're not even touching it or inputting the numbers. And that makes it easier to spend more than you'd like.

If you want to make it harder to spend on your favorite e-commerce sites, remove your saved payment information. Not only will it help curb your spending impulses, but it'll also make your financial information safer. Businesses large and small have found themselves vulnerable to hackers and data breaches as online shopping has grown in popularity. Keeping your payment info private, even if a company provides encrypted, secure payment processing, is an extra step you can take to protect your personal information from fraudsters.

HACK 38

Hit the Gym

Want to feel a rush that's a lot like the one you feel when you go shopping? Go for a run. Really! Exercise reduces stress, which is probably one of the triggers that makes you want to go shopping in the first place. The stress-busting effects of exercise last long after you leave the gym too, helping you build up resilience to those retail temptations.

Granted, exercise can eat up a substantial part of your budget if you belong to a pricey gym, participate in group classes, or subscribe to an online on-demand workout program. But if you're *not* already paying for one of these things, focus on what you can do to get moving for free.

- Lace up your sneakers and go for a brisk walk around your neighborhood.
- Find workout routines on *YouTube*.
- Check your city's recreation guides for free yoga or group fitness classes.
- Visit your local rec center to find group classes for as little as $2–$5 per visit.

This strategy isn't about getting buff or losing weight—it's just about replacing an unhealthy habit (reducing stress by spending) with a healthier one (reducing stress by moving around). Find an inexpensive physical activity you enjoy and schedule it into your week at regular intervals. Before you know it, you'll be looking forward to your workouts instead of looking forward to hitting the next big sale at the mall.

HACK 39
Start a New Hobby

It's hard to waste money when you're too busy to do it. A full financial re-evaluation is a great chance to pick up a new hobby, or maybe even an old hobby that's fallen by the wayside. The key is to choose a hobby that's not too expensive.

- If it requires costly equipment you don't already have, it's not a good fit.
- If it requires a lot of travel or up-front costs to participate, like some recreational sports leagues, it's not a good fit.

Free or affordable hobbies to consider include:

- Board games
- Jigsaw or crossword puzzles
- Sketching
- Baking
- Journaling
- Learning a new language
- Hiking or running
- Yoga (at home)

If you already have sporting or outdoors equipment, dust it off and hit the trail or court. Whether you pick up a hobby that's solitary or communal, you might find it's a good excuse to connect with friends, whether it's to discuss your latest activities or swap supplies.

For an extra challenge, track what you spend on your hobby and see how close to free you can keep it. For instance, if the nearest art museum doesn't charge admission on Tuesday evenings, round up your fellow art lovers and visit then.

Join a Buy-Nothing Group

Want the thrill of the bargain hunt without spending any money? Join a buy-nothing group. These local groups usually hang out on *Facebook*, and their mission is to allow neighbors to pass around things they no longer need and ask for items they desire.

Find your local group and sign up to get the lay of the land before making your first request or listing your first item to give away. There's no need to trade; simply offer items you have lying around and find you don't need anymore.

WHAT TO LOOK FOR

You might find that you can get free clothing, tools, event tickets, or even larger items like appliances. Toys and baby clothing tend to be popular in these groups, since kids often grow out of them before wearing them out. These groups are also a great way to get supplies for your hobbies, avoid spending on necessary (and unnecessary) items, and get to know your neighbors.

NOT A FAN OF *FACEBOOK*?

You can also look for a Freecycle email group for your area. These messages are a bit more transactional—members just send short email messages to the list containing their offer or request along with their neighborhood and details of the item. Freecycle groups are especially useful for giving and receiving moving and packing supplies, baby clothes and other items for kids, and furniture.

HACK 41

Use the Stranger Test

If a stranger offered you money, would you take it? What if they were also holding something you want to buy? Would you take the cash, or the item?

You'll probably be surprised at how often you'll choose the cash over the item. Don't imagine it's your friend holding the cash and the jeans, though—your friends know exactly how to sway you one way or the other, while a stranger doesn't care which one you choose.

HACK 42

Outsmart Pricing Tricks

Have you ever noticed a price tag that says "Originally $14.99. Now $12.99!"? It feels like you're getting a deal, but it's only a discount of two dollars. Retailers show you a higher price so that the lower price seems like a better deal.

Some retailers do this when an item hasn't even been discounted, saying "Compare to $85" before listing that store's price of $79. The item may be $6 more elsewhere, but that's not a reason to buy the cheaper one.

Whenever you see "manufacturer's suggested retail price (MSRP)," "compare at," or other similar language listed on a product tag, be wary of price anchoring. It's a cue to research the product via the manufacturer's website or other retailers. Remember that just because two prices are listed on a tag, doesn't mean you're getting a deal.

HACK 43

Avoid Temptation by Enjoying Convenience

Do you find yourself tossing snacks into your shopping cart right and left, even when you've carefully planned your grocery list and meal plan? Avoid the temptation by skipping the trip altogether and getting your groceries delivered to your door. All you have to do is select your items online, provide your payment information, choose a delivery window, and wait for your ingredients to arrive.

It's true that most of these services are not free. Whether you choose Amazon Fresh, Instacart, Peapod, or any other grocery delivery option, you'll probably pay between $7 and $12 per order. If you sign up for an annual membership, you might end up paying a little less per delivery.

But the true benefit here is the money you'll save by skipping the distracting add-ons at the store. You'll also save money on gas or other transportation, as well as the time you would have spent pacing the aisles.

HACK 44
Pay Yourself to Splurge

What if you could save and splurge at the same time? It might sound counterintuitive, but with a little bit of planning, you might be able to.

AN UNCONVENTIONAL STRATEGY

Once you've thoroughly considered an impulse or unexpected purchase and decided you really, truly want that item, dig a little deeper into your bank account. Do you have enough cash available to both buy the item and put the exact same amount into your savings account? If you're considering something small, like a donut to go with your morning coffee, you might say, "Sure, I've got $3 to put in my savings right now. I'm getting that donut."

BUT CONSIDER BIGGER TEMPTATIONS

As the impulse buys get more expensive, the math becomes a bit more challenging. If you've been eyeing a pair of boots that cost $100, you may not have enough money to be able to move another $100 into savings and still be able to buy groceries to last until your next paycheck. If that's the case, it's a sign that you probably shouldn't make this purchase right now.

On the plus side, if you transfer money to savings every time you make a purchase that's outside of your ordinary spending, you may find your savings balance adds up quicker than you could ever imagine.

HACK 45
Don't Shop When You're Tired

Whether you're heading to a job interview or competing in a sporting event, you want your performance to be its very best. Why not take the same thinking to your shopping?

Retail expert Paco Underhill says that you should never shop tired and never shop hungry. That's because we suffer from decision fatigue. When we're tired (probably at the end of the day), we've already made thousands of decisions of every size, from deciding what to eat for lunch to where to stand on the subway platform to which pair of socks to put on.

That's why you see some tech leaders wearing the same style of clothing every day—it's one less decision they have to think about, and they can focus their energy on more important tasks.

You may not be willing to adopt a uniform or eat the same sandwich every single day. But you can recognize when you're vulnerable to decision fatigue. Is it when you head to the grocery store on your way home, right before dinnertime? Is it while scrolling through *Instagram* when you're lounging on your couch at night?

If you shop when you're tired or hungry (either out at a store or online), you're more likely to make impulsive decisions that could lead to buyer's remorse. If you notice you're exhausted or peckish, hold off on your purchasing decisions until you feel refreshed.

HACK 46

Focus On Your Financial Goals

Have you ever gotten a new job, raise, or promotion and ended up wondering why you don't feel any richer? Lifestyle inflation is probably the culprit. You likely spent the "extra" money on what you previously thought you couldn't afford:

- Takeout lunches
- Trips to the salon
- A round of drinks

Sure, you can technically afford these extra expenses, but they're not getting you any closer to your financial goals.

If you find yourself earning consistently more money than you're used to, make gradual changes to your spending. Replace one aging appliance before renovating your entire kitchen. Remember that just because there's more money in your budget doesn't mean you need to spend it. Focus on your financial goals and don't let the thrill of extra spending money throw you off course. You deserve to treat yourself for your accomplishments, but don't neglect the guidelines you've set for yourself so that you can achieve even more down the road.

HACK 47

Pay Now or Not at All

The last time you purchased clothing online, you may have seen next to your payment choices a fancy new option: to pay for your cart in installments. That means you can apply for a loan right there on the retailer's website, with the option to pay for your purchase over three months, four months, or even longer. These services make it easy to apply in just a few moments and show you what your monthly payment could be before you even start the application process.

But that convenience could get you in trouble. Some installment plan services charge interest rates as high as 30 percent, but distract you from that fact by pointing out that there are no late fees or other "surprises."

Some services offer interest-free installments but drop a hefty interest rate on you if you don't pay on time. All this just to buy cosmetics, clothing, and shoes. Are these essential items in your budget, or discretionary categories?

The next time you're confronted with the option to pay now or pay later via an installment plan, think long and hard about how long you want to be paying for those sneakers that could get scuffed up on the very first day.

CHAPTER TWO
Be a Savvy Saver

Choose Two Savings Goals

Consider your goals in order of priority. Then, choose just two to work on at a time. While it's great to have several goals, working toward all of them at once will slow down your progress for each one. Imagine thinking about your next vacation when your vacation fund only has $20, then $25, then $30 in it over several months because you have so many other goals parceled out. Scale back and focus with intent on your two most important savings goals. Once you achieve your goal amount for one, switch it out with a new goal. Continue to rotate through goals as needed.

If you don't have an emergency fund, start there and work up to a financial cushion of three to six months of your typical expenses. From there, it's all up to you.

Get Free Movies at the Library

There's a lot to love about streaming TV and movies, but the downside is that none of those services are free. Why not cancel *Netflix* and *Hulu* and head to your local library? Even in this age of streaming, libraries carry plenty of movies and TV shows on DVD, including new releases that sometimes charge extra to access on streaming services.

You may have to wait a few weeks for the series or film you want to be available for checkout, and you typically only have about a week to complete your viewing. But the anticipation is worth it if you want to keep up with your favorite on-screen characters without a monthly fee. Just make sure to return the titles you borrow on time.

HACK 50
Save 10 Percent of Every Paycheck

Want to give your savings an extra boost? Strive to save just 10 percent more. At this point, you've probably set up automatic transfers to set aside money for retirement, build your emergency fund, or work toward other financial goals. What's stopping you from saving just a bit more?

The next time you look at your checking account, determine whether you can transfer 10 percent of your take-home pay to savings, even once you've already put money toward your other savings goals, debt payments, and fixed expenses. If your next paycheck is for $941.50, for example, could you transfer $94.15 to savings? What would you have to adjust in your budget to make it work? You may not be able to do this every time you get paid, but looking for opportunities to transfer 10 percent can help you build up a savings cushion that can be quite meaningful over a short time.

WHAT ABOUT SIDE HUSTLES?

This strategy works just as well. Maybe you make an extra $60 per week teaching piano lessons. Can you put $6 into savings before you allocate that money to any other parts of your budget? Don't worry if the amount feels too small to make a difference. The important part is that you scan your budget and bank account every few weeks to look for opportunities to save even more.

HACK 51

Automate Your Savings

If your company offers direct deposit, find out if you can split your paycheck into two or more separate accounts. It only takes five or ten minutes to fill out new direct deposit forms, and you'll be able to choose how much of each paycheck—either a percentage of your take-home pay, or a specific dollar amount—goes into which account. Some employers require you to submit voided checks to initiate direct deposit, while others only need your routing and account numbers.

You'll get used to seeing only the amount that goes into your primary checking account each pay period, instead of watching your whole paycheck get whittled down by transactions like rent, your grocery bill, and your transfers to savings. Making your savings automatic—and putting it somewhere you can't see it all the time—reduces your chances of falling short on your financial goals.

Round Up to Boost Your Savings

Want to replicate the feeling of dropping your spare change into a piggy bank? Sign up for a program that rounds up your debit purchases and puts that spare change toward your financial goals. Your bank might offer this for free if you have a checking and savings account, like Bank of America's Keep the Change program. But there are various apps that offer the same function.

- Chime rounds up your transactions to the nearest dollar if you're a customer who uses its debit card.
- Acorns allows you to round up your purchases and puts your spare change into an investing account (there's a fee of $1–$3 per month).
- Tip Yourself (now a part of the Earnin app) links to your checking account and creates a secure "tip jar" for savings. It's triggered by your own actions that you set. Log a trip to the gym, for instance? A dollar gets transferred to your tip jar.

Never, Ever Pay Bank Fees

With online banks growing and competing with traditional banks, there are plenty of options for storing your money. The average checking account fee is $9.60, according to *MyBankTracker*. What would you rather do with almost $10 per month? If you keep your money with an institution that charges monthly fees for your checking account, it's time to look for another bank.

It's easy to miss these fees when you first sign up with a bank. Many don't charge a monthly account fee if your balance stays over a certain amount, or if you are signed up for direct deposit. But those restrictions don't offer much flexibility if you want to shift your money to another account, have some big purchases coming up, or have irregular income.

Before opening a new account elsewhere, find out if you can convert your checking account to a free version at the same bank. If that's a no-go, search "best checking accounts" online to find options that don't charge fees—you might even find that some offer sign-up bonuses. Just be sure to choose a bank that's still convenient for you, whether it's in your town or online.

HACK 54

Get Cash Back

Even if you plan ahead for times when you need to have cash on hand, sometimes those cash-only moments crop up on you unexpectedly. Instead of turning to the nearest ATM, take a look around you for a supermarket or drugstore. Most of these retailers offer cash back at checkout for up to $40, $50, or sometimes even more. Of course, you'll need to buy something with a debit card in order to take advantage of this.

Does buying something on a whim cancel out the savings you get from not paying ATM fees? It depends on the situation, and this tip makes the most sense for when you're far from your own bank and its ATMs. Here's how to make the most of it:

- If you track your grocery list on your mobile phone, it'll be easy to reference that list to see if there's a small item you can grab.
- If you're not sure what's ready for restocking at home, pick an easy-to-carry item that you need on a recurring basis.
- If your efforts to make a sensible purchase fail, a beverage, pack of gum, or even candy might do in a pinch.

Just make sure to double-check that the cashier can give you cash back before you have them start ringing up your purchase, so you don't get to the last step only to find they can't give you the one thing you came in for in the first place.

Pay Your Bills Up Front

Think about the services you use that renew once or twice per year for a hefty amount, like, for instance, car insurance. The default option you probably see is you pay that bill over the course of several months instead of all at once. At first, you might be relieved to not have to pay up front. But if you can manage the entire bill in one fell swoop, you could save anywhere between 5 percent and 15 percent for paying in advance instead of monthly. If you don't see an option for this on your billing statement, call your service provider and ask if there's a discount for paying up front.

Beyond the savings, paying up front is usually a flexible arrangement. You may be ready to pay your annual premium or other service fee this time, but the next time that service renews, you can usually switch back to monthly payments if your financial situation has changed. You won't get the same prepayment savings if you do, but you won't have to deal with credit card or other interest fees in order to spread out those payments once again.

HACK 56
Keep the Best Interest Rates

Certificates of Deposit (CDs) aren't just the music you used to play on road trips. They're also a useful addition to your financial toolkit. A CD is a savings device that locks up your money for a certain amount of time, called a term. That term could be anywhere between a few months and a few years, and you can't access your money during that time without paying a hefty penalty.

In return for saying goodbye to your cash for now, CDs offer competitive interest rates—some of the highest available for savings accounts of any kind. When the CD matures (the term ends), you can take all your money back or renew for another term.

WHEN TO CHOOSE A CD

You don't want to store your emergency savings in a CD, since you want to be able to access that part of your savings quickly if necessary. But say you've started saving to purchase a house and think you might be able to save up the down payment in four or five years. You could put the money you have saved so far in a three-year CD so it can grow as quickly as possible due to interest, without risking that you'll dip into that fund to pay for a spontaneous vacation. At the end of the term, you can decide if you're ready to use that money, move it somewhere else, or you want to tuck it away again for another year or two.

HACK 57

Make Your Money Work for You

It can be tough to get motivated to save money when interest rates are low. If your bank isn't offering competitive rates for regular savings or high-yield savings accounts, consider opening a money market account.

A money market account works a lot like a savings account, but it allows you to make a few transactions by check or debit card each month. There can be a few drawbacks:

- Some money market accounts require an opening deposit of $1,000, $2,500, or more.
- You may be required to keep a certain amount in your account at all times.

But, in return for those inconveniences, you can often get an interest rate that's higher than other savings accounts by as much as 1 percent. And even if your money grows by 1 additional percent each year, that's extra money in your pocket for the long run.

HACK 58

Make Tuesday Your New Movie Night

Find out when your local movie theaters offer discounted tickets all day. Tuesday is a popular one, with many theater chains offering a "$5 Tuesday" promotion all day. All you have to do is show up and buy your tickets.

Some cell phone service providers offer a discount if you buy tickets through their customer portal, with tickets often costing somewhere around $5 rather than the usual $12–$15. You can also check the schedule for early showings. Sometimes the first show of the day is discounted even further than a regular matinee show.

HACK 59
Install a Browser Extension

You might be working to dramatically reduce your spending, but you can't go forever without doing at least some online shopping. We've come to expect that we'll be able to use a coupon code, either for a discount or for free shipping on our order. But how can you find them without wasting a bunch of time checking dead-end forums or sketchy-looking coupon portals? Instead of searching for coupon codes, install a browser extension that does it for you automatically. Examples include:

- Honey
- Wikibuy
- InvisibleHand

Some even tell you if an item is available for a lower price somewhere else. They're free to use and can reduce your reliance on those coupon codes and sale ads that are still crowding your email inbox. Start with one coupon extension and remember that you can always delete it and try another if you don't like it.

Team Up for Greater Savings

Savings clubs are popular in communities that may not wish to rely on traditional banks. They prove the power of a group in saving money for a goal. To do it, you need a savings goal, a group of friends who want to save the same amount, and someone who's willing to manage the finances of the group for the duration.

A SAVINGS CLUB IN ACTION

Say you and ten friends each want to save $1,000 over the course of the next ten months. Each month, you each contribute $100. On the same day you meet to turn in your $100 each, one of you takes home the full $1,000 pot.

Then next month, that person continues to contribute their $100, while someone else takes home $1,000. The "winner" rotates until everyone has taken home the full $1,000 that they've contributed over the course of the ten months, although some people will get their money early (which acts almost like an interest-free loan) and some people will get their money closer to the end of the cycle.

If you identify a group of people who want to participate, consider starting with a smaller goal so the stakes are lower. Once you complete a cycle, you can increase the amount you all save together.

HACK 61

Reap the Benefits of Loyalty

Every store seems to have a loyalty club or rewards program now. And while they don't make any sense if you only shop at a retailer occasionally—they just tempt you to shop—they make so much sense for places you shop with regular frequency.

- If you do all your grocery shopping at two supermarkets in your neighborhood, of course you want to get those members-only discounts.
- If you find yourself picking up the same items several times a year from the beauty supply store, you might be missing out on rewards points or coupons by not signing up.

The great thing about loyalty programs is that most of them are free, and more and more of them are becoming available to customers without requiring them to open a store credit card. That means if you end up not shopping at that store often or you move away from your favorite location, you won't have wasted any money or effort in your quest to save.

And don't forget the power of the humble punch card. Look for cards that offer a discount or freebie once you accrue a number of stamps or hole-punches at businesses like:

- Gas stations
- Car washes
- Hair salons
- Consignment stores
- Coffee shops

It's easy to lose and forget them, so keep your punch cards in an easy-to-grab spot, like your car's glove box.

HACK 62

Earn Rebates

Once you've applied the most valuable promo codes to your online order, make sure you're *also* earning cash back on your purchases. It's easy to get started through mobile apps as well as browser extensions.

HOW MUCH CAN YOU EARN?

It depends on where you shop and which shopping portal or app you use. You can earn anywhere between 1 percent and 10 percent—and sometimes even more—when you shop a specific participating retailer through *Rakuten*.

Meanwhile, Ibotta offers a dollar-value rebate for various products when you shop in-store (for example, get 25 cents when you buy a specific brand of cereal); it also offers percentage-back opportunities to earn in stores beyond grocery and big-box chains.

WHAT'S THE CATCH?

You might be wondering what the app gets out of this deal. It depends on the program. Retailers typically pay to participate by sharing a sliver of your purchase total with the cash-back portal. In addition, rebate programs make money by selling information about consumer purchasing. They may not use your personal demographic information, like age and location (check their terms and conditions to be sure), but they typically aggregate the buying patterns from their users to provide information about sales trends or product preferences.

To make sure the rebate program doesn't encourage you to spend more, make your shopping list before you log on to look for applicable rebates and cash-back offers.

HACK 63

Browse Your Local Pawn Shops

Pawn shops are frequently filled with treasures ranging from antique jewelry and quality electronics to sporting equipment and small appliances. You don't have to feel guilty about buying these items—there are plenty of people who chose to sell their items outright to these local businesses.

If you're looking for a specific brand or model of an item, call around to find out if any pawn shops nearby have it in stock. Check whether local stores have social media accounts or websites that catalog their more covetable items. Ask about purchasing warranties that go above and beyond the typical return policy. You'll already be saving up to half price on what you'd pay for that same item new.

HACK 64

Roll Your Own Coins

As much as we shift our financial lives to digital methods, we still end up with random piles of change: on your dresser, in the bottom of your handbag, in the cupholder of the car, etc. After a while, you might be tempted to round up all that extra change in a jar and take it to the coin counter at your nearest grocery store.

You're in the right mindset to think about taking that loose change and turning it into more useful currency. But some machines don't take a fee if you choose to take the value as a store credit for select stores.

Your bank will give you free coin wrappers, and it doesn't take long to sort and stack your change. The next time you need to visit the bank, simply take those rolled coins with you to deposit them.

HACK 65

Buy Refurbished Electronics

Do you want the latest, greatest version of that smartphone or other tech device but don't want to pay full price? You can save $50, $100, or more by picking out one that's refurbished. Refurbished items typically come from one of two places:

- Someone who owned and used that item sold it to a retailer or reseller
- Someone who bought the item, opened the box, changed their mind, and returned it

In the latter case, the retailer can't advertise the item as new. They list it as an open-box item and offer a steep discount to unload that product. Refurbished items are reviewed in detail by the party reselling them, and they get restored to factory settings before getting listed for sale.

ARE REFURBISHED ELECTRONICS LEGIT?

You can usually trust a refurbished item you see advertised by a major electronics maker. Some retailers that sell various products also offer an "outlet" section of their website where they list open-box and refurbished items. These sections are always changing, so it's worth checking repeatedly or setting up alerts. You'll also want to check prices for e-commerce resellers.

As with all purchases, do your research, comparison shop, and make sure any refurbished item you're considering matches the specifications (like screen size or amount of memory) you really want.

HACK 66

Visit Tourist Attractions for Free

Admission to your local museum, zoo, or cultural site can cost more than $20 for a single day of fun. But almost every one of those destinations offers a free or reduced admission day. Some offer the same day or evening each week, while some offer a monthly event.

Determine when their special admission days take place and what their prices are. You can probably put together a schedule with a free admission available almost every day of the week. Look for terms like:

- Free days
- Pay-what-you-wish days
- Discount days
- By-donation days

Keep a close eye on museum and other sites' calendars for events with partner organizations, as well. Smaller art galleries, animal rescues, or educational centers that partner with bigger museums may offer even lower admission rates or even be free to visit all the time.

You'll also want to keep an eye out for *Smithsonian Magazine*'s Free Museum Day, when museums around the country offer free admission on the same Saturday. You'll need to reserve your spot online in advance and be prepared for crowds.

HACK 67

Share Your Ride

Ride-hailing apps have made it easy to get an inexpensive ride around town. But after fees and tips, your Uber or Lyft rides can quickly add up to a considerable portion of your budget. Both services have even less-expensive options of getting a ride, offering you a discount for sharing your route with other users who are going the same way. But choosing an UberPool or a Lyft Shared ride can add considerable time to your trip, and you may not feel like chatting with strangers on your way home from the airport or dinner party. You can still save by looking for opportunities to share rides with people you know.

- Most ride-hailing services allow you to make two stops in one trip, so you can make an extra pickup on the way to dinner.
- Coordinate with your companions to start the night at a single location rather than meeting up at the venue if you're going to see a performance or sporting event.

It takes a little extra time to plan who's going to meet where in order to make the trip efficient, but you were probably going to spend a bunch of time texting those people anyway. You might as well spend a few minutes figuring out how you can all spend less money on transportation.

HACK 68

Be the Host with the Most

Instead of gravitating toward your usual nightlife haunts, invite your friends over for a night in. Host a potluck if you want a hearty meal or set out some simple snacks and make the night bring-your-own-beverage for a gathering that's even more gentle on your budget. If you want to create some structure, plan your evening around a sporting event on TV, or a card or board game.

The dress code is casual, it's not too loud to have a conversation, your pets are always welcome, and there's plenty of elbow room. The next time you want to get together, you can rotate to someone else's place, so you don't have to host every single time.

HACK 69

Save Money at a Repair Café

Don't throw away that piece of furniture, item of clothing, or kids' toy you think is broken. Take it to a Repair Café. Repair Cafés are free meetups where you can bring broken items from home. The meetup location has tools and materials on hand for your repairs, and category specialists are on hand to assist you in completing the repair your item needs. There are more than two thousand Repair Cafés around the world, and you can usually drop in without registering or making an appointment.

If your item is too big to bring to a café location, you can still attend—bring some photos of the issue and as many details as you can remember. You might run into an expert who can advise you. Every meetup is volunteer-run, and some groups request you provide a small donation if you're able. To find a Repair Café near you, visit RepairCafe.org/en/.

HACK 70

Pay Less for Prescription Drugs

Sometimes the prescription your doctor has ordered for you has a price far higher than you expected, even if you have health insurance coverage. Before you risk getting surprised at the pharmacy register, look online to see if there are any coupons or discounts available for the drug you need to take. Some pharmaceutical brands provide information for coupon programs on their website, so check there if your doctor's office or pharmacy doesn't have information about a discount program from the drug maker (your doctor, nurse, or pharmacist is often aware of these programs that help their patients save money!). You can also search on drug coupon sites.

HOW TO USE PHARMACY COUPONS

A good pharmacy coupon site is free to use and will provide pricing information for various grocery and drug store pharmacies in your area. If there's a coupon available for that drug, you'll be able to print it at home and take it with you when you pick up your prescription.

Just be sure to tell the pharmacist that you have a coupon before they apply the drug to your insurance plan. Sometimes you can use both together, but sometimes you can't. In that case, you'll be able to make a decision at the cash register whether to accept the price for your prescription plan or pay the retail price with the coupon you've found.

Going to the pharmacy to pick up medication can be an exhausting endeavor, especially when you're not feeling well. But a few extra moments spent searching online could save you $10, $20, or potentially far more.

HACK 71

Budget Your Utility Bill

If you live in a climate that features roasting hot summers and frigid winters, your heating and cooling bills can be a major stressor month in and month out. Instead of sacrificing your comfort by keeping your thermostat at a level that makes everyone in your household resent you, find out if your utility provider offers a budget plan.

A budget plan analyzes your past bills and averages your monthly usage. Then it bills you the same amount each month, all year round. You'll have to pay a higher bill during the spring and fall when you're not using your utilities as much, but that slightly elevated bill will be predictable. Then, during those extremely hot or cold months, you set the thermostat and forget it (bonus points if you use a programmable thermostat). There may be a fee to participate, so check those details before signing up. It may still be worth it if you value a steady monthly bill.

ONE CAVEAT TO NOTE

At the end of the year, if your usage varies widely from what your utility provider estimated, you may have to pay the difference. So, don't get lazy about where you set that thermostat, even though you're on a regular utility budget. Some programs also warn that if you end your service with the utility provider before your year is up, you'll need to pay for the difference in your usage. Budget plans like this are best for people who know they'll be staying in one spot for at least a year or two after signing up.

HACK 72
Clean the Back of Your Fridge

You've replaced your light bulbs with energy-saving options, you've lowered your thermostat, and you've insulated your home. But you still want to shave a few dollars off your energy bill. Look behind or under the fridge for a common culprit. You'll have to get a little dusty to complete this task, but it's worth it.

HELP YOUR FRIDGE HELP YOU

Find out where your fridge condenser coils are located. They're usually on the back of the fridge or underneath it, behind a small grate. These coils release heat from the unit so your food stays cold in the fridge. If your condenser coils are covered in dust, pet hair, or cobwebs, your fridge has to work harder to chill your groceries.

Take a vacuum attachment to the coils (you may have to remove a cover) for a quick cleaning; check the instruction manual for your model for specific instructions and maintenance tips. Do this every six months to keep your refrigerator running efficiently.

While you're at it, take a peek at the vents in your freezer. They blow out cold air and can get blocked up with frozen condensation. Wipe these vents with a damp cloth once a month or so to keep them clear. When you're done, you can reward yourself with some ice cream.

These two tasks take just a few minutes a couple of times each year but can do a lot to keep your food cool—and your power bill pretty chill too.

HACK 73
Turn Down the Heat

You may enjoy a long, hot shower, but you can probably survive with that water temperature just a few degrees cooler, right? Turning down the temperature on your hot water heater is a quick and easy way to reduce your heating costs all year long. Water heater manufacturers often set the temperature to 140°F, which is far hotter than the average household needs. By turning your hot water heater thermostat down to 120°F, you could save up to 10 percent on your annual energy bill.

That's because a too-hot water heater can waste energy in a major way:

- **Distribution losses:** heat escaping as the heated water travels through pipes from the water heater throughout your home.

Check the instructions for your water heater to learn how to adjust the temperature. Call a handy friend or neighbor if you don't feel confident making the adjustment yourself.

HACK 74

Save Money by Moving on a Weekday

When it's time to move to a new abode, you might schedule your movers or rental truck for Saturday. After all, you're off work and will have the entire weekend to transfer your stuff to your new place.

But since moving companies have the highest demand on the weekends, that's when their services or rental vehicles are the most expensive. The next time you compare prices, check a weekday—Monday through Thursday—date versus the weekend options (Friday counts as a weekend day in this case).

If moving during the week would be cheaper than the weekend by the equivalent of one day's pay, it's worth taking the day off and considering a weekday move.

HACK 75

Get an Energy Audit

Even if you turn off the lights whenever you leave a room, your home may have inefficiencies that can make your monthly bills higher than they need to be. Find out if your energy provider offers energy audits to pinpoint areas where you can increase your home's efficiency. These appointments are usually free, with a trained professional who can help you identify trouble spots, whether they're caused by your appliances or insulation or by your habits. The consultation only takes about an hour.

Participation can also make you eligible for rebates from your energy provider if you make significant improvements to enhance your home's energy efficiency. It's not just for homeowners—in many cases, renters can take advantage of these programs.

HACK 76

Use Ceiling Fans Strategically

An easy way to save money might be right above your head—it's your ceiling fan. Ceiling fans don't warm or cool a space; they move the air to make you *feel* warmer or cooler. A ceiling fan costs about a penny per hour to run, according to *Angie's List*, and you can use yours in tandem with your heating and air conditioning systems to actually save you money.

- If you want the room to feel cooler, make sure the blades are turning counterclockwise to move the cool air down toward you.
- To feel warmer, make sure the blades are turning clockwise to draw cool air up and bring warm air down toward your skin.

The US Department of Energy says you can adjust your thermostat by four degrees if you have a fan on in the room, and you'll feel just as comfortable. Doing this can reduce your energy costs by as much as 30 percent in the summer and as much as 15 percent in the winter.

Check your fan's installation manual or search for instructions online to learn how to change the fan direction; it usually just takes a flip of a switch on the unit. While you're up there, wipe down the blades to reduce the amount of dust in the room. Make a note to adjust the setting every six months or so and you'll be sure to have a comfortable room all year round.

HACK 77
Never Forget a Bill Again

The easiest way to pay your bills on time, every time, is to not pay them at all. Instead, set up automatic payments. This option is usually free, but the real savings comes from the fees it prevents you from dealing with. Once your bill is late, your phone or cable company typically won't chase you down with repeated emails to remind you that you're late. It'll be a month later when you realize the error and have to pay two months' worth at once—plus late fees—putting a major dent in your financial plans. Setting up auto-pay prevents errors even if you consider yourself a diligent bill payer. Why mess with fate when you can avoid late fees for free?

HACK 78
Stop Buying Books

Instead of letting yourself automatically click that "buy now" button and having your favorite author's latest title shipped to you ASAP, remind yourself of the power of your local library, with the help of a free browser extension.

The Library Extension app (www.libraryextension.com) can be added to Chrome and Firefox browsers. All you have to do to start saving is select your local library system. Then, when you browse titles on *Amazon*, *Barnes & Noble*, *Google Books*, or *Goodreads*, you'll get a notification if your library has that book. You'll also see how many copies of the title are available. Even if you have to wait for the book to become available at your nearest branch, you'll have made a wallet-friendly choice that doesn't interfere with your reading habits.

HACK 79

Spend Money to Save Money (and Time)

Some financial startups will do all the work of negotiating your phone, cable TV, and Internet bills for you. That means they wait on hold, haggle with customer service representatives, and seal the deal for you without you ever needing to say a peep. All you have to do is upload your latest billing statement.

In exchange for this service, you pay a portion of the achieved savings to the negotiation service; but then you continue saving all year long. Depending on how much they can negotiate your bill, the savings can add up to a significant amount. And consider the time you'll save by outsourcing this task.

HACK 80

Score Double Savings on Groceries

What's the best day of the week to shop for groceries? That depends on when the new sale circular goes into effect. Some stores make their sales even better by combining two weeks' worth of sales into one.

Say the sale week starts on Wednesday. Every Wednesday, the store will honor sale prices on items from last week's sale *and* the coming week's sale. You might need your store loyalty card, but there are no coupons to take advantage of double the number of items on sale. All you have to do is pick the right day to shop—and brace yourself for the crowds if everyone else is already in on the secret.

Not every chain does this, so you'll want to check the policies for the stores in your area.

Make Your Shopping Trips Count

Have you ever run to the store for a few items only to find that none of them are in stock? Instead of getting what you need, you return home, having wasted gas on an unsuccessful trip. Or, you continue your search, hoping the next store (or the next, or the next) will have what you need. That wastes even more gas.

Instead of simply hoping the store has what you need, check inventory before you leave the house. Many stores allow you to do this online, while others will require you to use their mobile app to check inventory. If an item is out of stock, you can check other locations and determine whether it's worth visiting another store to complete your shopping list. Take five minutes to check before getting in the car and you could save yourself a lot of time overall.

You can also use that inventory check to simply order the items and avoid traipsing around the store completely. Major chains like Walmart and Target allow you to place an order on-line and pick it up at the customer service counter or even at the curb—often as quickly as the same day. It's a savings trifecta:

- You save money by not paying for shipping.
- You get exactly what you need.
- You won't be tempted by other items if you don't go past the pickup counter.

HACK 82

Avoid Convenience Stores

Having essential items at the ready for your last-minute needs comes at a price. Researchers have found that convenience stores charge 11 percent more than grocery stores for the same item. Similarly, drugstores often charge higher prices than you'll find for the same item at a supermarket or big-box store.

If you regularly find yourself popping into the convenience store or the pharmacy, take note of that spending and start planning ahead for those purchases. It may take a bit more energy to drop into the grocery store when you only need a few items, but the savings might be worth the tradeoff.

HACK 83

Enjoy Fresh Herbs with Every Meal

You may not have space to have a lush garden, but just about everyone has space for a simple herb garden. All you need is a windowsill and a few seedlings from your local garden or hardware store.

Fresh herbs pump up the flavor in your favorite dishes, and you can collect exactly what you need from your own plants. Plus, you can make sure you never run out of your favorites.

If your plants get a little too overzealous, clip some to share with friends or neighbors. In fact, before you purchase herbs to grow at home, think about who you know who might already have herbs growing in their own home. Gardening enthusiasts—even those in very small spaces—are usually happy to share cuttings or smaller plants they've raised from their larger plants.

HACK 84
Shop Clockwise at the Grocery Store

Since more people are right-handed, a store layout that guides you to start on the right side of the store and work your way around, counterclockwise, encourages you to spend more. You're pushing the cart with your left hand and grabbing items with your right. Customers who follow along spend $2 more per trip to the grocery store, according to researchers.

Go against the grain the next time you go grocery shopping and navigate the store clockwise instead of counterclockwise. It won't be any harder to steer the cart, but you may feel less temptation to pick up extra items while you check off your list.

HACK 85
Fly on the Cheapest Days

Everyone loves to get away, but no one enjoys paying for the jet-set life. If you have some flexibility in your schedule, focus your search on flights during the middle of the week, when demand is lower. *CheapAir* has found that flights on Tuesdays are on average $85 cheaper than they are on the most expensive day of the week to fly, which is Sunday. Wednesday and Thursday flights are often considerably less expensive than options on Friday, Saturday, Sunday, and Monday.

Tuesday afternoon is the best time to purchase airfare, according to *FareCompare*. US airlines tend to start discounting their fares late on Monday or early on Tuesday, which sparks competition among them that settles down by Tuesday afternoon. You'll have the best selection of the lowest prices then.

HACK 86
Buy Lunch Twice a Week

If you abruptly switch from buying lunch every day to packing lunch every day, you're going to find yourself in a rut. No matter how good your intent is to change your habits and save money, you can't deny the irresistibility of a hot dish or crisp salad prepared for you fresh by someone else. To make it easier to transition to a leftovers-heavy life, set a realistic meal prep goal.

Pack your lunch three days each week, while leaving two days as free days during which you can go out for lunch or order delivery. By mixing up your week, you give yourself something to look forward to while still sticking to your goal of increasing the number of days you save money by bringing your own lunch.

Format the week however you desire:

- Bring your own lunch on Mondays, Tuesdays, and Wednesdays and splurge the rest of the week.
- Pack lunch on Mondays, Tuesdays and Thursdays, leaving Wednesday and Friday for takeout lunch.

However you organize the week, try to leave Friday as one of your "hot lunch" days. At the end of the week, your brain is tired, and your body might be too. You're allowed to make your Friday a little easier with takeout to help you stay strong until the stroke of five on Friday afternoon.

HACK 87

Shop Your Pantry
Instead of the Store

The best way to save money is by not spending any at all. Delay your next trip to the grocery store by a few days. Instead, raid your pantry.

- Open the cabinets and pull out anything that's been ignored.
- Dig inside the fridge and find perishables it's time to use up before they expire and go to waste.

You might be surprised what you can whip up instead of standing in front of the fridge complaining there's nothing to eat. As an added bonus, searching your pantry for ingredients can also help you find where you've doubled up on supplies over time. Take a few moments to organize those shelves so you know with a glance what you have—and what you don't need to spend money on this week.

HACK 88

Fill Your Gas Tank on Monday

The best time to fuel up your car is well before the light on your dash comes on. Instead of driving farther (and using more gas) to save a few cents per gallon, focus on the day of the week you fill up. A survey from *GasBuddy* found that the best day of the week to buy gas is Monday. Fill up on your way into work or on your lunch break with prices that are likely to be the lowest you'll see all week.

The worst time to buy gas is Friday, Saturday, or Sunday. As the end of the week nears, we tend to fill up our tanks in preparation for fun weekend plans or completing errands. If you can stop to top off your tank on Mondays, it could keep your week running smoothly for a bit less money.

HACK 89
Try Every Weird Tip Once

The further you get into the world of personal finance blogs and communities, the weirder the advice gets. It's not necessarily because all the advice is the same and we're desperate to mix it up. It's more because money advice is so specific to every person. What works well for your friend might be a nightmare for you. If you read a tip for saving money, try it once or twice and evaluate its usefulness to you before committing.

YES, TRY THIS AT HOME

Take this one for instance: Some people reuse tinfoil in their kitchens. Once they unwrap that extra piece of lasagna that was in the freezer, they wash the sheet of tinfoil in the sink, let it dry, fold it up and stick it in the drawer next to the roll of new foil. You can reuse a portion of aluminum foil two or three times or more, but only if you have the patience to wash, dry, and store it between uses. For some people, this routine means saving $5–$10 per year on this kitchen material. But you might see it as a waste of time after a few attempts.

If a tip doesn't work for you, don't worry that you're doing it wrong or you're just not frugal enough. Skip it and move on, experimenting with strategies and adopting those that work for you—not just the ones you feel like you *should* be doing.

Always Buy the Biggest Pizza

After many days of dining on the meals you've prepped ahead of time to save money, it's finally time to enjoy a hot, fresh pizza delivered by your favorite local spot. You've earned it! But which size pizza should you get?

If you're feeding a group, it's probably an easy decision to get a large pie. But if you're just ordering for yourself or you and a partner, you might wonder if you really need to spend more on a large pizza.

THE MATH SAYS SO

You might be surprised to learn that you should always buy the large pizza, no matter how many hungry people are hanging out at home. It's because of the geometry of the area of a pie. A 16-inch pizza is four times the size of an 8-inch pizza. To get the same amount of pizza with small or medium pies as you would with large pies, you'd end up paying far more for your entire order.

If you have access to a fridge or freezer, it's worth wrapping up the leftovers once you've had your fill and reheating slices when your next pizza craving hits. It may feel like you're spending more, but you're really maximizing the amount of pizza you're getting per dollar you spend. Plus, with your savings, you can kick an extra buck or two back in to get pepperoni or your other favorite topping. Consider it a reward for ordering smart.

HACK 91
Stock Your Garden for Free

Houseplants are all the rage right now, but the bigger they are, the more expensive they get. And if you're just getting started with lots of small plants, those can start to add up too. Instead of blowing all your money at the hardware store or garden center, find a free plant swap in your area. At these events, plant enthusiasts bring:

- Flowers
- Cuttings
- Entire plants already in pots

Not only will you be able to pick up some new greenery for free, you'll also be able to learn from other enthusiasts before you take your new leaves home.

If you don't have any cuttings of your own to offer yet, you may be able to pay a small fee to attend. Or, ask a friend who's a green thumb to take you along to share the fruits of their labor.

Tune In to New Skills

You don't have to be a trained mechanic to learn how to take good care of your vehicle. Learn how to do basic tune-ups for your vehicle to save major cash on regular maintenance. It may seem daunting if you haven't spent much time under the hood, but there are lots of free resources—from library books to *YouTube* channels—to help you get started.

Take the cost of an oil change, for example. Doing it yourself can cost as little as $25, while having it done by someone else can easily cost up to $100. Plus, think of the convenience of changing your own oil, filters, and fluids on your own. You can spend that time tinkering at home, instead of in a waiting room, and no one's going to try to sell you extras you don't really need if you're doing all the work yourself.

If you're nervous about following a tutorial, you may be able to get hands-on knowledge at a live class. Search for "free car care classes" in your area or visit your local library for help tracking them down.

KEEP CALM AND RIDE ON

If you steer two wheels instead of four, you're also in luck. The ability to do basic repairs on your bicycle can save you the $30–$75 you'll pay for a tune-up at your local shop. Find out if your area has a bike co-op that offers hands-on repair help for nominal fees. Local biking clubs may also help you connect with repair resources and you'll probably find fellow cyclists happy to guide you through your first few repairs.

HACK 93

Buy a Transit Pass

Reduce the cost of each ride on mass transit by paying in advance for a weekly or monthly transit pass. When you're just getting used to a new commute, it can be hard to gauge whether you can save by essentially buying transit fares in bulk. But if you take two trips per day (to work and back) during the week, plus any weekend trips, you're likely to save 20–30 percent for each trip overall.

Take the Los Angeles DASH bus, for one example. The city's transit department has a calculator to show how much you'd save with a monthly pass for unlimited rides. It only costs 50 cents each time you ride the bus, but if you ride twice per day almost every day of the month, you could buy a monthly pass for $18 and save $120 per year.

HACK 94

Take Out Your Cell Phone

Looking for a new place to live, either buying or renting? Do yourself a favor and look at your cell phone signal during your tour. Don't just check it once near the front door—make sure you take a peek at how strong your signal is in every room of the home.

If you're struggling to find a strong signal, it's worth thinking about the additional costs you may have to deal with after moving in—and it's even more important if you plan to work from home.

If you need to get a signal booster or "repeater" to extend the strength of your cellular signal throughout your home, you'll need to get one that specifically works with your carrier's signal. That could cost you $300 or more. A network extender that serves the same purpose can cost just as much.

Cut Insurance You Don't Need

Before you pick up your rental car, check to see what insurance benefits your credit card offers. Extra insurance benefits are usually available for cards that offer travel rewards, and you can only use these extra perks on travel purchases you make with that credit card.

SWEAT THE DETAILS

Check whether your card offers primary or secondary insurance for rental cars. If it only offers secondary insurance, that means it will only cover the costs of a collision or other damage after you file a claim with your primary insurance company. If your card only offers secondary insurance and you don't have a car insurance policy (say, you don't have your own vehicle), you may still need to purchase insurance from the rental car company.

You'll also want to research whether your credit card offers collision coverage, liability coverage, or both; it's common to have coverage from your card issuer for damage to your own rental car (collision) but not for damages to the other party. This information is listed in your credit card's guide to benefits that you received in the mail; you can also find this document in your online account for that card. If you have questions about what the insurance benefit does and does not cover, call your card issuer to clarify before heading to the rental counter.

And when it's time to pick up your rental, take that guide-to-benefits pamphlet with you. Some car rental agencies will ask for proof of your credit card insurance coverage if you decline theirs. Rental car insurance can add as much as $50 per day to your overall bill. Imagine what you could do with an extra $50 per day to spend on the fun parts of your journey?

HACK 96

Make Your Airfare "Typical" or "Cheap"

Have you ever searched for airfare on *Google Flights*? The site has lots of tools to help you find the best deal on airfare. But you'll miss one of the most helpful tools if you don't know where to look for it.

Don't just scan the prices and pick the one that looks the lowest. Click on an itinerary (you'll need to select a departure and a return close to your ideal for the trip) and scroll to the bottom of the next page. You'll see a chart that shows whether the price for that itinerary is cheap, typical, or high based on other flights on the same route. It will also tell you the typical range, so you know exactly what price spread to keep an eye out for.

If the flights you're seeing are on the lower end of the "typical" range or even "cheap," you can be confident booking your trip right away. If the fares are "high," wait to purchase or redo your search with different dates or even a different nearby airport selected.

Never Prepay for Gas

If you've ever rented a car, you know it can be a tense conversation at the counter. You want to be a responsible driver, but you also don't want to overpay for what can already be a pricey convenience.

No matter how many options the counter associate throws at you, never prepay for gas. When you do that, you're essentially paying up front for the rental company to refill the tank when you return the car. And you pay for an entire tank, even if you don't drive enough to get the needle down toward the *E*. There aren't refunds for prepaying, either, if you only drive a little bit.

On top of that, rental companies often charge higher per-gallon rates for gasoline than the stations located nearby. So even if you choose to pay per gallon for what you need when you return the car, you're likely to be paying several cents more per gallon than you would if you had done the errand yourself on your way back to the rental facility.

Next time you rent a car, tell them you'll fill the car up yourself. Then, take a note of nearby gas stations as you depart the rental facility with your temporary ride. You'll be happy you did when your trip is over. If you're really nervous about getting credit for your legwork fueling up before you drop off, take a photo of the gas gauge with your phone when you pick up the car, before you fuel up, and as you're dropping it back off.

HACK 98

Negotiate Car Prices by Email

The days of rolling up to the nearest car dealership and spending the afternoon haggling are long gone. If you haven't bought a car in a while, you might not know about the latest advancements in car shopping:

- Email
- Texting

Dealerships show available new and used inventory online, and you can input your contact information to ask a question about the vehicle or express your interest. Most dealerships will try calling you as soon as you submit your request, even if you check that you prefer to be contacted by email. Once you're connected to a sales associate, the ball is in your court to negotiate pricing—and you don't even need to have a conversation out loud.

These newer methods are useful if you get anxious negotiating or working with sales associates. You can plan your next question or statement carefully and you won't feel pressured into making a decision.

DON'T LIKE THE PRICE?

Go quiet for a few days and wait for the associate to follow up. Their next text message or email might offer the deal you're looking for. You'll still have to visit the dealership to do that mountain of paperwork and get payment settled, but you'll save all that negotiation time and skip the sweaty palms.

HACK 99

Haggle the Best Price

Choosing the right car for you and negotiating a price at the dealership can be a long and anxiety-ridden process. But the work isn't done once you agree on a price.

Next, unless you're prepared to pay for the vehicle in cash, it's time to talk to the finance office. Car dealerships are happy to offer you financing, but you shouldn't trust that your dealer has the best rate. Before getting too far into your car shopping process, check car loan rates from your own bank or credit union. Take proof of that quote with you when you go car shopping. Your dealer is likely to do their best to match the rate you were offered; if they can't, they'll help you complete the process to use the financing offer you have.

IS IT WORTH IT?

It may feel like a lot of work for an interest rate that's close to what the dealership might offer you. But consider that 1 percent of a $15,000 car is $150. Why pay an extra $150 for your new wheels if you don't have to?

Checking your credit for a loan does impact your credit score, and you may see it decrease by a few points while you're car shopping. But don't let that prevent you from doing your own research and shopping around. Credit bureaus can tell when you're shopping for a large purchase and will lump those preapproval inquiries into a single event on your credit report.

CHAPTER THREE
Get Debt-Free

Check Your Free Credit Report

There's only one place to get your credit report from all three credit bureaus—TransUnion, Equifax, and Experian—for free. To get yours, visit AnnualCreditReport.com.

You'll provide your Social Security number and answer a series of questions to verify your identity to gain access to your credit report from any or all of the bureaus. This report won't show your score, but it's actually more important than your numeric credit grade. It shows every credit account you've held for the past seven to ten years, along with your payment history. (If you don't see your most recent payment activity, that's okay—it takes lenders a month or two to send updates to the credit bureaus.)

Doing these checks also ensures that you haven't been a victim of identity theft or fraud. Review it for any errors or accounts you don't recognize. If there are discrepancies, you'll need to file a dispute with that credit bureau to get it straightened out (the bureau will have instructions for doing that at the top of your report). The more boring your report is, filled with decreasing balances and on-time payments, the better.

WHY IT'S IMPORTANT

Your credit report gives you a baseline for the health of your credit, so routinely check it like you would your health. You can access a free report once a year from each of the three bureaus, meaning you can choose to access them all at once (helpful for your first time), or stagger them throughout the year. Maybe you request your free Equifax report every January, then TransUnion in May and Experian in October. Whatever schedule you choose, mark it on your calendar so you don't forget.

HACK 101

Know Your Debt

The first step to getting out of debt is knowing what you owe. Log in to your credit card accounts online or look at your most recent mailed statement to find out how much debt you have and what your interest rate is. The interest rate often won't be obvious when you log in to your online account, so you may have to hunt around a bit or open the digital version of your last statement.

Create a spreadsheet or list of your cards, the balance and interest rate for each, and the monthly due date for each one. Do the same for balances and interest rates for any:

- Student loans
- Personal loans
- Car loans

Don't get overwhelmed when you do this—you're just taking inventory. You don't need to have all the answers for paying off your debt just yet; you only need to know the details of what you're working with.

Keep Your Oldest Credit Card

Don't close your oldest credit card if it doesn't charge an annual fee. The length of your credit history makes up 15 percent of your credit score; the longer your history, the better that part of your score gets. The length of history for that credit card adds to your "credit age," which is the average length of all your credit accounts. If you're just starting to build credit, you might only have a credit history of six months or a year. That doesn't make much of a case to other lenders who might consider you as a borrower. But if you have a history that's at least five or six years, a lender can get a better picture of how much risk it would take by lending to you.

Check Your Statement

If you're paying your credit card bill on time and usually pay off the entire balance, you may not feel like you need to look at every line of your statement. But reviewing your transactions from the previous billing period can help you catch any signs of fraud before it's too late to take action.

If you wait a month or more after a fraud event happens to contact your card issuer and file a fraud report with your local police, it's harder to prove you weren't the person who made the charges. If you can catch suspicious or unusual charges within a week or two of them taking place, you have a much better chance of the card issuer and any other party you must consult with standing in your corner to help you solve the problem—and help you get your money back ASAP.

HACK 104

Get Your Annual Fee Waived

There's so much competition among credit cards that it usually doesn't make sense to have one that charges an annual fee. But if you find yourself with one, you may want to call the number on the back of your card. You might be able to get your annual fee waived.

Many cards waive the annual fee for your first year before reminding you about it in year two. As your renewal date approaches, call and ask politely if it's possible to have your annual fee waived.

FOLLOW THIS SCRIPT

You might say something like, "I've been a customer for [however long]. I really like this card, but I'm considering closing it due to the annual fee. Is there anything you can do to waive that fee?" Even if the customer service representative can't cut the fee completely, they may be able to reduce it for you.

A CreditCards.com survey found that more than 80 percent of people who asked got their annual fee waived or reduced. If you have a high-end rewards card with an annual fee in the $450–$550 range, you may have less success than if you're trying this for a card with a lower fee. In that case, you may want to ask if you can switch to a card with a lower annual fee, or none at all. You'll earn fewer rewards, but you'll pay less for the privilege.

HACK 105

Track to Motivate

How close are you to paying off your debt? Search online for fun and interesting ways to track your debt payoff progress.

By tracking your progress in a visual format, you can glance at your progress and get an instant boost of motivation to keep going.

Whatever you choose, put it somewhere in your home where you can see it often. Don't be shy about visitors seeing it—it'll help everyone get talking about the importance of monitoring your money and your financial goals. It may even inspire others to pay down their own debt with more diligence.

HACK 106

Make Every Dollar Count

Ever opened a birthday card to find a $20 bill and felt a sense of endless possibility? That gift could turn into a night at the movies, the tab at your favorite lunch spot, or a portion of that new pair of sneakers you've been eyeing.

But what if you put every extra dollar toward your debt? Think of all the extra money you end up with each year from:

- Birthday cards
- Holiday gifts
- Commissions or bonuses at work
- Consigning clothing you no longer wear
- Other surprises

It may seem like the least fun way to use extra funds, but it can make a serious dent in your debt with minimal effort.

HACK 107

Score FICO for Free

Your free credit report has plenty of information about your credit history, but you'll notice it doesn't contain your numeric credit score. There are plenty of places online that will sell you your credit score—even FICO charges consumers about $60 to access their score from all three credit bureaus. Since FICO scores are the ones used most frequently by lenders, learn where you stand before applying for credit.

But don't pay those inflated prices when you can probably access your FICO score for free through your bank or credit card issuer. More than two hundred financial institutions offer their customers free FICO credit scores, including:

- Bank of America
- Barclays
- Citibank
- Discover
- HSBC
- SunTrust
- Wells Fargo

Many credit unions participate as well. To see your free FICO score, log in to your account and look for an icon for your score on your customer dashboard. It's the easiest $60 you'll ever save.

HACK 108

Never Be Late

If you pay your credit card bill late, you get up to a month of leeway before it gets reported to the credit bureaus and impacts your score.

But there's another negative to keep in mind: You could be slapped with a penalty APR of 10 points higher (or more) than your typical interest rate. The highest penalty APR that can be charged is 29.99 percent. Card issuers can't switch you to a penalty APR until your account has hit sixty days late, but they can put that higher interest rate on both current and future balances on your card.

Your card issuer is required to lift your penalty APR once you've made six months of on-time payments. But that penalty APR may still apply to your future balances for several months—be sure to check your card's terms and conditions for details.

There's also a negative impact right away when you don't pay at least the minimum payment on time: a late fee. Credit card issuers can charge up to $30 for your first late payment and up to $40 if you've had repeated late payments. While you can call your issuer and ask them to waive the late fee, it only works once or twice—you're not going to get much sympathy if you're a repeat offender. With automated payments and mobile apps for credit cards, there's no reason to pay late. The price is just too high.

HACK 109

Ask Your Landlord to Report Your Rent

Your rent probably takes up a big chunk of your budget, but it rarely gets included on your credit report (that is, unless your rent is always late). There are two methods to getting your positive payment history reported to credit bureaus:

- Ask your landlord to report your on-time payments via a service like *RentTrack*, *Rentler*, or *Cozy*. These companies allow you to pay your rent online to facilitate the reporting process with your landlord.
- Have your rent payments reported without having to ask your landlord. *RentTrack* and *Rentler* provide this service; you pay online and in some cases the service mails a rent check on your behalf. Not every option is free, but the nominal fees could be worth it each month if you're making a concerted effort to raise your credit score.

HACK 110

Lower Your Interest

Did you know your interest rate for your credit card might not be set in stone? If you have a consistent on-time payment history, try calling your card issuer to request a lower APR, or annual percentage rate.

Do a little research first: If your interest rate is already the lowest shown for the available range for your card, you won't be able to snag a discount. But say the interest rate range for your card is between 16 percent and 25 percent (the better your credit when you apply, typically the lower the rate). If you have a 23 percent interest rate right now, you may be able to convince your issuer to knock that down to 19 or 20 percent. That reduction may not seem like a lot, but it can make a huge difference in the long run.

If you have a high balance, an interest rate even just a couple of percentage points lower could potentially save you hundreds, even thousands, of dollars in interest, especially if you are only able to make the minimum monthly payments and it takes you a long time to pay down the balance.

This negotiation tactic doesn't work for personal, car, or student loans, as they all have a fixed term; it only works for revolving accounts like credit cards. You can search online for "APR negotiation script" for examples you can use when you make the call. Always be polite, and if you strike out, try again in a month or two. It never hurts to ask, especially when the outcome could mean saving thousands of dollars.

HACK 111

Aim for Excellence

The highest credit score you can get is 850. It's difficult (but not impossible) to get that if you have a shorter credit history or don't have enough types of credit in your profile. But once you achieve a credit score of 740 or higher, you're an excellent borrower. That status gets you access to the best interest rates and loan terms.

The reason 740 is the key number is because lenders can use a variety of credit scoring methods to evaluate your creditworthiness. Your score might be higher or lower depending on the scoring method, but once you exceed a 740, everyone just gets stuck into one main group of winners. So, don't worry about your numerical score as much as what contributes to it. If you're paying on time and watching your credit utilization, you're likely at that star level—or creeping closer and closer to it.

HACK 112

Set Smaller Goals

Don't let a large debt balance drag you into a pit of despair. Instead, break your debt into parts and attack those smaller goals one by one.

There's no wrong way to do this. Perhaps mentally you look ahead to the payoff date on one credit card at a time, or the amount you plan to put toward your debt each year.

You need to be aware of both the long and the short term in order to think of your debt payoff realistically, but if you can break down your debt into smaller payoff goals, you'll reduce your chances of getting discouraged halfway through because you feel stagnant.

HACK 113
Boost Your Credit Score

One frustrating aspect of your credit score is that lenders use it to determine if you're a reliable borrower, but your report doesn't show all your other good financial habits outside of credit cards or loans. What about your sparkling payment history for your utilities, your always-early rent payments, or your consistent cash flow?

Several programs can help you increase your credit score by adding elements to your credit history.

ULTRAFICO

Credit scoring system FICO allows you to opt into UltraFICO, which pulls in information about the balances for your checking, savings, and money market accounts to show that you have a consistent banking history. It doesn't replace your score if you already have enough credit history for a FICO score—it simply creates a new score with the additional information included. FICO says that seven in ten people who sign up find out they have an UltraFICO score that's higher than their regular score; you can choose to share your UltraFICO score with lenders when it's time to make your next big financial decision.

EXPERIAN BOOST

Credit bureau Experian allows you to connect your bank accounts, which it uses to pull your positive payment history for utility and phone bills. Then you can choose which accounts you include for your boost. Experian says that the average user sees their FICO 8 score increase by 13 points. Experian does warn that if your lender doesn't use the FICO 8 score (there are 10 FICO scoring versions), your boosted score may not reflect when that lender pulls your credit score.

HACK 114

Start an Avalanche
or Build a Snowball

There are two methods for paying off your debt. While one has an obvious monetary benefit, which one you choose really depends on your preference.

THE AVALANCHE METHOD

Start with the debt that has the highest interest rate and focus your efforts on paying off that one debt—by doing so, you reduce the amount of interest you pay in the long run. While you focus on that high-interest debt, you pay the minimum balance on all your other debts.

Once the high-interest debt is paid off, take all the money you were spending each month on that account and start paying that amount—plus the minimum you were already paying each month—on the next highest interest rate on your list. You continue this "avalanche" until you've worked your way down through all your debts.

THE SNOWBALL METHOD

In this strategy, you focus on the lowest balance first; once that lowest balance is paid, you roll that payment into the next lowest debt. The quick win of paying off a debt account motivates you to keep going, and you work your way up the list of debts by total amount instead of interest rate. You'll pay a little more in the long run because you're not chipping away at your interest with as much gusto, but you'll feel like you're progressing faster.

HACK 115

Kickstart with a Blizzard

Can't decide between the avalanche or the snowball? Combine the best of both into what's called a debt blizzard. This hybrid method starts with the best part of the snowball method: paying off your smallest balance to free up some cash to put toward your other balances. Then you switch over to the avalanche and focus on your debt interest rates from highest to lowest.

You can do a blizzard just once to get you started or come back to it whenever you need a boost of motivation on a long journey. See one of your balances creeping closer to zero? Zap it with a quick snowball, then go back to the avalanche.

HACK 116

Pay More Often

You may receive a monthly statement for your credit card, but that doesn't mean you can only make a payment once per month. Credit card interest is calculated daily, which means that the sooner you pay toward your revolving balance, the less interest you'll pay on your next statement.

Your credit card issuer charges your daily interest rate based on your average daily balance. The smaller your average daily balance is at the end of the billing cycle, the lower the interest you'll owe on your next statement.

You can make a credit card payment every day if you want, although that's probably a bit excessive. But don't hesitate to schedule twice monthly or even weekly payments to your credit card if it helps you stay motivated to chip away at your debt.

HACK 117

Hide Your Credit Cards

You might have heard the old tip that if you want to stop using your credit card, freeze it in a block of ice. But you don't really have to freeze your credit cards to put them out of sight and out of mind.

The best strategy is to leave your credit cards at home. If you typically reach for a credit card to pay for everything, see how you feel every time you reach for your debit card or even cash. You probably think for a second longer before swiping your debit card, right? Plan to have cash or a healthy cushion in your checking account before you run out for "just a few errands." If you can separate yourself from the idea that you always need a credit card handy for emergencies, you can break that habit of reaching for credit first.

HACK 118

Write a Goodwill Letter

Want to quickly raise your credit score? Write a goodwill letter. This is a letter that asks your lenders to remove any negative marks from your history—most likely, you'd do this if you had a former track record of late payments.

Your letter doesn't have to be long or detailed. Instead, explain in plain language if you had a particular circumstance (a hospital stay, a job loss) that made it difficult to uphold your obligations as a borrower. Acknowledge that it's your fault you fell behind and highlight the actions you took (or are still taking) to remedy the situation.

If you don't hear back within a few months, send a short follow-up letter highlighting your original request. Your lender may not take any action to benefit you, but it's worth the effort to make your case in your favor.

Look for Balance Transfer Offers

One of the quickest ways to accelerate your debt payoff process is to transfer credit card balances to a card with a zero-interest promotional offer. If you have a good payment history with a credit card you've already had for a few years, you might have a balance transfer offer on that card; you can also find balance transfer offers on new credit cards you might be eligible for. These offers usually last for anywhere between a year and two years before increasing your interest rate to one you're probably more used to, in the 16–25 percent range.

FIND YOUR BALANCE

It's like putting pause on your credit card balances. Your balances won't shrink, but they won't grow due to interest either. It's up to you to accelerate your payments as much as possible before the interest-free period ends.

It's best to take advantage of an interest-free offer when you know you can pay off the balance during that promotional period. For instance, if you can transfer up to $5,000 but only have twelve months interest free, it doesn't make sense to move your balance over unless the post-promotional interest fee would be lower than the interest rate you are already paying on your current card. But maybe you can transfer $1,000 with confidence to be able to make a dent in your debt in a quicker manner.

Try it once and see if it helps motivate you in your debt payoff process. If it feels too complex, leave your debts where they are and stay focused. Using balance transfers is an advanced trick a lot of people use to get their debt under control and kickstart their payoff plans, but it's not for everyone.

HACK 120
Partner Up for Accountability

If you're not working to pay off debt with a significant other, your payoff process can be a long and lonely road. Prepare to endure the marathon by enlisting an accountability partner. This might be someone who's also working to pay off debt, or someone whose financial habits you admire.

Once you find the right person, set parameters for how often you'll check in and in what format you'll communicate. If you're both working on a debt payoff goal, you'll likely find that your discussions go beyond a weekly check-in as you navigate the details of your journeys together. Knowing there's someone there cheering you on every step of the way can make a long slog feel a little lighter.

HACK 121

Reward Yourself

Once you've determined smaller benchmarks for paying off your debt, set rewards for yourself. A few ideas:

- After six months of making debt payments above your minimum amounts, you can go to the movies—and it doesn't even need to be a cheaper matinee show.
- Celebrate one year of your debt payoff journey by planning a hike with friends.
- Every time you pay a total of $1,000 toward your debt, you can get a manicure at your favorite salon.

Don't pick rewards as you go, because you'll start creating arbitrary goals for the sake of rewarding yourself. Plan ahead and write down your benchmarks and your rewards for achieving those goals. Share them with your accountability partner, who's likely to be just as excited as you are as you near your goals and corresponding rewards.

Remember Why You're Doing This

No matter the financial goal you've chosen, there's a good chance it's going to take you a while to achieve it. That's especially true when you're paying off debt. You're spending time thinking about interest rates, payment calendars, and everything you're giving up in exchange for a debt-free life.

Acknowledge that you're playing a long game by putting visible reminders around you:

- Make your phone lock screen an inspirational quote you cite often, or a picture of your dream vacation spot.
- Tape a handwritten reminder to your bathroom mirror so you'll think about what's motivating you every time you brush your teeth.
- Tuck a photo of your family into your wallet.

It doesn't need to be fancy; it just needs to be present in a place you'll look on a regular basis. Those small reminders can help reset your motivation on hard days, scrimp and save a bit more when you're feeling tempted to splurge, and light the path toward the end of those pesky debt payments.

Your accountability partner can't be with you 24/7. In those cases, you—armed with your motivational messages in whatever form you prefer—will be prepared for those moments you need a little extra strength.

HACK 123

Automate Your Payments

The best way to ensure you can pay down your debt on a zero-percent interest card is to set up autopayments. It's easy to figure out because you don't have to factor in compounding interest—you simply have to divide your balance by the number of interest-free months you have ahead of you. Schedule a recurring payment from your checking account, make a note on your calendar to make sure your payment went through without a hitch, and enjoy knowing you're making progress paying your debt without any extra interest fees.

It's helpful to set up these payments because as your balance decreases, you may feel compelled to pay it off altogether. But since you're not paying interest for a while, it makes more sense to stay the course and make consistent payments on your interest-free balance while working to bring down your balance on any interest-bearing accounts.

HACK 124

Pay Off Your Debt with Refunds

Ever returned an item you purchased online and been surprised when you see the refund hit your account a week or two later? Instead of celebrating your newfound cash by spending it, funnel any refunds you get into your debt payments. If you notice a ton of refunds coming back into your account (outside of the holiday season or a special event that required a lot of trial-and-error shopping), it may be time to skip back to Chapter 1 to re-evaluate your spending. Doing so could help you find even more money to put toward reducing your debt.

HACK 125

Claim Your Missing Money

The National Association of Unclaimed Property Administrators says that about one in ten people has unclaimed cash or property held by state governments. These funds could be money from a forgotten savings or checking account, refunds, uncashed payroll checks, rental or utility security deposits, or even contents of safe-deposit boxes.

GO TREASURE HUNTING

Search for your name in the state where you live (and states where you used to live or go to school too). It's as easy as visiting Unclaimed.org to find and search your state's directory for unclaimed funds.

The process for filing a claim depends on your state and the type of property, but you'll have to provide proof of identification and ownership, which could mean a pay stub or an old utility bill. Some states process unclaimed property claims in thirty days or fewer, but some take longer; you'll probably get a check in the mail unless you're getting actual property from your state.

Resist the urge to spend your "surprise" money on something fun, and instead deposit those funds into your debt bills. If you were "missing" any money, you probably won't be able to try this tactic repeatedly, but the one-time injection of funding toward your debt could shorten your payoff timeline by just a bit.

HACK 126

Repair Your Credit
with a Secured Card

If you've made mistakes in the past with credit, you may feel the need to boost your credit score. But how can you get approved for a new credit card if your credit score isn't great?

The answer may be a credit-builder loan or secured credit card. These products look and feel like regular loans and credit cards, except that you hand over money up front in order to access them. In the case of a secured credit card, you'll pay a collateral that's the same as your credit limit. You could pay $500 to open your card and be able to spend up to $500 on that card. After about a year, if you've proven you can pay on time and respect your credit limit, your bank may graduate you to a normal credit card; you'll get that initial $500 back.

For a credit-builder loan, you'll take out a loan, but you won't receive the money—your lender will instead put it into a CD or other savings vehicle for the duration. You'll make monthly payments plus an interest fee each month until the loan is paid off. Then, your lender will release the amount of the loan (along with the interest that accrued during that time), and you'll get that cash.

The downside is that you need cash on hand in order to open one of these accounts. But if you can gather a few hundred bucks and have a year to work on building your credit, one of these options could get you on positive footing with your bank as you prove you're a reliable customer. Your credit score will reflect your improvement.

HACK 127

Track Down Your Student Loans

Having a hard time getting organized so you can pay off your student loans? The first step is to track down all those loans, along with other financial aid awards you may have received over the years. If you can't find the paperwork or emails for all your aid packages, visit the National Student Loan Data System at StudentAid.gov. You'll be able to see all the federal financial aid you've received, and the terms for each loan.

You'll need your Federal Student Aid (FSA) ID to log in and see the status for each of your loans. This review can help you formulate a plan for approaching your repayment, or help you decide if refinancing your loans is an option for you.

HACK 128

Never Skip a Payment

If you routinely make payments larger than the minimum for a loan with a fixed term, you'll probably end up with a billing statement that says there's no payment due. It's confusing because you know you still owe money, so why doesn't the lender want you to pay that money? This is actually a courtesy—the lender is showing you that you're caught up, so you've essentially bought yourself time.

If you take that "grace period" you created for yourself, you'll lose all the momentum you created by scheduling substantial payments. Even if a loan with a balance says there's no payment due, continue to make your planned monthly payments to keep chipping away at that debt. Just because your debt has a fixed term of a set number of months or years doesn't mean you can't pay it off early and enjoy your freedom from debt.

Never Let Your Student Loans Default

No one wants to get behind on their bills, but your student loans should take priority if you find yourself struggling to make ends meet. If your federal student loans go unpaid for 270 days (about nine months), they enter default. The consequences of letting your loans go this long is that you lose your eligibility for some federal repayment programs, and you could be sued or taken to collections. The federal government can even garnish your wages or take your tax refunds until you're caught up.

If you're nearing the nine-month mark on a student loan that has fallen behind, make a payment as soon as you can to avoid going into default. Even if you can't come current on what you owe, making a payment shows your intent to get caught up. Call your lender and explain your situation to them—they may be able to put you into a payment plan that fits your circumstances better, or help you pause your loan payments through deferment or forbearance.

ALREADY IN DEFAULT?
Getting back in good standing will take some time. The primary way to do this is with loan rehabilitation. You'll need to show your responsibility by making nine on-time payments over ten months. Once you do so, your credit report will show your late payments, but won't show that you were in default.

HACK 130

Choose the Right Repayment Plan

Federal student loan repayment plans can be confusing to decipher. The Department of Education provides a repayment estimator (https://studentaid.gov/loan-simulator/) to help you determine which payment plan or plans may work best for your situation. Here's a short guide to your options:

- **Standard repayment plan:** You'll pay a fixed amount each month for a period of up to ten years. Everyone is eligible for this plan.
- **Graduated repayment plan:** Your monthly loan payment amounts increase every two years, and you finish paying your loans in ten years or fewer. Everyone is eligible for this plan.
- **Extended repayment plan:** You'll pay your loans in twenty-five years or fewer. Payments can be fixed or graduated. You must have more than $30,000 in Direct Loans to be eligible for this plan.
- **Revised Pay As You Earn Plan (REPAYE):** Your monthly payment amount is recalculated each year; you'll pay 10 percent of your discretionary income each month. If your loans aren't paid off in twenty years (twenty-five for graduate programs), any amount that's left will be forgiven. You may have to pay income tax on the amount that's forgiven.
- **Pay As You Earn Repayment Plan (PAYE):** You'll pay 10 percent of your discretionary income each month. If you haven't repaid your full loan in twenty years, the remainder will be forgiven, and you'll pay income tax on that forgiven amount.
- **Income-Based Repayment Plan (IBR):** Your monthly payment is recalculated each year and will be either 10 or 15 percent of your discretionary income, depending on when you

received your loan. The remainder gets forgiven after twenty or twenty-five years, again depending on the date of the loan, and you might have to pay income tax on that remainder. You must have a high amount of debt compared to your income.

- **Income-Contingent Repayment Plan (ICR):** Your monthly payment is either 20 percent of your discretionary income or the amount you'd pay on a twelve-year fixed payment plan depending on your income. The amount gets recalculated each year and the remainder is forgiven after twenty-five years, with income tax due on the remainder. Any Direct Loan borrower can choose this plan.

- **Income-Sensitive Repayment Plan:** Your monthly payment depends on your income. Your loan will be paid off within fifteen years. This plan is only available for Federal Family Education Loans (FFEL).

HACK 131

Make Payments Every Other Week

Your student loan interest doesn't get plunked onto your balance once a month. Instead, it accrues on a daily basis. That means the lower you can shrink your loan balance, the less interest you'll pay—and the more money you'll save while you're working to pay back your loans. If you get into the habit of making a student loan payment every other week, you'll end up making that payment an extra two times. That adds up to thirteen "monthly" payments in a year, instead of twelve. Paying in this way shaves months off your repayment period too.

Consider a $20,000 loan balance with a 7 percent interest rate. You're just starting your ten-year repayment term. If you pay biweekly, you'll pay your loan a little more than a year early and save almost $950 in interest. Just make sure your payments are automated (so you don't have to remember which weeks require you to pay your loan), and make sure that your total payments submitted for that month add up to at least your minimum monthly payment.

COMPARE YOUR INTEREST RATE TO THE MARKET RATE OF RETURN

If your only debt is student loan debt, you might feel torn between trying to pay it off as soon as possible and not prioritizing it at all. But there's an easy trick to help you figure out which part of your finances should take center stage:

- If your interest rate for your loans is more than the return you could get by investing, focus on paying off the loans to minimize the amount you'll pay between the principal and interest.

- If the interest on your student loans is less than your expected return, you should stay the course with your regular loan repayment schedule and prioritize investing instead. Your money will earn more over time than you would save by paying your loan early.

A conservative rate of return for an investment portfolio is about 6 percent. If you're paying 7 or 8 percent interest on your student loans, get them paid off ASAP. But if you're only paying 2–4 percent interest on your loans, it's a no-brainer: Focus on investing now so you're more comfortable down the road.

HACK 132

Check If You're
Eligible for Forgiveness

If you work in a public service field, you may be able to have your federal direct student loans forgiven, tax-free, after ten years through the Public Service Loan Forgiveness program (PSLF). Qualifying work includes careers in local, state, or federal government (including law enforcement), public schools, and non-profit organizations. To be eligible:

- You don't have to work at the same job for all ten years, but you must have your employer certify your employment each year.
- You also must make on-time payments for the entirety of that ten-year span under a standard repayment plan or an income-driven repayment plan.
- Once you've made your 120 payments, you can apply for forgiveness.

PSLF was created in 2007, and the first student loan borrowers became eligible for forgiveness in 2017. It's still difficult to get your loans discharged because many applications get rejected for missing information or not meeting program requirements. To learn more about the restrictions and requirements for this program, visit https://studentaid.gov/manage-loans/forgiveness-cancellation/public-service. There, you'll be able to use the Federal Student Aid PSLF Help Tool, which leads you through prompts to determine your eligibility for PSLF and help you submit the required forms. The only plans that protect your eligibility for the Public Service Loan Forgiveness program are REPAYE, PAYE, IBR, and ICR (see hack 130). If you have private student loans, your payment plans will differ.

HACK 133
Never Buy Rewards

Earning points or miles on a credit card makes it even more fun to spend money. But the excitement of earning while you spend can catch up with you quickly.

The urge to spend in order to earn rewards especially increases when you consider sign-up bonuses. These introductory offers lure you with the promise of a certain number of points or miles (we're talking in the 20,000–60,000 range) if you spend a certain amount of money within a specific—and short—time frame. If you don't typically make enough charges on a card to hit that minimum spend, you're pretty much signing up to go into debt in exchange for a free flight or hotel stay. Before swiping a rewards card, check your motivation and make sure your spending is in line with your budget.

HACK 134
Max Your Credit Card Rewards

Planning a trip after you've earned points or miles on your rewards credit card is the best part of having one in your wallet. But before you book flights or a hotel room, find out how to get the best value for your points. Some credit cards offer a rewards portal that allows you to book travel; if you do this instead of transferring your points to a travel partner, your points could be worth 25–50 percent more.

Some credit cards offer a higher value for points used in their portals, but the flights and stays you find there are more expensive than if you transferred your points to the airline or hotel directly. But unless you're booking a spontaneous getaway, you probably have time to do your research before spending those hard-earned points.

HACK 135

Never Let Your Rewards Expire

Do you know when your credit card points or miles expire? Do they even have an expiration date? A Bankrate survey found that 29 percent of people have let their credit card rewards expire, and only 33 percent of people could recall their rewards balance. Every credit card, airline, and hotel has its own rules regarding expiration dates, so don't assume it's the same for all your rewards cards and frequent traveler programs.

Check the terms and conditions of your rewards program to find out when and if your earned points or miles expire; if they do expire, note if there are actions you can take to delay that expiration.

HACK 136

Find the Best Places to Earn Rewards

If you carry several rewards credit cards, you may wonder which one offers the most points for which category. Some give you more points for purchases at gas stations, restaurants, flights, or any other combination of categories. If you can't keep them all straight, enlist an app. Reward tracking apps identify businesses near you and recommend a card to use based on how that business is categorized.

- Max Rewards and Birch link to your accounts to give you the most holistic view of your rewards card lineup.
- If you want an app that doesn't link up with your accounts and simply provides information based on the cards you select from its list, try Maxivu.

The best part? They're all free.

HACK 137

Spread Out Your Balances

It's best not to carry a card balance from month to month. But if you must carry a revolving balance, spread your spending across your credit cards, rather than using just one. The credit utilization rate impacts 30 percent of your credit score. As soon as you spend more than 25 percent of your available balance on any one credit card, your credit score will start to go down by as much as 50 points. The closer you get to your credit limit on that card, the more your credit score will go down.

Instead, make smaller purchases on your cards so the balance on none of them exceeds that important 25 percent. Of course, in an emergency, this might not be possible. But if you're just using your credit cards to fill a temporary gap in your finances, keep a close eye on your credit limits and your utilization rate.

Consider Your Options for Medical Bills

Medical debt is one of the leading causes of bankruptcy in the United States, and it impacts people who have insurance as much as it does people who don't. If you have a stack of outstanding medical bills on your kitchen counter, don't ignore them. Read the fine print, or call the billing department to determine what payment options are available to you. You may be able to get a discount on your bill for paying the entire amount at once.

If the amount isn't something you can tackle in one payment, ask about starting a payment plan. Medical billing offices often offer interest-free payment plans for up to six months or a year, depending on the amount and their policies. It's as easy as asking, "Do you offer payment plans?"

You don't need to have a sad story lined up for why they should cut you a break—remember this is just business. If the biller doesn't offer an interest-free payment plan, they may recommend the next-best solution for you. For instance, they may offer payment plans for a fee, but that fee may be lower than your credit card interest, making it a better deal than charging your medical bills or risking a late fee. In short, don't just take the printed bill you've received as the end of the story. Make time to have a conversation with the billing office to find out what your options are and see how you can get those bills paid off fastest.

Reallocate Your Credit

Closing a credit card can lower your credit score because your amount of available credit across cards decreases. But if you know which question to ask your credit card issuer, you might be able to avoid that.

Ask to have your credit limit transferred to another card with the same issuer. This can be especially helpful if you want to ditch a credit card that has an annual fee but has an impressively large credit limit. If you can get at least a portion of that limit transferred to another card, you can feel more confident closing that card and washing your hands of that annual fee. Your score may fluctuate slightly for a few months depending on the length of time you held the now-closed card, but your positive utilization should bolster your score for the long run.

Take the Shortest Possible Loan Term

It used to be normal to get a car loan for either three years or five years. Or you'd get a thirty-year mortgage—*maybe* fifteen, if you were really in control of your finances. But now, loan terms seem to be longer than ever before. The average car loan for new vehicles is almost seventy months, and you can actually find mortgages available for forty or even fifty years.

THE LONG AND THE SHORT OF IT

Longer loan terms seem attractive because by stretching out the length of the loan, you can make lower payments each month. But instead of taking the loan term that gives you the lowest payment, you should choose the one that keeps you in debt for the least amount of time you can afford. Doing so allows you to gain equity faster, if you're paying for an item like a car or house.

It also reduces the amount of interest you pay. Consider a car loan for $20,000 at 5 percent interest. If you pay it off over sixty months (five years), you'll pay $2,645 in interest. That same loan for eighty-four months (seven years) will cost you $3,745 in interest.

Don't let a lower monthly payment fool you into paying more interest over time. Do your math before you shop to know how much you can really afford to pay and how quickly you can reasonably do it.

Skip the Extended Warranty

Making a sizable purchase like a computer or home appliance? The retailer will remind you that the manufacturer of the item probably only offers a one- or two-year warranty and encourage you to purchase an extended warranty from them. An extended warranty can give you peace of mind, but you may not need to buy one if you're making the purchase with a credit card. Check your card's guide to benefits to see if it offers extended warranties on purchases. In some cases, your card will give you a spare year after the manufacturer's or retailer's warranty; some cards will double what's already offered.

If you need to make a claim, expect to present the receipt for the item and documentation of any warrantees or guarantees made by the product's manufacturer. Since the ink on many receipts fades over time, save a digital copy of the receipt image along with the original. Stick all your receipts and user guides in one designated spot so you don't lose track of them.

HACK 142

Ask for Help

If you're having trouble making ends meet, don't avoid your debt to the point where you end up behind on payments. Asking for help is hard, but it can save you money in the long run and a lot of stress and heartache.

First, if you're struggling to pay your minimum debt payments on time, call your lender and ask if there's a hardship department or hardship program you can speak with. If you have an obvious circumstance like unemployment, an illness or hospital stay, natural disaster, or a family crisis, your lender may be able to put you on special terms for a few months to help you get back on your feet. You may have to provide documentation proving your hardship, and your lender may require that you agree to special terms, like a reduced or paused interest rate, in writing.

Participating in such a program could cause your credit score to go down since your credit utilization will go up if you're paying less or not paying at all for several months. But it's better to have your score decrease for this reason than to end up with a credit history loaded with negative marks due to late payments and fees.

FOR LONG-TERM HELP

If your struggle is more than temporary, you might consider debt counseling. Don't trust advertisements that claim to offer quick and easy debt relief. Instead, search for accredited counselors through the National Foundation for Credit Counseling or the Financial Counseling Association of America. Debt counselors can provide education and guidance to determine the best path to eliminate your debt over time. In some cases, you may be a good candidate for a debt management program. In these programs, your debt isn't reduced, but your program may be able to negotiate a lower interest rate for you. Your debt counselor will manage all your debt payments and you'll make one payment each month toward your debt. Some programs charge a monthly fee of about $30 to participate. There's no cost to chat with a debt counselor or access resources that can help you get organized, so don't hesitate to reach out to a respected organization if you're in need of support.

Use Reward Points to Buy Gift Cards

If the holidays are approaching, it might be worth bolstering your gift-giving fund by using some of your credit card rewards. Much like some credit card issuers offer increased point value when you book travel through its rewards portal, you can often shop for other items through these same portals. That means you can buy gift cards alongside various merchandise.

If your rewards portal increases the value of your points by half a penny, you could end up buying a gift card and getting some of that card's value as a "free" bonus. It's a better option than choosing to get cash back, as that often has the lowest value of all the methods of redeeming your rewards. Buy gift cards to a few stores you know you'll shop during the holidays and you could cross a few items off your list without having to actually spend any more money.

Ask for a Better Sign-Up Bonus

The best way to earn credit card rewards quickly is to get a sign-up bonus when you first open your card. These bonuses usually require that you spend a certain amount of money in the first few months using the card in exchange for far more points than you could earn normally on the same purchases.

But what if you sign up for a card, get a decent bonus, and then find out the card is now offering an even better bonus for new customers? You may be able to ask for an adjustment. If it's been ninety days or less since you opened your account, call your card issuer or bank and tell them you noticed that even-newer customers are being offered a better bonus than yours. Ask if they'll adjust it to match—they just might do it. (You can also make this request via your bank's messaging portal or live chat, if you don't want to call.)

But before you make the ask, make sure that you can achieve the higher standards that might come with a better sign-up bonus. If you need to spend an extra $2,000 to get that extra bonus of several thousand points, you will want to ensure you plan to put $2,000 worth of charges on your card before time runs out.

HACK 145

Choose the Best Travel Credit Card

The best card to use for meals and other expenses while you're traveling isn't necessarily the one that offers the best reward earning potential. It's more important to choose credit and debit cards that tout no international transfer fees. These fees can range from 1 to 3 percent of your purchase total every time you swipe a card to pay with another currency.

The same goes for taking money out of ATMs—you'll pay the same percentage on top of any ATM fees your bank charges (and whatever fees that ATM charges). When you're finally on that big international vacation, you don't want to have to worry about those small percentages that add up quickly. Put as many charges as possible on a card that has no international transaction fees.

HACK 146

Always Pay in Local Currency

You've chosen a credit card that doesn't charge international transaction fees, but now you're sitting in a café and the register is giving you two options for paying your bill: the local currency, or your home country's currency.

This heightens the case for carrying a card without transaction fees. It makes the decision, if there is one, easy—always choose the local currency. But it's also a reminder to look twice before you sign off on any bill when you're traveling internationally. You want to make sure you get what you're paying for, and in the currency you feel most comfortable handling.

CHAPTER FOUR
Make More Money

Find Out What You're Worth

It's hard to negotiate your salary or ask for alternative workplace perks if you don't know what you're worth. To get a better idea of your true market value, use a salary calculator to find out how much you *should* be earning. You can do this on sites like *PayScale*, Salary.com, or *Glassdoor*, to name a few. You can also search for industry-specific reports on compensation, as many fields share salary guides for various roles.

If you find that your market value is well above what you're currently making, don't despair. You can use that information during your next annual review, when you're interviewing for a new job, or if you've simply decided to have a compensation conversation with your supervisor.

Take Your Address Off Your Resume

You'd think listing your mailing address on your resume would be an obvious component, right? But if you're looking for a job outside of the region where you live right now, employers may skip you in favor of a local applicant.

If you're applying to jobs far from home, you have two options to make sure your resume doesn't get lost in the shuffle:

- Don't put a location on your resume at all. You might include the location of your previous roles, but don't stick your mailing address at the top—it'll only draw attention to it.
- List your address as "Relocating to: New York City" or whatever city the company is located in—but only if you truly intend to move there.

HACK 149
Build Your Public Portfolio

You can't rely on a well-written resume to get you a job these days. You need to be easy to find online. Specifically, you need digital proof that you're progressing in your career.

The easiest way to do this is to set up an account on *LinkedIn*. Include details about your current and past jobs, but don't forget to list your accomplishments, instead of just your usual duties. It's easy to upload or link to examples of your work within your *LinkedIn* profile. If your work isn't visual, describe the challenges and tasks along with your results under each role.

If your work would benefit from a separate portfolio outside of *LinkedIn*, it's easy to set one up on a simple website through *WordPress*, *Squarespace*, or *Wix*. All have free options and have templates you can choose to show off your designs or other samples of your work.

HACK 150
Use Every Vacation Day

Do you use all your vacation days your employer offers? If you don't, you're not alone. A Bankrate survey found that only 28 percent of people use every single day of their available paid time off. Even if you can't afford to take a lavish vacation—or go away at all—you should still be sure to take all your vacation days each and every year.

This rule applies especially for people who can't roll over their days into the following year or get paid for unused vacation time if you leave your job. If your paid time off (PTO) is "use it or lose it," not using it means you're essentially working for free.

Even if you love your job, at the very least, schedule some staycation time for yourself to enjoy the sights near your town—or even just hang out at home with a good book or your favorite hobby. You deserve it!

HACK 151

Learn a Skill You Can Sell

Ever think to yourself, "If only I knew how to do this one extra thing, I could get a promotion"? As you get settled into your career, you might wonder how you can keep growing your skillset. Continuing education can be a big part of that advancement.

It doesn't have to cost a lot of money to pick up additional skills that can enhance your value. Your company might offer access to courses through *Lynda* (which is becoming *LinkedIn Learning*), *Skillshare*, or another online learning platform. Some libraries even offer free subscriptions to the classes on these platforms, although you may need to visit your local branch to access them.

You can also investigate class offerings at your local community college, or sign up for a free online class called a MOOC (Massive Open Online Course) offered by a top-name university. There might even be a club of enthusiasts who offer free or inexpensive classes and workshops in your area, whether you want to learn how to code websites or practice a language.

Learning about a new aspect of your industry or a skill you can apply to your daily work not only gives you a boost of confidence. It also looks great on your resume when it's time to apply for a job or promotion. Or, you may find that your newly honed skills help you sell the products or services you offer in your side hustle. Either way, you'll be putting your best foot forward and showing your value while you stretch your brain a bit.

HACK 152

Get Credentials in Your Field

Want to level up your career beyond a particular skill? Consider earning credentials for your industry or type of work. An advanced degree could propel your career to new heights, but so can earning licenses or certifications. They can help you earn more in your career, and the best part is, your boss might cover the tab.

You might already be familiar with certifications in your industry, especially if you're looking for learning opportunities, as in your industry-related professional groups or a local networking group. You can also return to MOOC.org, which offers certification programs alongside free online classes. Its certifications typically aren't free, but many offer lengthy courses for a few hundred dollars. If your employer won't cover the cost, you may be able to chalk it up as an investment in your own professional future.

HACK 153

Don't Give the Government a Loan

It's nice to get a tax refund from Uncle Sam, but that refund is essentially an interest-free loan you gave to the government over the course of the year. Instead, you could find a few more dollars in every paycheck, all year long. It's your money—why wait to get it?

The IRS has made it easier to get your estimated tax withholding correct when you file your W-4 form with your employer. The form has five steps to determine your tax liability. You don't have to file this new form unless you start a new job at a new company. But if you think you have too much income tax taken out of your paychecks, you can ask to update your W-4. The IRS has a tax withholding calculator (www.irs.gov/individuals/tax-withholding-estimator).

HACK 154

Always Negotiate a Job Offer

Hiring managers usually leave some wiggle room in their initial offer anticipating you to ask for more. If you take the first offer, you could be leaving thousands of dollars on the table. And if you don't negotiate when you first get a job offer, it could be harder to earn more down the line.

If your new employer only typically increases salaries by 2 or 3 percent per year, it could take years for your salary to catch up to the point you could have started at in the first place. And if you sell yourself short, your salary could suffer not just in this job, but in future ones too. If you can't negotiate monetary compensation, ask about vacation days, remote work, or other add-ons that could make the role worth it for you even if you can't max out the salary range for the job.

HACK 155

Let Strangers Rent Your Time

Do you want to rent your time? If you consider yourself a people person or have special skills or activities you want to share with others, consider letting people rent your friendship.

RentAFriend.com claims it has more than six hundred thousand "friends" available for hire worldwide. The platform charges a membership fee for people looking for companions. People offering their time set their own rates, and users pay them directly; rates tend to be around $25 per hour.

Plus, depending on what your new friend wants to do during their time with you, you may get to see a museum, movie, or sporting event for free; you may even get to dine on their tab. If you're looking to expand your social circle, this could be a good way to meet new people while also making a few bucks along the way.

Use a Job Offer to Get a Salary Boost

If you're having a hard time getting your boss's attention to negotiate a raise, it may be time to enlist an outside influence: a counteroffer. If you can get a better job offer, you may be able to use it to get a raise in the job you already have. You don't need to share what company the other offer is with—just simply state why it's compelling and what factors would make you consider staying with your current firm.

While you don't want to give your current employer an ultimatum, laying out what your current company can do to match your offer can help you get a much-needed salary bump. Of course, make sure you're serious about staying with your current employer, but also know what it would take to lead you to jump ship if your company isn't able to counter. Some companies have a strict policy not to provide counteroffers if an employee has an offer elsewhere, so ask a few trusted colleagues at your current job about that before you start going on interviews.

Set Your Hourly Rate

When you got your very first job in high school or college, you probably spent a lot of time focusing on how much money you made per hour. You knew that working a couple of extra hours could make a big difference in your paycheck. But when you get a job that has a set annual salary, it's harder to figure out what your time is worth in hourly increments. But doing so can help you determine how best to spend your time—and when it's worth spending a little money for the opportunity to make even more.

HOW TO DETERMINE YOUR HOURLY RATE

Check out your latest pay stub. You'll probably find that your paycheck is for a certain number of hours, even if you don't have to punch a time clock. Usually, that pay stub also lists out the rate for each of those hours worked.

Otherwise, you can simply divide your pre-tax pay by the number of hours you typically work. Doesn't your time—and your money—seem more valuable once you know what you're getting paid for each hour spent on the job?

HACK 158
Outsource Time-Sucks

Once you know your hourly rate (see hack 157), you can figure out if you have the financial space to outsource some tasks. Imagine the household tasks you hate to do; maybe you dread mowing the lawn, preparing meals, or mopping floors. Imagine someone was paying you your hourly rate to do that dreaded task. Does it make you want to do it more, or still avoid it? Or, could you pay someone else to do that same task, probably more efficiently than you can, at what might even be a lower hourly rate?

Spending money to do the chores you hate may not seem like a hack for making more money, but thinking smarter about your money and your time could eventually lead to an income bump. If you pay someone to do the tasks you dislike, you can spend more time focusing your energy on the work that makes you money. If you're in a salary role, maybe you can use that time to learn a new skill or work toward a promotion. Or you can get more rest so you can be sharper at your morning meetings.

It's especially important to consider outsourcing if you work for yourself or have a side hustle. If you can make more money doing what you're good at and pay someone to do some of the other stuff, you can still come out ahead; and you have a richer portfolio of work to show for it too.

HACK 159

Know Your Target, Alternative, and Reservation

When you receive a job offer or are offered a raise, it's important to be strategic in how you negotiate your salary. If you give a knee-jerk response, you could be selling yourself short. Before responding to the anchor—that's the initial offer that's made in a negotiation—consider the following:

- **Your target:** This is your ideal total compensation, from salary to insurance, 401(k) matching, or vacation time, to any other benefits.
- **Your BATNA:** This stands for the Best Alternative to a Negotiated Agreement. It's the next best thing if you can't get your target compensation.
- **Your reservation point:** This is the worst-case scenario you'll accept. If you're considering a new job offer, your reservation point is most likely the first salary you're offered. If you're asking for a raise, you might have a minimum in mind you'll accept that would keep you happy in your current role. It's helpful to think about your reservation point before even receiving a job offer.

PREPARE BEFORE BATTLE

Don't rely on your memory to serve you as you work toward an agreement, whether you're negotiating by phone or by email. Write down your target, BATNA, and reservation points and list out the factors that are most important to you, including salary, benefits, and other perks that could be leveraged.

And don't feel pressured to accept an offer up front; employers expect that you'll need to take a day or two to consider an offer, even if you've been negotiating for a while.

HACK 160

Add Up Your Benefits

If you're looking for a new job, it's not enough to compare your current salary to what a potential employer is offering. Consider your total compensation. This calculation includes your base salary, any bonuses you're eligible to receive, paid vacation and sick leave days, medical and other insurance coverage, and retirement plans. It might also include gym memberships, a cell phone plan, home-office stipend, commuter benefit, tuition assistance, or childcare. This all gets added up in a total compensation statement. If you haven't received one, you can ask your human resources department if there's one available for you.

Asking about your total compensation statement shows that you care about recognizing all the positives of working where you do, beyond the dollar amount you receive on a regular basis. You might be surprised at what your benefits are worth when you add them all up!

HACK 161

Let Your Job Pay You to Exercise

Some jobs offer reimbursement for your gym membership fee or coordinate with a local gym where you can attend for free. If you participate in programs like step-count challenges, you might be eligible for a free fitness device. Even better, some workplaces reimburse you for the cost of your insurance if you exercise. Each time you visit the gym, you ask a staff member to sign off on your attendance; if you visit a certain number of times in the course of a month, you may be eligible for a reimbursement of a portion of your health insurance premium.

Keep an Eye on the Job Boards

Even if you're happy in your current role, it's still a good idea to periodically check job listings for roles in your field. Doing so can help you learn a few key things that could help you earn.

First, those job listings give you an idea of what the competition is looking for in its candidates. A job listing for a role close to yours at a similar company can tip you off as to whether that company might be paying more for the role. Look closely at the job duties and requirements to see how the listing stacks up to yours. See duties on the list that aren't on your job description, but that you're regularly doing? Be sure to note that during your next review.

It also provides hints for what your next move could be as you progress in your career. Looking at jobs that are one level above you can help you prep for skills, certifications, or other factors that can aid in you getting hired or promoted.

Finally, it never hurts to be on the lookout for a new opportunity. You never know when the "perfect" job will open in your field—but it'll probably happen when you least expect it. Don't wait until you're unhappy in your current role to go looking for something better.

This doesn't have to be a time-consuming task. Set up a few job alerts on *Indeed* or *Glassdoor* and have them go to your personal email. You can "search" for a better job in just a few minutes a day.

HACK 163
Get a Mentor

If you want to excel in your career, you need help to get there. That doesn't just mean a supportive boss and great coworkers—it also means getting a mentor. This might be someone in your field or a person with general business experience who can guide you through critical moments. A good mentor is part cheerleader and part advisor who can remind you of your worth, all while challenging your assumptions about how you move through your career.

Studies have found that mentored employees are more likely to get higher compensation and more promotions. Plus, they feel more committed to and fulfilled by their career, which can only help when it's time for those conversations regarding compensation.

EXPLORE INTERNAL OPTIONS, BUT DON'T STOP THERE

If you work at a large corporation, you might find that there's an in-house mentorship program in which you can participate. But a mentor doesn't have to be someone who works at your company. To find a mentor, look to your existing professional network or within networking groups you frequent. A professional association for your industry may even have a formal mentorship program to match you with a mentor compatible with your goals and interests.

It can be hard to quantify the results of working with a mentor. It may not be until you look back on your career later that you see the impact of your relationship in the form of raises, promotions, and accolades. And who knows—your mentor may still be there to cheer you on.

HACK 164
Skip Your Commute

The average one-way commute in the United States is just over 26 miles, according to the US Census Bureau. If your job requires spending most of your time in front of a computer, instead of in meetings or working one-on-one with clients, you may be able to negotiate to spend less of your workday on that commute. Working from home does more than just reduce your time spent between home and work. It also helps you save money on gas, for one—an employee who works from home half the time can save anywhere between $450 and $4,500 (wow!) on the costs of commuting, from gas to tolls and meals outside the home, according to Global Workplace Analytics.

And, it helps you be more effective during your workday. Research has shown that remote and telecommuting employees are less distracted, miss fewer days at the office due to illness, and are more likely to be willing to try out and use new technologies to aid in their work.

To find out how much money you would save by telecommuting, try *SkipTheDrive*'s calculator (www.skipthedrive.com/how-much-money-can-you-save-by-telecommuting/) or search online for "telecommute savings calculator" or "remote work savings calculator."

HACK 165

Brag a Little

Performance reviews at work are usually stressful. When you look back at what you've accomplished, all your projects and tasks can blur together, making you wonder if you actually achieved anything at all.

If you can easily identify how you've excelled in your role, you have a better chance at nabbing a raise at review time. To do this, don't rely on memory. Keep a running list of work-related accomplishments, large and small. It may include projects you've completed, metrics you've met, or new skills you've learned.

HACK 166

Work Off Your Student Loans

When you check out job listings, one benefit that may surprise you is student loan repayment. More and more companies are adding repayment assistance to their roster of employee perks— about 8 percent of companies offer this benefit. Employers usually have a cap per year of $1,000 to $2,000, with a lifetime cap somewhere around $10,000.

Some participating companies base your benefit on what you pay toward your own student loans and match it up to a certain point. You probably won't be able to pay off your student loans altogether with this help, but you may be able to accelerate your repayment timeline. Just keep in mind that it's considered taxable income on your annual return, although Congress is trying to make at least a portion of that contribution tax-free for employees.

Track Your Mileage

If you drive your personal vehicle for your job duties or a side hustle, you need to document every mile you drive. If you're lucky, your employer reimburses you for miles you track and submit. But even if you're not so lucky, you can deduct that mileage from your annual income taxes.

Tracking your mileage used to mean keeping a handwritten log in your car and remembering to keep up with the task. But now, there are lots of apps available to do the heavy lifting for you—and many of them are free. Try Hurdlr, TripLog, or Stride; each app has a free version and only charges for premium features.

Sell Your Junk Mail

You can actually gather up your junk mail like credit card offers, restaurant flyers, and other advertisements and exchange them for gift cards.

The program is run by SBKCenter.com, a market research company. It sends you prepaid envelopes, into which you can tuck your junk mail as you receive it. After a few weeks, seal up the envelope and send it off to get points in exchange for your mail. Once you earn 2,000 points, you get a prepaid gift card that you can use like a debit card. It's that easy!

You won't be able to change your lifestyle if you apply to this program and start "selling" your mail. Panelists typically earn a few $20 gift cards per year. But surely you can think of a few things you'd like to do if you had a few extra twenties in your wallet?

Find Extra Money in Your Paycheck

Instead of digging wrinkled coupons out of your pocket when it's time to pay at the drugstore, make your money go further by actually having more of it to spend. If your employer offers a Flexible Spending Account (FSA) as part of your benefits, you can set aside pre-tax dollars to use on a variety of health-related expenses. That means that if you're in the 25 percent tax bracket, for example, you'll get a full dollar to spend instead of your after-tax 75 cents.

Each time you get paid, an amount of your choosing gets put on a debit card. You can use that money for doctor visit copays, prescription drugs, birth control, chiropractic and acupuncture visits, first-aid supplies, contact lenses, prescription glasses, and more. (Some programs require you to pay up front and then reimburse you. Either way, you should keep your receipts according to your program's guidelines.) Your employer will have a list available of qualified expenses for which you can use your FSA funds.

The tricky part about FSA accounts is that there's a limit for how much you can contribute per year—about $2,750—and you have to use all that money in the same year you contribute it. Your employer may allow you to roll up to $500 into the following year or offer a grace period of two and a half months into the next year, but that's not mandatory. It's up to you to accurately predict how much money you should put aside for your medical expenses that aren't covered by your insurance and use it accordingly.

Find the Perfect Side Hustle

If you can, pick a second gig that doesn't look anything like your nine-to-five job. If you sit at a computer all day, for example, don't become a transcriptionist or pick up work as a virtual assistant. You might be more energized getting on your feet working in a boutique or out walking dogs. Remember that variety is the spice of life, even when it comes to making a little extra money, and don't assume that the most lucrative side gig is the best fit for you. The best side gig is one you can tolerate and even enjoy doing for as long as you want to rake in those extra bucks.

Deliver Groceries, Packages, or People

Who *doesn't* have a side hustle driving for a ride service? The average ride-hailing driver makes about $10 per hour after expenses. If that doesn't seem like enough money to deal with chatty passengers or strange hours, consider the alternative: delivering items.

Amazon Flex drivers make about $19 per hour delivering packages in their neighborhoods. Grocery delivery drivers for services like Instacart make about $11 per hour, and takeout delivery drivers for companies like Postmates make about $15 per hour.

All these services make it easy to sign up, so you can test a few out and see which you like best—and which brings in the most income. There are also lots of forums online where current drivers discuss the platforms they use and their experiences.

HACK 172

Start a Seasonal Side Hustle

Don't want to worry about maintaining a side hustle all the time? Choose a seasonal one that allows you to make some cash in a shorter period. These seasonal gigs will probably take place outdoors. Adore watching the leaves change? Rake leaves for a few weeks in the fall. Love when it snows? Shovel driveways or sidewalks for neighbors who don't want to do the task. In the spring, you could offer yard prep and garden-starting services for people who want help fostering a lush lawn.

If spending time outdoors doesn't excite you, find an indoor activity that does. You could offer your services as a day-of party assistant during the holidays when people are hosting guests and have plenty of chores to go around. Or, if you make a unique craft, market it for a specific holiday or season.

Running a side hustle for a few months out of the year can help you bring in extra cash without going through the requirements of setting up a formal business (you'll still need to report your extra income to the IRS, though). Once you know what you want to do, you can promote your services on *Facebook*, *Nextdoor*, *Instagram*, or even *Twitter*. Offer a small discount if your friends recommend your work to others. Friends and neighbors are likely to remember you and your amazing seasonal services year after year. And a seasonal schedule ensures you get plenty of rest after all your hard work.

HACK 173

Become a Notary

In this digital age, there's still plenty of paperwork that must be signed by hand. And notaries are ready to witness and authenticate those documents—for a small fee. Becoming a notary public is a side gig that you can add to your repertoire without a ton of training, and it's an additional source of income you can take just about anywhere you go.

What you earn will depend on the state where you live. Some states allow notaries to set their own fees, while others have standard fees for various types of documents. But some states also allow you to charge clients for your mileage, or an extra fee if you perform services for a marriage. On average, you'll probably make $10–$20 per hour of work.

It doesn't take much money to get started, so you'll recoup your startup costs quickly. Typically, you'll pay $100–$200 to take a class and pass an exam according to your state's regulations; you'll also need to pass a background check and have your fingerprints taken. Then, you'll get a surety bond, which is basically insurance that covers you if you make an error in your duties. You pay a fraction of what your bond is worth to get it, usually between 1 percent and 15 percent of the bond amount. You'll pay any fees your state requires to file certification paperwork, and you have to buy your notary seal and record-keeping kit. You can find out more about the process and how to qualify to become a notary via the National Notary Association (www.nationalnotary.org).

Show Off Your Hometown

Do you have an interest in history, culture, or architecture? Do you love showing people around town when they come to visit? Being a tour guide could be a great side gig for you. Companies in towns large and small offer walking tours, ghost tours, and even brewery tours—and they need people who can engage with a crowd to lead them. Tour guides can make about $15 per hour and sometimes get tips at the end of the tour.

If there's not a tour company hiring in your town, you might be able to host your own tours. Beyond lodging listings, *Airbnb* also offers "Experiences" to travelers who want to learn from locals during their visit. You set your own rates, and *Airbnb* keeps 20 percent.

Leverage Your Second Language

If you speak more than one language, you can communicate with family and friends, and wow people you meet with your talents. But you might not know that people who can speak more than one language can earn more at work. Bilingual people earn about 2 percent more per year than people who speak just one language. That might only add $1,000 to a $50,000 salary, but over the course of your career, it could add up to significant additional earnings.

It helps if you know a language that's less common in your region, as it can add major value for an employer who may not have someone on staff already who speaks that language. But whether you're fluent in Russian or Spanish, it's worth pointing out to potential employers—or even your current boss—that you've got additional language skills to share.

Get Paid to Share Your Home

You don't need to have the fanciest home to be a host on *Airbnb* or *Vrbo*. You just need to have some extra space to host guests. If you're willing to have guests stay with you for at least part of the month, the earnings can really add up. One survey found that hosts in fifteen cities who listed one bedroom in a two-bedroom apartment could cover 81 percent of their rent via *Airbnb* bookings.

Of course, it takes work to get these results—beyond having extra space, you'll need to have the time to keep your place squeaky clean and change all the linens between guests. And, not everyone is allowed to offer short-term rentals on platforms like *Airbnb* and *Vrbo*, so check your local laws.

Stick with a Short-Term Rental

Don't want to feel like you're always "on" as an *Airbnb* host? Consider hosting guests for just a few days each year. Typically, when you make income by renting out space, that income is subject to taxes. But the IRS has an exemption: If you rent out your home for fourteen days or fewer, you're exempt from paying taxes on the money you make. That means you can take advantage of big events happening near your home—maybe a big sports game, music festival, annual parade, or college graduation weekend—and host guests during these times when hotels and other rentals may be booked or overpriced.

Of course, check your local regulations before doing this, and make sure your renters or homeowners insurance will cover any incidents that may arise during that brief period.

Tutor Students Around the World

You don't have to spend afternoons at the library to tutor students anymore. Now you can do it from the comfort of your own home. Online platforms hire tutors to help students around the world practice their English language skills. You typically don't need a teaching or language arts background—just enthusiasm and a good handle on the basics of the English language. And if you do have a teaching background or certificate, you can make up to $20 per hour, with some platforms offering bonuses after you teach a certain number of classes. Due to time zones, you may need to teach at strange times of day, like early in the morning or late at night. But that makes it easy to fit tutoring into your schedule before or after work.

Hang with a Pet

Don't want the burden of taking care of a pet 24/7? Or maybe you already have some furry friends of your own but have a "the more the merrier!" mindset. Pet sitting might be a good side gig for you.

If you're a natural with animals, you usually don't need any special skills—just time and the ability to get to your client's home to pick up their pet or provide in-home care. You can sign up for a pet-sitting platform, or apply for a part-time job with a local pet-sitting company. The benefits of going either of those routes—instead of just putting up flyers in your local coffee shop—is that pet-sitting platforms and established companies have insurance specifically for the risks that come with pet sitting and walking dogs. That means that you can focus on making money instead of covering overhead expenses.

HACK 180

Get Cash for Last Year's Phone

Online platforms allow you to see a quote for selling or trading in your phone before you commit to the deal. You enter details about your device's specifications and its condition, and if you accept an offer, you typically have a few weeks to mail your item with a prepaid mailing label. That gives you time to purchase your new phone or a replacement device if you're trying to generate funds for an upgrade.

Check websites like *Gazelle*, *Swappa*, and *Decluttr* to see how much money you could make from your devices. Look around to see if you have any extra old phones tucked into your junk drawer. These websites will still pay you a few bucks for those phones, even if they're a few years old.

HACK 181

Sell Your Stuff to Your Neighbors

You'd be amazed at how many people will be interested in buying everything from your old furniture or car parts, to your clothing and even houseplants.

If your neighborhood has a robust *NextDoor* community, list your items individually or announce a full-blown garage sale. *Facebook*, meanwhile, even allows payments to be sent through its messenger platform, making it easier to trade items on its *Marketplace*. Being able to see interested buyers' profiles on *NextDoor* and *Facebook* can also ease your nerves if you're anxious about meeting strangers from the Internet. You don't have to exchange your items for cash at home either—most police departments are happy to have you meet buyers in their parking lots.

HACK 182

Sell Your Books, DVDs, and Video Games

If you're reading this book at home, take a look around the room where you're sitting. Chances are, you have some books you'll never read again, DVDs you haven't touched in years, or video games you finished playing a long time ago. Why not make some money selling these gently used items? While the resale market for used books, music, movies, and games may not be as lucrative as it used to be, there are still plenty of people who want some fresh entertainment without paying full price.

Some resale platforms let you scan item barcodes with your smartphone and give you an instant quote; they often cover the cost of shipping your items to them and pay within a few days. Others allow you to sell movies and video games directly to your peers, taking a cut of your revenue for the convenience. And there's always *Amazon*, which makes it easy to list your item and price it according to demand.

If your item is hard to find, like a first edition book or collector's item, you may be able to get top dollar by putting it up on an online auction site, as enthusiasts are always watching for items they can add to their collections.

Of course, you can always go to your favorite used bookstore or video game shop to sell your wares in person. But don't start browsing there while you wait, or you may be tempted to spend your profits.

Pay Attention to
Class Action Settlements

What do customers get when big companies do them wrong? Sometimes a lot of money. When businesses make false claims about their product, violate customer privacy, or even when they experience a data breach, the result is often a class action lawsuit—meaning that many customers come together to sue the company. A few key plaintiffs represent the whole "class" so that thousands of people who were impacted by the bad business practices don't have to go to court.

Typically, the company defending its products or practices doesn't admit guilt but does agree to a settlement. That settlement can take many forms, including in some cases, coupons toward future purchases. But in many cases, you are rewarded with a check.

But you can't get that cash unless you know what class action settlements are available, and whether you were impacted by the case. One website that compiles information for current settlement opportunities is TopClassActions.com. You can also usually learn about class action settlements during your local news station's "consumer corner" segment.

Not every settlement opportunity will apply to you, but you'd be surprised at the number you're eligible to claim. You give up your right to sue the company in the future if you file a class action settlement claim, but the odds of you taking up a case against a major corporation were probably slim to begin with.

Get Paid for Your Opinions

Companies are always looking for regular people to help them evaluate new products. They hire marketing companies that run focus groups to allow people to test products, share their opinions, and point out opportunities for improvement. While you probably can't make a living off focus groups, you can get up to $200 to participate in a single focus group session.

This side gig is best for people with flexible schedules, as many focus groups take place during the day. There's usually an initial survey or questionnaire before you attend to make sure that you don't have a conflict of interest (for instance, if you work for a toothpaste company, you'd probably be excluded from a focus group about dental care products).

Legitimate focus group hosts never charge a fee for access to their opportunities. To find focus groups near you, search "your city + focus groups" or check the directory on FocusGroups.org.

HACK 185

Get Paid to Sleep Over

Maybe you're not into dogs and cats, but you're cool with house-plants. You could work on the side as a house sitter. Many house-sitting gigs don't pay, because you get to stay in the client's home for free. It can be a great way to take a budget-friendly vacation or even a staycation. But there are opportunities to get paid for house-sitting too.

The pay depends on the services required and how long the resident is gone, with sitters charging anywhere between $10 and $80 per day according to HouseSitter.com. Sitters who can care for and stay overnight with pets tend to earn more, but you can still command a decent rate if you can look after plants, bring in the mail, take out the trash, and maybe do some light cleaning. You can find house-sitting gigs on HouseSitter.com, Care.com, or through local social media networks.

HACK 186

Use Your Hands to Make Extra Cash

Do you have a knack for DIY tasks? Maybe you love to clean. You may be able to make extra income by picking up assignments through online platforms.

Your options are wider at some sites, where "taskers" can do everything from cleaning and home improvement jobs to moving furniture, delivering items, or performing personal assistant tasks. You can even spend an afternoon putting together furniture with the aid of illustrated directions. You'll set your own hours and rates to be matched with jobs near you. The site generally keeps a portion of the fee you charge for each job.

HACK 187

Rent Your Garage, Shed, or Yard

What's in your garage? Are you using the space, or is it just...sitting there? What about your shed? You can make money sharing spaces you don't use often.

To make money renting out your extra space, you just have to be willing to relinquish a bit of access to it. Rental platform *Spacer* says users who rent their garages earn about $250 per month. Your driveway could bring in $200 per month, while an outdoor space could earn you as much as $175 per month.

Of course, if you use a platform like *Spacer* or Neighbor.com, be aware you'll share some of your earnings with the platform. Want to deal locally? Put up an ad on social media or consider running a small ad in your local newspaper or neighborhood newsletter.

Become a Shopping Detective

Become a mystery shopper and get paid to shop, dine out, visit breweries, or visit lots of other places.

It's the perfect side gig if you have great attention to detail and a good memory. Mystery shoppers complete a task at their assigned location, then file a report or fill out a questionnaire immediately after "doing the shop," as the pros say. Once your report is processed by the company you're shopping for, your expenses get reimbursed. On top of that reimbursement, you get paid to complete the assignment. While the pay can be low—think $10 or less per hour of work—the addition of free meals, merchandise, or experiences makes up for the low rate.

WATCH OUT FOR SCAM "OPPORTUNITIES"

There are a ton of scammers out there claiming to have mystery shopping opportunities for you. Legitimate opportunities won't charge you a fee, and you'll find legit companies listed by the Mystery Shopping Professionals Association (www.mspa-global.org). You can also check Secret Hopper for opportunities doing mystery shopping at breweries, BestMark if you're down to test drive cars or visit casinos, or Market Force if you want to go to the movies on someone else's dime. Mystery shopping won't dramatically boost your income, but it's a fun way to make some extra cash while trying new spots around town.

HACK 189

Let Strangers Rent Your Car

If you don't drive much—maybe you convinced your boss to let you work from home more!—there's potential to make extra money by renting your car to other people. It may sound like a risky proposition, but there are a few platforms that exist to facilitate this peer-to-peer exchange.

Turo allows you to set your own pricing and vehicle availability, and you keep between 65 percent and 85 percent of the rental fee, depending on how much damage insurance you choose (*Turo* covers the liability insurance). The company says the average user earns about $700 per month by listing their car. You get paid a few days after each rental.

Getaround suggests how to price your car, and in some cities, it offers predictive pricing that fluctuates depending on demand. The company takes 40 percent of every rental fee, which covers liability and damage insurance. You pay $99 up front to have a device installed that allows your car to be unlocked with the company's app, plus $20 per month to use that device. *Getaround* says the average user makes about $500 per month, and you get paid monthly.

HACK 190

Wrap Your Car

Next time you're on the road, keep an eye out for vehicles with logos painted across the side. They might be a regular commuter like you, driving the car and getting paid to drive that rolling advertisement. Car wraps are advertising decals that look flawless once a pro installs them, and you may be able to make $200-$500 per month to add one to your car.

There are lots of scam car wrap companies out there, so keep in mind that a legitimate one will never make you pay a fee for access to its opportunities. But do keep in mind that every legit car wrap agency will have its own requirements for eligibility, like:

- Minimum number of miles per day
- Average distance per day
- Car make or model
- Car age (the newer, the better)
- A clean driving record

If you're already on the road as a part of your regular day, why not make some money doing it? You can even apply with some agencies if you're an Uber or Lyft driver, in order to multiply your earnings. To find car wrap opportunities near you, start with Wrapify, which operates nationally, or Carvertise, which operates in many major cities. Heard about a company near you that pays for car wraps? Look them up in the Better Business Bureau directory to ensure there aren't any troubling complaints against the company—and always be on the lookout for those scammers.

HACK 191

Switch Banks for the Bonus

Just because your bank gets the job done doesn't mean you need to stick with it forever—or that you can't have accounts at more than one bank. By selectively opening new accounts, you can earn cash that can quickly add up to a few hundred bucks.

Banks sometimes offer new account sign-up bonuses for checking or savings accounts—and sometimes offer more when you open both types of account. Naturally, there are a few requirements. You have to be a new customer, and usually you have to either meet a minimum initial deposit or set up direct deposit into that account.

The latter can be a hassle, so you won't want to try to sign up for every new customer offer you see. But if you haven't opened a new account in a while, it could take just a few minutes to open a checking or savings account and funnel a portion of your paycheck into your new account to meet that direct deposit requirement. Perhaps you could even use your new account as a place to tuck away extra-special savings you're planning to use for a trip or other big occasion.

If you take advantage of one of these sign-up offers, be sure to read the fine print to make sure your new account doesn't come with monthly maintenance fees or even an account closure fee. Note any important dates related to your account opening and bonus eligibility. You don't want to miss out on your bonus cash after doing all the work of getting set up as a new customer!

CHAPTER FIVE

Plan for the Future

HACK 192
Blow Out Your Money Candles

Everyone wants to set big new goals that start on January 1. But when it comes to money, the start of a new year might not be the best time to make a resolution. You've just completed a year's worth of financial transactions, and especially after the holiday season, your wallet might be feeling a little drained. It can be difficult to make heads or tails of your finances after a month and a half of parties, food, and other indulgences.

Instead of making a financial resolution for the new year, set money-related goals each year on your birthday. Your birthday is a time of year when your ambition is high–you're reflecting on the past year's achievements and can see lots of possibility in the year to come. So after you blow out the candles and put away your party hat, spend some time reviewing your finances and setting some goals–large or small, they're all important!–for your money.

Once you have a goal or two for the new year, write them down somewhere you can refer to often. Whenever you pay bills or consider a large purchase is a good time to check in with those goals and see if you're on track.

HACK 193

Go On a Money Date

Couples can choose to manage their finances in a variety of ways, but whichever you choose, there's one necessary requirement: You need to communicate. If you don't talk about your money, you won't be able to make smart financial decisions as a group. That's why it's important to have money dates with your partner.

You might choose to have these meetings monthly, quarterly, or even twice a year, depending on your goals. Use your time together to review your progress, talk through any conflicts that have popped up, and prepare for the months ahead. These meetings don't have to be formal, and you can make an agenda that suits you. Order takeout, sit together at the kitchen table while you eat and talk, and then take to the living room to unwind with a movie after your meeting. Or, maybe you focus on business first, then go for a run after to clear your minds.

Whatever works best for you, be sure to make notes about what you discussed and what you'll want to check in on next time you chat. It may feel awkward and formal at first, but before you know it, you'll look forward to your money dates with your partner.

Merge with Caution

One of the biggest decisions in your life will be whether to marry and who to do it with. But before you tie the knot, it's worth talking about how you'll manage your money as a couple.

There's no "right" way to merge your finances as a couple. A few options to help you kickstart your own discussion:

- **Merge everything:** Become joint partners in every account, from debit to credit to everything in between.
- **Partial merge:** Create a joint account for expenses that serve you both, like housing, transportation, and funneling money toward your savings. You might send part of your paycheck to this shared account via direct deposit or transfer money manually.
- **No merge:** Keep your money separate and share money only when necessary. For instance, if your partner pays the rent, you might transfer your half to them each month.

The method you choose isn't as important as the fact that you choose a method at all. Couples benefit greatly from discussing their preferred financial management system before they walk down the aisle.

Choose Equitable over Equal

If you decide to share expenses with your partner, you don't have to split everything fifty-fifty. Each share of the finances doesn't need to be equal if there's a noticeable difference, but it should be equitable.

For instance, say you make $60,000 per year and your partner makes $40,000. Both you and your partner feel fulfilled in your careers, and you make salaries that are on par with your peers. To make those salaries work for your household budget, you should pay 60 percent of the expenses, and they should pay 40 percent.

Taking the example one step further, if your rent is $1,000 per month, that means you pay $600 and your partner kicks in $400. It takes a bit of figuring out, but once you're set up, it's easy to contribute equitably and adjust as needed.

Determine Your Investing Risk

In general, stocks are riskier investments than bonds, but their volatility can bring a larger return—which means more money for you. And as you get older, it's recommended that you gradually shift your portfolio from more stock-heavy, to one that leans more on less-risky, more stable bonds.

How much is enough of each for your portfolio? An easy way to determine your balance of stocks to bonds is to start with 100 and subtract your age. For example, if you're twenty-eight, you might invest up to 72 percent of your portfolio in stocks, with the remainder in bonds. But by the time you're thirty-eight, it's time to drop that stock allocation to 62 percent.

HACK 197
Go Mortgage Hunting

There are two steps to the process of getting qualified for a mortgage.

STEP 1: GET PREQUALIFIED

It only takes a few moments and gives you an idea of the amount of mortgage you may be able to get from a particular lender. In many cases you can do this without a full credit check.

STEP 2: GET PREAPPROVED

If you like the rates a lender offers, you can get preapproved, which means you'll submit to a full examination of your credit and finances. Once you're approved, you get a letter confirming you have a mortgage offer. If you move forward to get preapproved, ask your lender if you can lock in your rate; it preserves your interest rate for a while in case rates go up while you're house hunting.

HACK 198
Get Financially Fit

You might be familiar with your employer's workplace wellness program that reimburses your gym membership fees or provides healthy snacks at the office. But some companies go a step further and offer financial wellness programs for their staff members.

The programs can take many forms, including access to financial counselors or financial planners, retirement planning workshops, access to financial management platforms, online lessons for topics from budgeting to investing, and even debt management programs.

Employers offer such programming because it's widely known that money is notorious for causing high levels of stress. By reducing some of that stress, companies can encourage good money management behaviors and put employees' minds at ease.

Most financial wellness plans are operated by a vendor (not your boss), so you know that your personal and financial situation is kept confidential. If you're not sure, ask to see your program's written confidentiality policy.

HACK 199

Get Free Money from Your Boss

After taxes and other deductions are taken out of your paycheck, you might feel like you don't have enough money left to be able to save for retirement. But if your employer offers a 401(k) plan with a match, you're missing out on free money. Having a 401(k) is already a smart move because it's a tax-advantaged retirement account. Your contribution gets funneled over to your retirement savings before taxes are taken out of your paycheck, so once you get used to the adjustment, you won't even notice that your checks are a bit smaller. If your employer offers a match, they'll typically offer it up to a certain percentage of your salary. That means that you can contribute as much of your salary to your 401(k) as you want (up to the annual limit), but your employer will only match a certain percent of that.

For instance, imagine you make $40,000 and contribute 3 percent of your salary to your 401(k). You'll contribute $100 per month. If your employer matches up to 3 percent of your salary, your employer will *also* contribute $100 per month. Now imagine you contribute 5 percent of that same salary to your 401(k), which comes out to $167 per month. But your employer will only contribute $100 per month—3 percent of your salary.

On the other end of the spectrum, if you don't contribute up to the employer match limit, you're missing out on free money. Picture that same salary. If you only contribute 2 percent, you and your employer each only contribute $67 each month. That's like leaving a $33 bonus from your boss on the table. A few percent may not seem like a big difference, but your larger contribution will really add up.

HACK 200

Don't Watch the Market

Knowing the latest stock market movers and shakers makes you sound brilliant when you're chatting around the water cooler. But knowing too much about what's going on in the markets could negatively impact your portfolio's growth potential. When an event is fresh in your mind—like a stock market dip—you're nervous that it's going to happen again. And that could convince you to change your investment strategy to be more conservative.

If you're investing for the long term, like for retirement, resist the urge to get too caught up in what's happening in the financial world every moment. Sure, it can benefit you to keep up with investing trends. But be wary of making decisions because you got fired up over something you saw on a news broadcast. You probably don't need to make any quick changes to your portfolio.

HACK 201

Start with a Robo-Advisor

Robo-advisors are digital platforms that provide financial planning services, but instead of working with a human through your computer, you work mostly with the computer itself. Based on your needs, the robo-advisor can help you manage your portfolio and work toward your goals.

Check out Betterment, Wealthfront, Personal Capital, and Ally Invest. Some robo-advisors have account minimums to get started ranging from $500 to $25,000, but still many of them let you get started with no account minimum at all.

HACK 202
Pay Taxes Now to Save Later

While 401(k) tends to be the default option for employer-sponsored retirement programs, you may be able to choose a Roth 401(k). While you contribute funds to your 401(k) before taxes, you put after-tax money into a Roth 401(k). But then, it's tax free from there on out—even when you start taking out money for retirement.

Why's it such an attractive idea? Because you get taxed at your tax rate today, not the one you reach in your sixties. If you decide not to retire until well into your sixties or even your seventies, you'll be taxed on withdrawals from your regular 401(k) at the rate of your salary at that point.

If you withdraw money from your account early, you are only on the hook for income taxes on your earnings—not your original contributions—on top of a 10 percent penalty.

HACK 203
Use Your Investment Time Machine

Want to give your IRA an extra boost? Contribute to last year's limits. IRAs allow you to contribute from January 1 through April 15 of the following year. That means that if you're doing your taxes in March, you still have time to put money in your account and have it count for the previous year. Not only does this help you maximize your savings for each and every year that you have an IRA, it can also give you a boost if you get a raise or have another windfall.

If you contribute to a traditional IRA, make any additional contributions before you do your taxes, since those contributions are tax-deductible. Otherwise you'll have to submit an amended tax return later to reflect your full contribution for the tax year.

HACK 204
Work for Yourself?
Don't Forget to Save

Just because you don't have access to an employer-sponsored retirement account doesn't mean you can't invest with similar tools. There are a few retirement accounts available especially for you, and they're easy to get through a regular investment brokerage like Charles Schwab or Vanguard.

- **SEP IRA:** SEP stands for Simplified Employee Pension. If you're self-employed or have just a few employees, you can contribute up to 25 percent of your compensation or net self-employment earnings to a SEP IRA. You can deduct your contributions, but distributions are taxed as income when you withdraw money later.

- **SIMPLE IRA:** It's called the Savings Incentive Match Plan for Employees, but you can open one if you're self-employed too. You can contribute up to about $13,500 of your earnings pre-tax each year, but you must also contribute from your net self-employment earnings.

- **Solo 401(k):** If you're self-employed and don't have any other employees, you can open a solo 401(k), sometimes called an individual 401(k) or a one-participant 401(k) plan. It allows you to contribute pre-tax funds as both employee and employer. You can contribute up to $19,000 as an employee; on the employer side, you can contribute up to 25 percent of your compensation. And if you'd rather pay taxes now than later, you can open a Roth 401(k).

To get your "net self-employment income," subtract your business expenses from your revenue. Then, multiply the answer by .9235 (92.35 percent) to find out your net income.

Invest In the 5 Percent Rule

You've heard that you should diversify your portfolio, but how varied do your investments really need to be? Play it safe with the 5 percent rule of investing. The rule states that no more than 5 percent of your portfolio should be locked up in one particular investment type. If you were investing in individual stocks, for example, you would want to invest no more than 5 percent of your money into a single stock.

If you invest not via individual stocks but through products like index funds or exchange-traded funds (ETFs), it can be slightly more difficult to determine the 5 percent rule; but it's not impossible once you know where you look. You'll want to check the holdings for each fund. Mutual funds are assumed to be diverse by design, but some of them can get lopsided in favor of stocks, bonds, or even precious metals.

You can also use the 5 percent rule to ensure your portfolio doesn't rely on any one sector. Some funds focus on a particular industry, like healthcare or real estate, for example. But you don't want your portfolio's success to ride on either of those industries. Keep your allocation for each sector to 5 percent or less.

Of course, there's an exception to every rule. One mutual fund can take up more than 5 percent of your portfolio if the holdings *within the fund itself* respect the 5 percent rule. You might choose a highly diversified index fund to take up a substantial chunk of your portfolio, while supplementing with smaller allocations to a few other funds.

HACK 206

Choose a Target

Perhaps you're looking at different types of mutual funds you can choose for your portfolio, and you're just feeling overwhelmed or confused. No need to fret—there's an easy solution to get your money invested ASAP so it starts to grow: a target date fund.

All you have to do is pick the fund for the year you expect to retire. You don't have to pick the exact year you turn sixty-five—target date funds usually increase years by fives—just pick a date that's close to the age you think you'll retire. That mutual fund is managed with the people in that retirement date range in mind.

HOW A TARGET DATE FUND CHANGES AS YOU AGE

For example, if you're in your twenties and choose a target date fund for around the time you turn seventy, your target date fund is likely to be filled primarily with high-risk, high-reward investments, like stocks. Each year, it'll get a little bit more conservative until you near your retirement date, by which point you'll probably see that it's mostly invested in bonds and other stable investments.

The drawback of a target date fund is that it's not tailored exactly to your personal financial situation. But it's a solid set-it-and-forget-it starting point for many beginner investors. You might start with just a target date fund at first, then slowly start to reallocate your investments to other types of funds, or even a few different target date funds. Remember, you're not locked in for life when you choose a fund like this. It's simply a good place to get started.

HACK 207

Double Your Money

Do you know how long it will take your money in an investment or savings account to double? It might have never occurred to you to even wonder. But a simple equation could help you determine if your money is in the right place based on your financial goals.

It's called the rule of 72. All you do is divide 72 by the interest rate for your savings account (or the anticipated rate of return for your investing vehicle). If the interest rate on your high-yield savings account is 1 percent, it'll take—no surprise here—seventy-two years for your money to double. If your interest rate is 2 percent, it'll take thirty-six years for your money to double. A 10 percent return rate on an index fund—maybe the markets are having a great couple of years—will require a little over seven years for your money to double.

You should not use the rule of 72 to feel bad about how slow it may feel your money is growing. What you should use it for instead is to motivate you to make sure your money is in the right place at the right time. If the interest rate for your savings account drops below 1 percent, and you see lots of other banks offering 2 or 3 percent, moving over to a competitor could dramatically reduce the amount of time it takes for your money to accrue interest. Or, the rule of 72 could be a reminder not to hoard too much money in a liquid savings account when you could be earning so much more by investing it.

HACK 208

Celebrate Your Money Anniversary

Look at your investment portfolio too often and you'll work yourself into a frenzy about the performance of each and every one of the index funds, ETFs, and other investment vehicles you're relying on for your future comfort and prosperity. But if you never look at your portfolio, you basically have your head in the sand. You can't make smart decisions for your finances if you're not paying attention at all.

Find a happy medium by reviewing and rebalancing your investment allocations once each year. It doesn't matter when you do it—the start of the year, right after Tax Day, your birthday—it just matters that you make time to regularly review your portfolio. When you do it, check in on the following areas:

- **Your Money Goals:** Are you contributing enough of your income to your retirement account? Experts usually say to aim for 15 percent.
- **Your Portfolio Performance:** Regardless of any big peaks and valleys you see on the line graph for the past year, are your investments generally growing?
- **Your Age and Risk Tolerance:** Do you have a mix of stocks and bonds that fits the level of risk you're comfortable taking on right now?
- **Your Fees:** Your annual check-in is a great time to review the expense ratio for each of your investments. An expense ratio of more than 1 percent means it's time to move on.

Don't Overlook Money Market Funds

Money market funds—not to be confused with money market *accounts* from Chapter 2—are known for their reliability for investors who don't want to take on a lot of risk. Only a few money market funds have "broken the buck" (meaning they lost money) since these funds were first created in the 1970s.

The tradeoff for not subjecting your money to a lot of risk is that money market accounts don't provide a huge potential for return. In fact, they're often close to the same rate of growth you'll find for high-yield savings accounts. The difference is that money market funds earn dividends. When you buy shares of a fund, you're basically giving a short-term loan to an organization. When that company or government pays back the loan—with interest—you get that interest as a dividend, which you can withdraw as cash or reinvest into your fund.

Money market funds keep it simple—one share equals one dollar for every fund. Funds frequently require a higher minimum than a savings account to get started, but you can withdraw your money at any time. Money market funds aren't FDIC insured like a savings account, but since the risk of poor performance on these accounts is low, it's not likely that you'll see a notable loss. One downside of money market funds—they usually don't keep up with the rate of inflation, so your money loses value if you leave it there for a long time.

HACK 210

Don't Forget to Actually Invest Your Money

It's a big misconception that once you set up automatic contributions to your 401(k) or IRA, your work is done. But it's really just beginning. When you contribute cash, it sits in what's called a settlement fund until you decide what to do with it. Since your settlement fund is a money market fund, it earns interest, but only a small amount. This money isn't invested in stocks, bonds, or anything else. You have to choose how to invest those funds.

If you're enrolled in a 401(k), it's likely that the plan administrator automatically enrolled your cash into an index fund or other diversified option. But if you're investing on your own, say through an IRA, no one's going to do this for you. Make a point to log in to your account to make sure you've chosen one or a few holdings. Then, once you've chosen your holdings, check your scheduled contributions to make sure they're going directly into the holdings you want to focus on growing, instead of into the settlement fund.

YOUR SETTLEMENT FUND IS A SAFE SPACE

Your settlement fund is where you receive dividends or trade earnings, so don't be alarmed if you see a bit of money in there. Depending on how your account is set up, these earnings are likely reinvested into your holdings. Other than that, you don't have to worry too much about what's in your settlement fund and why. Just keep contributing to your selected holdings and watch your money grow.

HACK 211

Become a Homebuying Pro

If you're thinking about buying your first home in the next few years, take advantage of free first-time homebuying classes. A class can teach you the lingo you need to know *and* help you qualify for first-time homebuyer programs that can save you money on your first place.

Classes tend to run about $40–$75 and last between four and eight hours, either in person or online. Look for one that's approved by the Department of Housing and Urban Development (HUD). If you take an online class, you'll probably be required to complete the curriculum in a time frame of about a month.

Once you complete a class, don't lose your certificate or other documentation. It'll be required for many first-time homebuyer programs that provide down-payment assistance or low mortgage rates. Some programs require that your class be completed in the past year or two.

HACK 212

Keep Company Stock Out of Your Portfolio

Your retirement account is sponsored by your company. Why not fill it up with your company's stock? This is a bad way to invest. You already spend eight hours a day working there (at least)! Don't invest twice in the company by holding a bunch of your company stock and hoping business stays brisk.

Companies love to give out stock, either as part of your compensation plan or as the default investment option for your 401(k). So keep an eye out for opportunities to minimize your risk by investing in more reliable options like index funds.

If company stock is the default option for your 401(k), it should be easy to switch it to another option offered by your plan. If company stock is a part of your compensation, you may have to wait until you've been with the company for a few years until you're fully vested.

HACK 213

Ask Your Employer for Lower Fees

Your employer's 401(k) options may be limited to a few dozen fund options. That might give you enough flexibility to choose a direction for your investments, but what if all the expense ratios look too high? It's worth asking your employer if there are other options for you. Ask your human resources department if it's possible for your company to add another option through your plan administrator. If there's potential for you to keep more of the money you earn, there's potential for your coworkers too—so everyone should be happy about the potential change.

HACK 214

Ditch PMI ASAP

If you make a down payment on a home that's less than 20 percent of the cost, you'll need to get private mortgage insurance. This kind of insurance protects your mortgage lender if you skip out on your loan. It usually costs up to 2.5 percent of your total annual mortgage each year, but you can get rid of it once you've paid off 20 percent of your home's value. It helps to request this yourself, because lenders must (by law) let you off the hook once you've paid 22 percent of the purchase price. Why wait for them to stop billing you?

You may also be a candidate for lender-paid mortgage insurance (LPMI). It's designed for people who don't plan to own their home for the full length of the mortgage, allowing them to spread the PMI over the length of the loan so you pay less up front (but more over the total length of the loan, if you decide to stay).

Go On a Retirement Treasure Hunt

How many jobs have you had since you were eighteen? Even if they didn't all offer retirement plans, there's a good chance that you've had at least one 401(k) under a previous employer. If you're not sure you took care of that account when you left your job, it's time to double-check your history for lost 401(k) accounts. Doing this is important because you may have had a job in the past where your employer contributed on your behalf even if you didn't.

WHERE TO LOOK FOR OLD 401(K)S

Your employer. Check through the paperwork from your old job for any information about a retirement account. If you have information about your plan administrator, contact them for account login info. You may need to contact your previous employer's human resources department for direction, otherwise.

Your state's unclaimed property office. Your employer may have cashed out your account if the balance was small, leaving the cash in limbo. Check MissingMoney.com—and see Chapter 3 for more details about getting unclaimed funds back.

The National Registry of Unclaimed Retirement Benefits (www.unclaimedretirementbenefits.com). You can search for plans in your name using only your Social Security number. If there's a match, you enter your contact information so your employer or account custodian can find out what you want to do with the money.

Once you find your retirement plan, you can choose to roll it over into an account you already have, leave it in its current account, or take a cash distribution. Obviously, continuing to invest that money is your best move.

HACK 216

Wed Wisely

Can you guess how much a wedding costs in the United States? The average is about $30,000, with weddings in pricey places like New York City and Miami coming in with much higher averages. But just because you want your friends and family to witness you committing your love to one another doesn't mean you need to break the bank to do it.

A few options for reducing the cost of your reception without sacrificing the fun:

- Get married in the off-season for your area (winter and early spring are usually your safest bets)
- Consider a venue that has everything you need on site, like a restaurant
- Host a wedding brunch or lunch instead of the pricier dinner meal
- Offer beer and wine instead of a full bar—or skip the booze altogether
- Have champagne and desserts instead of a full sit-down meal
- Explore the cost of a buffet versus a plated meal
- Skip spending extra on chair covers

Ask your friends and family for ways they saved money on their own weddings. They'll be sure to have recommendations of venues and vendors that fit your style and are in your price range. Remember that the amount you spend doesn't reflect how much you love one another. And if you can only afford a small party now, you can renew your vows later on and have an even bigger celebration if you choose.

HACK 217

Get Vested

When your employer puts money in your retirement account by matching the amount you contribute, it doesn't mean you have the right to that money right away. You may hear the word "vested" used by your company's HR department—that's a word for who owns your money. If you're fully vested from day one, you can take every penny that's been contributed to your 401(k) by you or your employer whenever you leave. Other companies will require that you work for a certain amount of time before being fully vested, meaning you own all the money you contributed, but not all the money your company contributed, until you have worked the required amount of time.

THE TWO KINDS OF VESTING

Cliff vesting: Your employer can make you wait up to three years to own the contributions it has made to your 401(k).

Graded vesting: Your employer can grant you partial ownership of the funds it has contributed, increasing that level over the course of a few years. In most cases, your employer must declare you fully vested within six years of your job starting.

The vesting schedule probably isn't the sole reason to take or leave a job. But if you've been thinking about a career move in the near future, it's worth checking your vesting schedule to make sure you'll get to keep all the money you see in your 401(k).

Don't Rob Your Retirement

Often parents, wanting the very best for their offspring, take early distributions or loans from their retirement accounts in order to help with college costs. But doing so puts you at a severe disadvantage. You may still be dealing with your own student loans, but the reality remains that your own children can—and will, if necessary—take out their own student loans to pay for school. But there's no similar option for you to take out loans to fund your retirement.

That's why it's so important to prioritize your own savings. You can't predict what shape their education will take, and you definitely can't bank on them getting rich and taking care of you in your old age. So, play it safe and prioritize your own retirement savings over their college fund.

Save for Graduate School

Did you know that you can benefit from a 529 plan even if you don't have children? You can use it to save for your own education, whether it's graduate school, continuing education courses, or a career change that requires additional training.

Contributions to 529 savings accounts are exempt from federal taxes. Every state offers at least one option for this type of savings account.

If you know you're going to go back to school at some point, saving with this type of tax-advantaged savings account can help you start to plan for those nerve-wracking tuition costs. But beware: If you withdraw these funds for a use that's not educational, you'll have to pay a 10 percent federal tax penalty.

Prepare Your Baby for College Costs

Even though you may (and should) prioritize your own retirement savings over your child's education fund, you can still make it easy for your family to save. Savings plans called 529s are investment accounts designed specifically for education expenses. Adults typically open them for their children, grandchildren, or other young relatives to help them save for college, but if you're over eighteen, you can also open one for yourself. While you can participate in a 529 that essentially buys prepaid credits to use at participating colleges, your better option is most likely to go with a 529 savings plan. You invest your funds sort of like you would in your 401(k). Then, when it's time to send junior off to college or trade school, that money is tax free as long as it's used toward tuition, housing, equipment, books, or other costs of attending. 529 funds can also be used for $10,000 worth of K–12 tuition per year.

529 PLANS MAKE GIFT-GIVING EASY

Anyone can contribute to a 529 plan, and there are no caps to how much a beneficiary's account can receive in a year. That makes it a great thing to have around for when your aunts, uncles, or parents ask, "How can we help you save for school for Junior?" because you can provide the information for them to contribute. And 529 balances are typically counted as assets belonging to the parent when it's time to apply for financial aid, so the amount of aid your student gets won't be reduced dramatically if you've done a great job helping them save.

HACK 221

Aim for 80 Percent in Retirement

How much money do you need when you retire? The reason it's so hard to determine the right amount is because it's different for everyone.

Experts say to plan for a yearly retirement income of 70 percent to 80 percent of your pre-retirement income. That's because you'll have fewer expenses—you won't be commuting to work every day, for starters. You won't be paying social security or Medicare taxes. And you won't be saving for retirement anymore.

Some financial planners think that mentally preparing to "spend" 80 percent of your salary per retirement year is too high, and that it encourages you to overspend as you get used to life in retirement. They have a point, but a benchmark like this gives you a goal to work toward.

HACK 222

Save Money on Financial Planning

Maybe you're ready to work with a human (vs. robo) financial planner, but you're worried about the cost. One of the ways you can get the most convenient service possible and save a bit of money is by working with a virtual planner. Instead of meeting in an office, the certified financial planner (CFP) or other advisor connects with clients through some combination of online video chat, phone, and email. This method keeps you from having to take time to travel to your advisor's office and to plan your meeting times around your working hours or theirs; and if one of you moves to another city or state, you'll still be able to work together.

HACK 223

Make Sure Your Money Lasts

If you've done everything right on your way to retirement, when the day finally comes you might feel like you deserve to splurge with a bit of your well-saved money. But there's a rule of thumb you should follow for your retirement account withdrawals if you want to make that money last.

Experts advise that you withdraw no more than 4 percent of your retirement funds each year if you want to make sure your money lasts for thirty years. Play around with this math, and you'll get a good idea of how much money you really need to save for retirement for the lifestyle you want.

HOW THE 4 PERCENT RULE WORKS

For instance, say you've saved $500,000 for retirement and your last day of work has finally arrived. Multiply 500,000 by .04 and you'll learn that you can take out $20,000 each year and still have plenty for future years. If that isn't enough for you, you'll know you need more in order to retire. The 4 percent rule on a savings of one million would allow you to withdraw $40,000 per year.

IT'S ONLY AN ESTIMATE

The math isn't perfect, but it gives you a rough number to shoot for depending on how much money you think you'll need for expenses when you retire. Many people don't just use this rule for life in their 60s, 70s, and beyond, though—if you've heard of the FIRE movement (Financial Independence, Retire Early), many of those people are hoping to amass as much money in their younger years as possible, so they can start withdrawing that 4 percent earlier, while maintaining strong financial footing.

Create a Backup Investing Account

If your employer offers a Health Savings Account (HSA) in tandem with a high-deductible healthcare plan, it may be worth considering, even if you think you're healthy enough not to need this savings account. When you contribute money to an HSA, you're not required to use the funds in a certain time frame, like you are with a flexible spending account. But while you're waiting to use these funds, you can hold them as cash or invest them like you would contributions to your 401(k) or IRA. That means you can basically use your HSA as a backup retirement account.

Your money grows tax-free, and your withdrawals for qualified healthcare expenses are tax-free too. If you withdraw the money for non-health reasons, you pay income tax plus a 20 percent penalty tax. But if you wait until age sixty-five to withdraw the money for non-health expenses, there's no penalty. You just pay income tax on your withdrawals, just like you would with a 401(k) account.

There are limits to how much you can contribute to your HSA each year—around $3,500 for an individual and $7,000 for a family. But if you can max out that contribution alongside what you put into your other retirement accounts, you can set yourself up to be more comfortable down the line—and to cover any medical issues that may come up prior to retirement.

HACK 225

Protect Your Finances with a Fiduciary

When it's time to work with a financial planner, it's important to find one that intends to take care of your money. CFPs and chartered financial analysts (CFAs) come in two main varieties: fee-only planners, who charge you a flat rate for their services; and commission-based planners, who earn a portion of the financial transactions they make on your behalf. Fee-only planners pledge to act in your best interest, monitoring your money and helping you make decisions regardless of whether the decision will benefit them. They earn their income based on charging a flat or hourly rate, or from a percentage of your assets that they manage.

CHOOSE FIDUCIARY OVER SUITABILITY

Being a fiduciary is voluntary. Commission-based financial advisors are only required to adhere to the "suitability standard," which means that the financial planner may not be as clear about their processes and aren't obligated to monitor the health of your accounts after a trade is made. They don't need to disclose conflicts of interest. Their income is based entirely on the products they sell you or accounts they open.

It's easy to see why you'd want to work with a fiduciary, so ask if they are fee-only or commission-based first when screening potential financial advisors. To find a fee-only fiduciary near you, search the XY Planning Network (www.xyplanningnetwork.com) or FeeOnlyNetwork.com (www.feeonlynetwork.com).

HACK 226

Let Your Money Be Boring

Your money should be boring. Financial experts tend to agree that the best way for your portfolio to grow is slow and steady over the course of many years—not with wild ups and downs that make you sweat. There is no secret that, if followed, will make you rich now and long into your golden years. Instead, it's a matter of saving, investing in inexpensive funds instead of individual stocks, and monitoring—but not reacting—to your portfolio performance. That's it!

HACK 227

Lock Down Your Credit

If you're even considering buying a home, get serious about your credit score. Get your score as high as possible, then maintain it—even for as long as one to two years. A boring yet healthy credit profile is exactly what lenders want to see when considering your mortgage application.

That means you should skip applying for a new credit card or car loan in the year or two leading up to your home purchase. You should strive to pay off as much debt as possible, and make sure any late payments get covered up in your credit history by a long string of on-time payments. If you work to fortify your credit score with plenty of time before you do apply for a mortgage, you can make sure there are no surprises when you see the rates available based on your credit report.

HACK 228

Get Your FICO Mortgage Score

There are many different ways to calculate a credit score. But you can reduce your chance of surprise if you have a good relationship with your bank or credit union. Going this route can help you get your score without paying for it.

Ask your banker if they can access your FICO score specifically for mortgages. You may also be able to request your score for free from a housing counselor that's approved by HUD. There are a few variations that lenders can choose for mortgage applications, but it's a far smaller pool than the dozens of methods you could see used otherwise. Doing this will give you a good idea of what you're working with and whether you need to raise your score before applying.

HACK 229

Request a Rapid Rescore

If you've been working hard to boost your credit score, you may have noticed it can take a while for paid debts to reflect in your score—sometimes up to forty-five days. But if you're anxious to start the process of buying a home, you may be able to accelerate the process.

It's possible through what's called rapid rescore, which is typically used to correct credit reports that have errors. You can ask a lender to do that if your score isn't matching up where you think it should be. You won't see a drastic change in your score, but even a boost of 20 points can get you a better interest rate. Doing so doesn't *guarantee* you'll get a better rate on your mortgage, but a better credit score never hurt anyone, did it?

Make a *Big* Down Payment

Even if you plan to make a small down payment on a home, you can use the savings you've built up for closing costs or even moving costs. Some lenders want to see that you have a few months of mortgage payments on hand before granting a loan. In fact, it's common for lenders to ask for copies of your tax returns and bank statements when you apply for a mortgage. The process of "account verification" allows them to see not just how much money you have, but also how long you've had it. If you have large deposits that suddenly show up in your accounts, the lender may even ask about the source of those funds to make sure you aren't inflating your ability to pay back a home loan.

Pay Points Now to Save Later

Maybe you already have a solid interest rate offer for a mortgage, but you'd like to pay even less interest over the course of your loan. It might be possible if you have extra money you can use to buy points. When you do this, you essentially pay off a bunch of interest on your mortgage in advance to get a lower interest rate. One point usually equals .25 percent off your mortgage interest rate (say, reducing it from 4.25 percent to 4 percent). To get that special discount, you'll pay 1 percent of your mortgage amount. You pay these points at closing, which is why it's important to have cash on hand after your down payment and your other closing costs.

HACK 232
Figure Out Your PITI

The people who tell you that you could have a monthly mortgage payment for less than your rent may not be looking at the right numbers. To get a better idea of how much buying a home would really cost each month, you need to know your PITI:

- **Principal:** The monthly main amount you pay on your mortgage (the part that makes the amount you owe go down).
- **Interest:** The monthly interest you pay on your mortgage loan (this gets rolled together with the principal for your overall mortgage payment).
- **Property Tax:** The taxes you pay on your home to your local government. The payment schedule depends on where you live, but the first few months usually get rolled into your closing costs. Often, you pay this as part of your bigger mortgage payment and your lender submits it to your city when due.
- **Insurance:** This is either your homeowners insurance or your homeowners association fee. If you're getting insurance for a home that's not in an association, you will need to pay up front for the first year, but you may be able to shift to monthly payments after that first year.

Why is it important to know how these four items add up to your monthly homeownership costs? Because if you don't know your PITI, you could be getting in way over your head in a house you can't truly afford. Lenders want to see your PITI as 28 percent or less of your income. And let's face it—you don't want the costs of owning a home to eat into your budget by too much more than that anyway.

HACK 233
Buy a House for Less

Finding an affordable home to purchase can be a long and frustrating process. Looking at foreclosed homes may open up new possibilities, but it also comes with risks. To get started without getting overwhelmed, look for homes that are in foreclosure in your area on HomePath.com. It's a program from government-sponsored mortgage company Fannie Mae that helps it sell the homes on which it has foreclosed. A lot of the homes are move-in ready, though conditions vary. Buyers may be eligible for one or both of two programs that can make the process of buying a home easier. The first is the HomeReady mortgage program, which allows low down payments. Meanwhile, the Ready Buyer program lets qualified buyers get a refund on up to 3 percent of their closing costs.

The other government-sponsored mortgage lender, Freddie Mac, has a similar program called HomeSteps. Freddie Mac provides cleaning and lawn services before its homes are put on the market. The Home Possible mortgage program allows down payments as low as 3 percent.

With both programs, investors are not permitted to make offers for the first several weeks the property is on the market, ensuring that people who are buying a primary residence get first dibs, instead of investors who have lots of cash to wave around.

HACK 234

Save Thousands on Your Mortgage

Once you sign all the paperwork and finally get to hold the keys, you might hope the stress of buying a home is over for a long, long time. But paying attention to mortgage rates in the months and even years after you buy could help you pay off your home faster by refinancing. When you refinance, you replace your current mortgage with a new one for the amount you still owe. You have to qualify for refinancing by having your credit reviewed by a mortgage lender, and you complete the entire closing process you went through when you first bought a home. You'll pay another round of closing costs, which might make the prospect of refinancing less attractive since you'll have to have at least a few thousand dollars on hand. But it could be worth it in the long run, if mortgage rates have decreased considerably. For instance, if you took out a thirty-year mortgage on a $300,000 house at 5 percent, then refinanced two years later at 4 percent, you could save approximately $32,000 in interest. Doing so would also reduce your mortgage payment by about $220 per month.

Of course, a lot depends on the market and how interest rates fluctuate. Talk to a mortgage broker to get an estimate of your potential up-front costs as well as a rundown of the potential savings you'll reap down the road. And remember, the later you refinance, the more equity you'll have in the home and the smaller mortgage you'll have to take out, so you won't necessarily have to saddle yourself with another thirty-year mortgage. Ten or fifteen years may be enough.

CHAPTER SIX
Protect Your Money

HACK 235

Put Your Credit on Ice

Want to make sure no one opens new credit in your name? It's as easy as requesting a freeze. A credit freeze prevents lenders from checking your credit, which in turn means that no one can use your personal information to open a credit card or take out a loan. You'll still be able to check your credit report, and you can still use your existing accounts when your credit is frozen.

Credit bureaus used to charge fees every time you wanted to freeze or unfreeze your credit. But now it's free for everyone. To freeze yours, visit each credit bureau's website—Equifax, TransUnion, and Experian—to create a free account with each. You'll log in to that account whenever you want to make a change to your freeze status. Remember to unfreeze your profile with each bureau before you apply for new credit!

This is one of those money tasks that takes a few minutes to set up but serves you in the long run. You probably don't even apply for new credit that often yourself, so there's no reason *not* to freeze your credit.

HACK 236
Set Up Banking Alerts

One of the easiest things you can do to keep your money safe is set up your notifications for just about every sort of event that could take place in your account. It's easy to set up alerts to make sure you're the only one using your cards or accounts in the ways you want to use them—and make sure no one else is meddling in your banking activity.

When you log in to your bank account, credit card, or other financial account online, you'll find a security section that allows you to toggle on or off alerts for any number of activities. You can usually choose to have these notifications sent to your email inbox or to your mobile phone.

Consider a few baseline alerts for your accounts:

- **Low balance alerts:** You'll get a notification when your balance drops below a level you specify.
- **Purchase alert:** You'll get an alert each time a purchase is made over a certain dollar amount that you set.
- **Fraud alert:** You'll get a message if your bank detects unusual activity on your account. These messages can be helpful if you avoid answering numbers you don't recognize to avoid robocalls.

HACK 237
Choose Better Passwords

While banks and other financial institutions have plenty of measures in place to keep your account secure, you need to do your part too. That means choosing good passwords for all your accounts. Don't default to your pet's name or the street where you grew up—make your passwords a pain for hackers to guess.

Passwords should be:

- **Complex:** Don't just use lowercase letters. Mix it up with capitals, numbers, and punctuation too. "moneyhacks" is a bad password. "M$neyH!ck5" is better.
- **Long:** The longer they are, the longer it takes for a hacker to figure out the right combination of numbers and letters.
- **Unique:** Don't reuse the same password for a whole bunch of accounts. If you do, when a hacker figures out your password for one account, it's like they've found the key to your entire financial life.

As an extra precaution, set up two-factor authentication on any account that offers it. Doing so will require you to enter a second password—a short, numeric code sent in an instant to your mobile phone—to complete the login process.

Cover the ATM PIN Pad

ATMs are pretty secure, right? After all, they require your card and your PIN to complete transactions. But scammers can still take advantage of you at the ATM even after they install a skimmer on top of the card slot. They may *also* install a pinhole camera that records you entering your PIN number.

So beyond the usual safety tips for visiting ATMs, like making sure the area is well lit and noting the presence of security cameras, you should also do one extra step: Cover the PIN pad when you enter your number. Use your hand, your bag, your hat—anything that blocks the view of the numbers you're pressing to any secret cameras that may be hoping to snag your info. You might feel silly next time you're taking out cash, but you'll be glad knowing your account is a little less vulnerable.

HACK 239
Avoid Tax Phishing Scams

As the ways we manage our finances online evolve, scammers are getting smarter in their efforts to get your personal information. These criminals often use phishing scams to take advantage of consumers, often by posing as the IRS, banks, or other financial professionals.

Phishing scams often come by email, saying you've violated a law, are delinquent in filing or paying your taxes, or need to fix a problem with your account. When you click a link or attachment in the email, scammers can gain access to your computer—and all of your financial and personal information.

Whether it's tax season or any other time of year, be skeptical of any emails, text messages, or phone calls you receive from anyone claiming to be from the IRS.

The IRS will never:

- Demand immediate payment of any kind
- Threaten to have you arrested
- Ask you to pay any entity other than the US Treasury
- Make you pay your taxes with a prepaid debit card, a gift card, or a wire transfer

To make you even more certain: The IRS usually contacts you about any issues with your taxes by regular mail first—and sends several notices before escalating any issue. And you always have the opportunity to question or appeal the amount you owe. So be skeptical of any contact from the "IRS" that doesn't come by mail. If you receive a suspicious message from someone claiming to work for the IRS, report it to www.irs.gov/privacy-disclosure/report-phishing. You can even forward suspected scam emails there too.

HACK 240

File Your Tax Return
As Early As Possible

If you're someone who dreads Tax Day and waits until the last minute to file their taxes, you may want to change your ways. The longer you wait to file your annual tax return, the greater the chance that someone could claim your tax refund for you.

It sounds like something out of a crime movie, but it happens more often than you might think. Fraudsters who gain access to your Social Security number can create a tax return and file it in your name—and then take any refund you are owed. When you finally get around to filing your tax return, you find out that someone has already done so for you. The result is a huge headache to sort out your identity theft with the IRS, the Federal Trade Commission, local police, and the credit bureaus.

A few tips for avoiding this type of tax fraud:

- Check your mail often to grab any tax forms as soon as they arrive.
- File your tax return as soon as you have the necessary forms.
- Check your credit report regularly for any unusual activity.
- Get an IRS Identity Protection PIN at www.irs.gov/identity-theft-fraud-scams/get-an-identity-protection-pin. You can sign up to get one of these six-digit PINs for free from the IRS. You'll use it any time you file tax forms to verify your identity alongside your Social Security number. It's not available nationwide yet, but tax filers in about half of the states can get one.

HACK 241

Don't Do Financial Tasks
on Public Wi-Fi

You might decide that instead of checking in on your finances from home, you'd like to visit your favorite coffee shop instead. But that may not be a great place to log in to all your bank and credit card accounts to check your balances.

Public Wi-Fi networks are more vulnerable to hackers, which means your accounts are more vulnerable—even if you have rock-solid passwords and are logging in via secure websites.

If you *must* check your financial accounts while you're out and about, use your data plan to access them from your phone instead of the Wi-Fi on your laptop or tablet. Hackers can still tap in to cellular networks, but it's more difficult for them to do so. If you really want to use your laptop to review your finances in public, consider using your phone's data plan to tether that signal to your computer.

Your best bet—just work on your finances at home, *then* go out for coffee with the newspaper or a good book.

HACK 242

Don't Click on Text Messages from Your Bank

If you get a text from an unfamiliar number claiming to be your bank, that's a big red flag. It may be a scam technique that takes you to a fake website made to look just like your bank's mobile login screen. When you enter your credentials to see what "unusual activity" your bank wants you to address, the scammer takes it and takes over your account.

Banks are on the lookout for these types of scams, but as criminals get more sophisticated in imitating financial institutions, you can't be too careful. If you get a message from your bank that you think is a real issue you need to address, use your bank's secure mobile app or type in its web address yourself—don't click on any links provided.

HACK 243

Make a Will While You're Healthy

Wills aren't just for people who have spouses or children. Even if you're single, a will can help your loved ones settle your estate. And it's not just about money either. A will can provide instructions for who will care for a pet; it can list recipients for items of sentimental value, like family photos or diaries. Your will can even help you leave a legacy, if there's an organization to which you'd like to leave funds.

If your finances are fairly simple, it can cost between $1,000 and $2,000 to have a will drawn up by an attorney. If you're short on cash, you can go the assisted-DIY route online through legal service platforms which cost significantly less.

Never Give Out Your PIN

It may seem like the easiest tip in the book to protect the PIN you use to access your bank account or take money from an ATM. But scammers know how to wear you down and take hold of this information. It's up to you to be aware of their methods to resist their attempts.

In what's called an imposter scam, the caller will claim to be someone you know in order to get you to give them money. For example, you might get a call from someone claiming to work at your bank. They may ask you about a fraud alert and ask you to confirm or provide details about your bank account. You might even get a text message the caller "generated" to confirm your identity—but watch out, because those text messages are often used to trick you into letting the caller reset your account password. And if they ask for your PIN and you *still* think this person is a helpful bank representative, you could have some serious fraud and identity theft on your hands.

The Federal Trade Commission says never to give out account numbers or numbers that identify you (like your Social Security number) to someone who calls you. If the caller has those numbers or a portion of the digits and asks you to confirm, don't do it. Hang up and file a complaint with the FTC at www.ftccomplaintassistant.gov.

When in doubt, don't share any bank-related info by phone. If you suspect there may be an issue with your bank account, call your bank using the number on the back of your debit or credit card.

Kick Up Credit Card Fraud Help

See something on your credit card statement that just doesn't add up to what you thought you spent? It might be fraud—or it might be a simple mistake.

Take a closer look at the transaction date, location, and amount. If you were overcharged or charged several times for the same amount, it's probably an error on the merchant's part. You can file a dispute to have your credit card issuer investigate the problem—and you can usually do that right from your statement when you're logged in online. You can also file a dispute if the product or service you paid for was never delivered, or if your refund for a return wasn't processed.

WHEN TO OPEN A FRAUD INVESTIGATION

Meanwhile, if you see charges from vendors you don't recognize or amounts that you don't remember spending, it's more likely to be fraud. In that case, don't use the dispute form—pick up the phone and call your bank or card issuer.

Disputes can take a few weeks to investigate, while fraud teams can start working on your case immediately. But it's up to you to know when to make the call, if your bank doesn't pick up on the problem first.

HACK 246

Consider Spending Extra
for Wedding Insurance

Wedding insurance can cover issues related to your ceremony or reception site, weather, and vendors. Your vendors will typically have insurance for liability if someone gets hurt during your celebration, but check with them about their cancellation or postponement policies. If they're rather strict, it may be worth getting a wedding insurance policy to cushion the blow if for any reason you need to delay your nuptials.

Wedding registry website *The Knot* says wedding insurance costs between $150 and $500, based on how much coverage you need. If your vendors don't offer a lot of liability insurance and you are worried your aunts and uncles will get hurt cutting a rug on the dance floor, consider paying more for liability insurance. But keep in mind: Your wedding insurance does not typically cover a change of heart by either partner about to be wed.

Protect Your New Car Purchase

If you're buying a brand-new car or truck with a loan, you may want to get gap insurance. Cars lose up to 20 percent of their value in their first year on the road. That means that if your new car gets totaled or seriously damaged in the first year you own it, it may have already depreciated so much that you could still owe more money than your insurance company declares it's worth. Gap insurance covers the difference between what your insurance company will pay and what you may still owe on your car.

Gap insurance adds about $20 per year to your insurance premium, according to the Insurance Information Institute. Your car dealership will likely offer this coverage to you when you're working through payment details, but you can save money by using your own auto insurance company.

Insurance carriers typically drop your gap insurance automatically once you've had your car or truck for a year or two, but you should routinely compare what you owe to your car's value to be sure of whether you still need your gap insurance.

HACK 248
Hold On to Your Gains

It's a good idea not to be too active in your investment strategy. But the time may come when you may want to do some buying and selling to switch things up in your portfolio. When you do, keep in mind that you'll have to pay capital gains taxes.

A capital gain is the profit you earn when you sell an investment for more than you paid for it. There are short-term and long-term capital gains, and they both get taxed. If you hold an asset for a year or less, that gain gets taxed at your regular income tax rate. But if you hold your investment for a year or more before selling, you only have to pay long-term capital gains taxes. The rates vary depending on your taxable income but are lower than your regular income tax rates.

If you're investing for the long term anyway, this may not come into play for you. But before you make any quick decisions with the assets in your portfolio, check the calendar to make sure you won't pay a higher tax rate than you absolutely need to.

Don't Be Fooled by the January Effect

Each January, the stock market tends to kick things off with an encouraging performance. There are a few contributors, but one of them is that investors sell off a bunch of stocks in December before that tax year ends, then they put that money back into other investments in January.

When you see the markets doing well in January, it shouldn't prompt you to suddenly invest more or to start moving around your allocations. You may find that your portfolio gains value in January, but that shouldn't be a signal to sell high and increase your risk with newer investments. Instead, focus on the long haul. If you want to increase how much you contribute to your investments in January, it's a great time to evaluate your priorities for the coming year. But don't count on a boom market to get you rich overnight.

HACK 250

Don't Get Duped by Funeral Homes

When you're grieving, it's easy to overspend. The federal government has rules to help make sure you don't pay more than you want to when it's time to plan a funeral, whether it's pre-planning for your own or handling someone else's affairs. The Federal Trade Commission's Funeral Rule requires funeral providers to give you itemized price lists for their services. That list must include casket prices. Funeral providers are also required to give you this pricing information over the phone. Once you choose products or services, funeral providers must give you a written statement of your total due that itemizes each charge.

Look Up Your Insurance Profile

By now, you know how important it is to check your credit report regularly. But did you know you can also access your financial risk profile? Your LexisNexis Risk Solutions report contains information about your financial history—much of it a repeat from your credit report—but also may include information about your education, property sales, traffic violations, and professional licenses, if you have any.

This information can be used to help companies decide whether to raise your insurance rates or insure you at all. For instance, your LexisNexis profile includes a CLUE report—comprehensive loss underwriting exchange—that helps auto insurance companies determine how risky you are to insure.

HOW TO GET YOUR INSURANCE PROFILE

You can get one copy of this report each year for free. All you have to do is visit https://consumer.risk.lexisnexis.com/request and provide the necessary information, including your Social Security number or your driver's license number.

The process takes longer than checking your credit report—once you submit your request, you'll wait for a letter in the mail with instructions for how to complete the process. Review your report for any errors or issues that look unfamiliar; errors could cause you to pay more for insurance or even be denied altogether. You'll want to dispute any issues as soon as you can to keep your profile in tip-top shape.

Like a credit report, you can also freeze your LexisNexis report. Doing so can prevent someone from taking out an insurance policy using your personal information; it can also protect your profile from mistakes if you have a common name.

HACK 252

Avoid Permanent Life Insurance

A permanent life insurance policy is just that: You pay a premium every year until you die, and once you die, your family gets cash. There's also a savings side to these policies—whole life and universal life insurance are ones you've probably heard of before. But…

The premiums are expensive because they go toward maintaining the policy *and* go toward building up your own cash fund from which you can borrow (or sometimes make withdrawals). Permanent life insurance can cost several thousand dollars each year, while the premium on a term life insurance is more likely to be in the low- to mid-hundreds each year. And since you pay that pricey premium up until the day you die, it can be hard to keep up with the tab. Most universal life policies, for instance, never pay out because payment lapses—and so the coverage lapses too.

HACK 253

Protect Your Final Wishes with a Trust

Want to make life even easier for your loved ones down the line? Set up a trust along with your will. When you die, the executor of your will has to go to probate court, where the contents of your will are made public—and that process can take up to a year. Set up a trust to make the process more private (and faster too). When your will is filed in court, it will just say that everything in the will is inside your trust, which gets to stay private. That can help your loved ones settle your estate faster and get your assets to where you want them to be.

HACK 254

Buy Term Life Insurance Early

If you're considering life insurance, *term* life insurance is probably your best bet. With this setup, you pay a premium for a certain number of years—twenty years is a common term—and if you die during that term, your family gets cash. If you're alive when your term expires and you want to continue having life insurance, you can usually renew your policy.

Your cost depends on how much coverage you get; experts tend to recommend you get coverage for ten times your annual salary if you have dependents like children. At a minimum, you'll want enough coverage to cover any debts you have, like a mortgage.

Have access to life insurance through your employer? You may think you don't need this tip at all. But if you leave your job, you probably won't be able to take your life insurance coverage with you. If you find yourself out of work for a while or join a company that doesn't offer life insurance in its benefits package, you'll want to consider getting your own policy.

HACK 255

Buy More Life Insurance Than You Think You Need

When you consider buying term life insurance, don't just stop at the first quote you get. It's important to compare several different plans. You might be able to get more insurance for a lower price.

The reason is because insurers put their coverage into groups. For instance, if you want life insurance for somewhere between $50,000 and $100,000, you'll pay a little bit more per year than the next rate group of $100,000 to $150,000, and so on. It's like buying in bulk for life insurance.

Each life insurance company sets their own coverage and pricing groups, which are known as rate bands. So, if you only want $100,000 of life insurance, you might actually pay more for it with one company than you would for $150,000 of coverage with another company.

Don't put on blinders and only look at the amount of insurance you think you need. Consider all the coverage available to you and see which fits into your budget best. You might be surprised at how much life insurance you can really afford.

HACK 256

Get an Insurance Discount

When you compare prices for insurance policies, don't forget to check with your affinity groups. Don't think you're in any of these groups? You might be surprised.

Here are a few examples of affinity groups:

- Alumni associations
- Professional associations
- Service clubs
- Honor societies
- Military organizations
- Recreational clubs

Insurance companies like these groups because there's something about them that makes their customers less risky to insure. It could be a level of education, a shared profession or industry, or approximate activity level.

Beyond offering special rates to members of these groups, insurers may offer additional perks. These might offer pricing guarantees, introductory rates, or bonus coverage levels. Keep in mind that you may need to access insurers' offers through the members-only website for your group, or by using a specific offer code provided by the group.

If you'd prefer to work with a different insurer rather than the one offered by your group, you can always ask if your preferred carrier can match its price.

HACK 257

Protect Your Salary

Imagine how you would perform your job duties if you got in a major accident. In the best-case scenario, it's likely you'd have difficulties doing routine tasks—even if you typically just sit at a computer all day. That's why it's important to consider purchasing disability insurance if your employer doesn't offer it.

Disability insurance provides for a considerable portion of your income—usually somewhere between 50 percent and 70 percent—if you can't work. Depending on your policy, there will be a cap for how much money you can receive per month and for how long you can continue to receive it. Short-term disability covers about three to six months out of work, while long-term disability insurance can provide coverage for several years.

SHORT-TERM DISABILITY VERSUS LONG-TERM DISABILITY

If you don't have a strong emergency fund set up, it can be worth considering getting short-term and long-term insurance because the latter usually requires a waiting period before the policy starts to pay out; short-term coverage can fill the gap. If you're out of work for a year, for instance, you don't want to have to wait until month three for your policy to kick in. When you compare your options, look for policies that are "noncancelable," meaning your policy can't be turned off by your insurer on a whim, and that are "guaranteed renewable," meaning you can renew your policy each year without a new medical exam.

Whether short term or long term, you can expect to pay a premium of 1 percent to 3 percent of your income each year for disability insurance.

HACK 258

Cover Your Own Occupation

Browsing your options for disability insurance? Make sure you select a policy that provides "own occupation" or "regular occupation" coverage. This ensures you'll get benefits from your policy if your injury or illness prevents you from performing your current occupation. If your policy doesn't specify this or says that it provides "any occupation" coverage, your benefits could be denied if there's any other job you could perform that replaces the same amount of your income as your policy would.

Say, for example, you work as a manager in a retail store. After your accident, it's hard to walk around the store and lift heavy objects like you used to do. Without own occupation coverage, your insurer could say that you should be able to work a desk job that doesn't require walking around or lifting anything. But if you've always worked on the sales floor managing a team, could you imagine trying to quickly transition into a desk job at the same time you're recovering from an injury?

You'll pay more for own occupation coverage because it's more flexible in how easily it provides benefits. But it's worth the added expense for the comfort of knowing that if you get hurt, you won't have to rush into an unfamiliar role just to make up some of your income. In addition, you'd probably be able to get your disability benefits, even if you are able to return to the workforce in a different role.

HACK 259

Grab an Umbrella (Policy)

One extra layer of insurance protection that's worth considering is an umbrella policy. Its name has nothing to do with actual umbrellas—rather, it refers to its purpose, and fits over the top of the policies you already have for your car or home. This insurance kicks in if you exceed the limits of your regular insurance policies for your car, home, or other assets. It's often referred to as excess liability insurance, and can come in handy if you get sued by someone with whom you're involved in an insurance claim.

It can be a good idea for people who do the following:

* Are landlords
* Coach a sports team
* Volunteer frequently with or serve on the board of a nonprofit
* Participate in high-risk sports
* Own a pool or hot tub

Umbrella insurance doesn't cover your own injuries or damages, but does cover others' injuries or damages, along with your legal defense. A $1 million umbrella insurance policy costs between $150 and $400 per year.

HACK 260
Name Names on Your Financial Accounts

When you open a new account related to your finances—whether it be for life insurance, a retirement account, or any number of other purposes—you probably get asked who you want to name as a beneficiary. Whoever you name gets the funds from that account after you're deceased, and it's typical to list a family member, friend, or other loved one. But while accounts like 401(k)s and IRAs will prompt you to name beneficiaries, you should also be on the lookout for opportunities to name beneficiaries for other accounts, such as regular old checking and savings accounts.

Naming someone as a beneficiary doesn't mean they get access to your accounts when you're alive—it just means that they can deal with your accounts when you pass away. Naming a beneficiary allows your selected person to access your accounts with just their identification and your death certificate, rather than waiting for the entire process of your will being read or your estate being handled in court. It can make life a lot easier for whomever you name to handle your finances when you die.

HACK 261
Go Window Shopping

One of the worst things you can do for your finances is get too comfortable. Companies that provide financial services know the power of inertia. You're not likely to pick up and change companies unless there's something super appealing about a competitor, or if something makes you really upset with your current company.

That means your insurance company can raise rates on you even if you've been a loyal customer for years. The practice is controversial. Some insurance carriers are known to buy consumer data about you to determine how sensitive you are to price increases. They use this data to figure out how much they can increase your rates when it's time to renew without you reacting. Then, at the same time they raise your premiums, they may say you're getting a discount or a special rate for being a loyal customer. The catch is that sometimes that discount is made up just to make you feel valued. The practice of using data for price optimization is frowned upon by regulators, but it's hard to prove insurance carriers do it.

Other carriers who don't participate in price optimizing will nudge your premiums upward while giving discounts to new customers because they know you're unlikely to move on. So, before you renew your policy without a second glance, compare your renewal rate to what you're seeing for new customers at the same company—or what you might be able to get somewhere else. You might not feel like moving where you do your business, but for the right price, you'd probably be willing.

HACK 262
Hold On to Your Car Keys

If you rely on your vehicle to get to your job, you want to make sure you protect it. That means you'll want to avoid lending your car out to people who aren't on your insurance policy.

Most car insurance policies will cover anything that happens to your car while anyone is driving it, as long as that person has permission to drive your car. But in the event of a collision, you and the borrower both have to deal with the consequences.

Even though your insurance will cover the accident, your premium is likely to go up. If the damage to the others involved in the accident exceeds your insurance limits, the driver who was in your car at the time may have to make up the difference with their own insurance. And in the worst-case scenario, if your friend doesn't have their own insurance, a serious accident could leave you on the hook for all damages, even if it exceeds your coverage.

It sounds mean to say no when someone asks to borrow your car. But if neither party can afford to pay the consequences in the event of an accident, it's best not to do it at all.

HACK 263
Create an Emergency Folder

Having important documents organized isn't just helpful if you die suddenly—it can also be a huge help if you take ill and need help managing your finances. To make life easier for any loved one who may step in unexpectedly, it's a good idea to keep your important documents and financial information in one central location in your home.

Perhaps you already have a file cabinet or file box set up for your essential documents. You can either add to it or set up a specific binder or envelope that contains the following:

- Your will, advanced medical directive, and/or estate plan
- Instructions for a funeral or other service
- Information for your insurance policies
- A list of recurring expenses, due dates, and which accounts you use to pay them
- A list of financial accounts and their purpose
- A list of passwords to access your online accounts (or your log-in to your computer or login for your online password manager)

If you choose to keep your documents in the cloud, consider downloading a copy of its contents to a portable drive, and storing that in an easy-to-reach spot at home. Your documents should be easy to access, and more than one trusted person should know how to access them in the event of an emergency. Once you've gotten organized, don't get complacent—review the contents once per year to make sure everything is up to date. While it was once recommended to keep all this information in a safe-deposit box, fewer banks offer this service these days—and you'll want your documents accessible immediately, not only during bank hours.

HACK 264

Consider Final Expense Insurance

Consider getting final expense insurance, sometimes called burial insurance. This coverage helps your loved ones deal with the immediate expenses related to your death, including medical bills and the cost of hosting a funeral.

There's no medical exam for final expense insurance, and your coverage likely won't exceed $50,000, which makes paying the annual premium more affordable. Premiums start at about $5 per month, depending on your age. If you're a new customer, there may be a waiting period before your loved ones can access your coverage in the event of your demise. Some policies even allow you to receive up to half your benefit while you're alive, if you develop a serious illness.

You can typically get a better deal on burial insurance as part of a regular life insurance policy, but if your finances are fairly limited, this coverage could help you bridge the gap if you pass unexpectedly.

HACK 265

Buy Travel Insurance, but Only Sometimes

Among the many boxes you tick when buying a travel ticket, you might encounter an option to buy travel insurance. It usually costs just a few dollars and claims it'll protect you if you need to cancel your trip. But unless you're taking an expensive trip, it may not be worth paying extra for this coverage.

For one, it's more cost-effective to buy your own travel insurance than to buy it as an add-on to a ticket. If you have a rewards credit card, it's more than likely that your card—as long as you use it to reserve your ticket—comes with enough protection to cover you if you need to cancel your trip and have nonrefundable tickets. If you change your mind at the last minute, you'll miss out on a refund either way. But if you get sick and need to cancel your trip, your credit card will probably reimburse you for tickets for which you can't get a credit.

ONE NOTABLE EXCEPTION

If you're traveling internationally or are embarking on a trip of a lifetime, take note: If you don't have medical insurance that works internationally, the coverage you'll get from a travel insurance policy will be a huge help and will cover more causes and effects than your credit card. But, as always, do a little price comparison first, and don't just check the box on the airline or tour company's booking website just because you feel like you're supposed to buy it.

HACK 266
Review Your Health Insurance Plan Every Year

Maybe you've seen a notice or two about open enrollment season for your health insurance. If you're already insured, you might not think you need to pay attention to open enrollment. But even if you love the insurance you have now, you still need to review your insurance options every time open enrollment comes around.

If you get insurance through your employer, there may be new options for your insurance coverage for the coming year, or your employer may have removed some options. If anything's changing to your current coverage, you'll want to switch to comparable coverage. Open enrollment is also the only time each year that you can make changes to your coverage, unless you have a major life event that qualifies you to make changes. You can add a flexible spending account, change your contribution to one, switch plans, add dependents—and you only get a period of about a month during which to do it.

It's a similar situation if you buy your own insurance, either outright or through the government exchange. During open enrollment, you might find that there are new plans available to you. Oftentimes you'll find similar coverage, but at a cost that's more appealing.

Find out when open enrollment takes place for your healthcare plan and make a point to review your current coverage about a month before that period begins. Think about what you like about your coverage—the cost, the convenience, maybe the prescription drug program—versus what you don't like. Are your doctors in network in your current plan? If not, that's one big reason you might consider switching things up. But if you go into open enrollment unprepared, you might find yourself stuck with a decision you regret for an entire year.

HACK 267

Learn the Difference Between HMOs and PPOs Once and for All

Do you know the difference between an HMO and a PPO health insurance plan? If not, you might be choosing coverage based on the price alone—and that could cause headaches later on when you're feeling under the weather.

An HMO is a health maintenance organization. You see your primary care doctor first whenever you have a health issue, and if they decide you need to see a specialist, they give you a referral for that care. You have to see the in-network specialist you get referred to, or else you may have to pay for the visits yourself. Copays are typically lower with an HMO.

A PPO is a preferred provider organization. You can choose from a variety of in-network healthcare providers without having to check with your primary care physician first. You can choose to see an out-of-network doctor, but you'll pay more out of pocket (but usually not the entire cost of the visit).

There's also a third type you may see: POS, or point of service. You work mainly with your primary care physician but can choose an out-of-network option if you need to see a specialist.

HOW YOUR CHOICE AFFECTS YOUR PREMIUMS

HMO plans are typically less expensive than PPOs because your choices are limited to your network. According to the Kaiser Family Foundation, the average monthly cost for a single person on an HMO is $548 per month, while the average monthly premium for a single person on a PPO is $567 per month. Ultimately, the right plan for you will depend on your medical needs and your budget.

HACK 268

Get the Most Expensive
Deductible You Can Afford

Want to pay the lowest rate possible on every kind of insurance from car, to renters, to health insurance? Take the highest deductible you can afford.

Your deductible is what you're responsible for paying after insurance takes care of its part. Depending on the type of insurance, your deductible could be anywhere from $250 (for a basic renters insurance policy) to $4,500 (for a health insurance policy). And those deductible levels depend not only on what type of policy it is, but also the insurance company from which you're getting a quote.

HIGHER DEDUCTIBLES MEAN LOWER PREMIUMS

The basic rule of thumb is that the higher your deductible, the lower your premium that you pay per month or year. That's because by volunteering to take on more of the costs of an incident on your own, you signal to the insurance company that you're a less risky client. Because you're so willing to take on that financial risk yourself, you get rewarded with a lower price.

Of course, don't sign up for a car insurance policy with a $1,000 deductible if you only have $250 in your emergency fund right now; if you do need to file a claim, you don't want to end up in debt trying to come up with money for your portion of the bill. But if you have a robust emergency fund, turning to that first before filing an insurance claim can help you save a lot in up-front costs.

HACK 269

Talk to Your Parents about Their Money

It can be hard to talk about money with your peers. But with your parents? That can be even harder.

It's important to know that your parents are set up to afford their lifestyle—or any lifestyle—well into their golden years. And you also need to know their final wishes for when that time comes, so you or another sibling can handle their estate accordingly. Not knowing about your parents' finances is like having your hand over your eyes while watching a scary movie. You know something bad is about to happen, but you're not quite sure what it is.

The easiest way to start talking about money with your parents is to talk about your own. Just made a will? That's the perfect time to ask your parents about theirs. But it goes beyond wills to living arrangements, long-term care, and planning ahead for medical emergencies.

Talk about Long-Term Care Plans for Mom and Dad

The average monthly cost for a private room in a nursing home is almost $8,000, according to the US Department of Health and Human Services. It may be too late to get long-term care insurance at a price that isn't prohibitively high, so you'll want to know about your parents' income, expenses, and if they have any debt (including a mortgage) in order to factor care into their long-term finances.

If you do end up providing 50 percent or more of the financial support your parents need in retirement, you can probably claim them as dependents on your taxes and get the dependent care credit.

Think about Long-Term Care Plans for Yourself

Long-term care insurance can be expensive, but it could be worth buying if you want your money to go further in retirement. This kind of insurance offers more options for when you get to the point that you need daily assistance in your home or a facility that health insurance doesn't cover.

It's recommended that you select your policy sometime between age fifty and sixty to get the best rates while you're in good health. You'll need to pay for care up front to be reimbursed by your policy, but having that policy could give you peace of mind as you enter your later phases of life.

HACK 272
Leave a Legacy

You might assume that your wealth must go to a family member or other loved one when you die. But many people choose planned giving to make sure that a favorite charity or nonprofit organization benefits from their estate. To do so, you typically name an organization in your will or trust and specify the terms of your gift. Then you send a notice to that organization of your intent to leave a gift when you pass.

You might not consider yourself a philanthropist yet, but think of it this way—instead of having a mindset of "You can't take it with you when you die!" about your money, consider sharing your wealth with an organization you'd like to support in a major way.

HACK 273
Don't Let the Market Upset You in September

Just as you shouldn't get caught up in January's stock market highs, don't be discouraged by September's lows. Don't make any rash moves with your portfolio. You'll recover some of that value as the markets move into the autumn months.

If you truly have money to spend on investments, September is a good time to buy. Think of stocks as being on sale during September. Buy a few shares now, and you'll probably find you can afford more than if you decided to buy on a random day in, say, March. Investors call this "buying the dip." The extra buys may take a while to start earning in your portfolio, but at least you'll have gotten a deal on them. If you decide to just hold on to what you've already got, that's okay too.

HACK 274

Take an Inventory

When you buy renters or homeowners insurance, tucking your policy into a file folder and into a drawer isn't enough. You need to be ready with documentation of what's in your home in case you need to make a claim. Having a list handy can help move your claim along more quickly so you can get the cash you need to rebuild.

The easiest way to get started without feeling overwhelmed by this task is to make a video for each room of your home. All you need is your smartphone. Go around the room, talking about what's in it and any important features of those items. Open cabinet doors and record what's inside. Open drawers and talk about what you see in there. Upload these videos to a cloud storage service that you can access from anywhere in the event you don't have your phone or computer.

USE YOUR VIDEO TO MAKE A LIST

Then, write out a list of what you own in each room. Describe each item and include model numbers and/or serial numbers for electronics. Record when you purchased or received each item and how much it cost when you bought it. If you know what it would cost to buy a comparable replacement item, list that too (maybe you got a record player as a gift, but know that a new one from the same brand would cost you $300).

Review your list annually to make sure it's up to date and make a new room-by-room video if needed. Beyond proof of your belongings, this process also helps to ensure that you have enough coverage based on the quantity and value of your belongings.

HACK 275
Value Your Valuables

When you're buying renters or homeowners insurance, you're probably thinking about the big things, like being able to replace your furniture and TV if a tree falls into your living room. But you should also be thinking about the items that might be vulnerable to thieves. Valuable items worth more than a certain amount often aren't covered by your insurance policy unless you insure those items specifically. This is often called personal property insurance, scheduled property coverage, or an endorsement.

Some examples you might have at home:

- Jewelry, like an engagement ring or family heirlooms
- Fine art
- Specialty electronics, like a digital camera or high-end computer
- Tools and equipment

Insuring your personal valuables typically costs about $25 for each $1,000 of coverage you need. If something happens to that item, you won't need to pay a deductible. But make note of whether your insurance policy covers the replacement value of an item or the actual cash value of the lost or destroyed item. For items that are replaceable but may depreciate (like electronics), you want to make sure you can get as close to an exact replacement as possible—so you want to look for replacement value over cash value.

Don't forget your documentation! For unique items that may have been passed down to you, you should expect to provide a copy of an appraisal to your insurer, so they have proof of the estimated value of the item. If it's a new item like a top-of-the-line camera, you may need to provide proof of purchase to document the value.

HACK 276
Save Claims for Big Mishaps

Homeowners and renters insurance policies are there to help if something goes wrong and you need to pay for repairs or replacements. But you should take caution not to make too many claims on your policy. If you make too many claims—or even if you make a single claim that you could have handled yourself—you may find that your premium rises a great deal.

A few instances where it's not wise to file an insurance claim:

IF YOU MADE A CLAIM RECENTLY
Homeowners typically make claims once every nine or ten years. Filing a claim more often is a big red flag to insurance companies, even those who have provided your coverage for a long time. Unless you have a major incident, avoid filing an insurance claim if you've already filed one in the past three to five years.

WHEN YOUR DEDUCTIBLE IS HIGHER THAN THE DAMAGE
If you have a $1,000 insurance deductible and a baseball comes through your living room window, will it cost more than $1,000 to replace the glass? If not, then pay for it yourself and save yourself the hassle.

WHEN IT'S NORMAL WEAR AND TEAR
These policies aren't for replacing worn-out computers or roofing shingles that come loose from age. You need to be ready to pay for those upkeep expenses yourself. File a claim for a wear-and-tear issue and you're likely to get denied.

HACK 277
Prepare for Disasters

If you live in a region that's prone to natural disasters, you may need to pay more for additional insurance to protect your home, whether you rent or own. The typical insurance policy does not cover earthquakes or related shifts; nor does it cover flooding due to storms.

Earthquake insurance covers damage to your property, loss of use of your residence, and clean-up costs. As a bonus, earthquake insurance typically covers sinkholes, if one happens to open up on your property. It doesn't cover damage to your home itself. You can probably add earthquake insurance to your current policy, but you can also buy a separate policy for earthquakes. Your cost will depend on your location's risk of earthquakes and how much coverage you want, but you'll pay a minimum of $5 per month.

Meanwhile, some renters or homeowners insurance policies cover water damage from pipe and sewer backup, but no standard policy covers damage from rain and natural flooding. Most flood insurance policies come from the federal government's National Flood Insurance Program (NFIP), which says that just 3 inches of water in a 1,000-square-foot, one-story dwelling could cause more than $11,000 in damage. You can get coverage for your belongings, including appliances, carpeting, and items of value, and/or building coverage, if you own your home. Your annual cost will depend on your area's flood risk, but providing an elevation certificate for your address may help lower your cost. The NFIP's FloodSmart.gov website says coverage for contents starts at only $99 per year, while coverage for a building and its contents starts at $325 per year.

HACK 278

Think Twice Before You Loan Money

When you're in a solid financial spot, it's natural to want to help others. But if a friend or family member asks to borrow money from you, you should think carefully about your answer. Spotting someone $10 for lunch is a lot different than a request to borrow $100, $1,000, or beyond.

If you think you can count on this person to pay you back and decide to lend them the cash, type up an agreement. It doesn't have to be fancy, but should spell out the date, amount, and repayment schedule. If you want to be a financial stickler, you can require your borrower to pay interest; you may decide that's too much work to worry about. Make sure you both sign it. If the borrower doesn't pay up on time, you can refer back to your agreement.

In all cases, you should assume the money you're lending to someone is a gift; if they repay it, be pleasantly surprised. Thinking about loans to friends and family in this way helps you think about whether you really have the money to spare, or if helping a friend would put yourself in a financial jam.

HACK 279

Check Your Child's Credit

Have you ever thought about checking your child's credit report? Probably not, because they shouldn't have one until they start to actually use credit. But child identity theft does happen, and if it goes unchecked, it can have lasting effects.

A few warning signs that your child's identity has been compromised:

- You get mailed credit card offers in their name
- You get a notice from the IRS concerning your child's name or Social Security number in relation to income taxes
- Debt collectors call looking for your child

If any of the above occurs, contact each credit bureau–TransUnion, Equifax, and Experian–to request they search for your child's credit file. You'll need to prove your child's identity and your own in order to do this. If your child has a credit file, you'll need to work with any lenders listed on their report, the credit bureaus, and the Federal Trade Commission to remedy their records.

If you're not suspicious of child identity theft, it's still a good idea to use your child's Social Security number as little as possible and ask about privacy measures anywhere that it's a required identifier.

HACK 280

Keep Scammers and Solicitors Out of Your Phone

If you hate getting phone calls from telemarketers, you probably know to sign up for the National Do Not Call Registry (www.donotcall.gov). This list, maintained by the Federal Trade Commission, blocks salespeople from calling you, but it doesn't block scam calls. And it doesn't block charities from calling to solicit donations or political groups from calling you before an election.

Often scammers—and even legitimate organizations—can make their calls from afar look like they're coming from your area code. That can make it hard to tell when you should pick up a call or let it go to voicemail. And on those occasions where you *do* pick up, it's easy to get cornered by a caller asking for donations for a charity you may indeed want to support.

To make dealing with these calls a little easier, pick a time of day when these calls can't interrupt you. A great time to do it is after dinnertime when you're winding down from the day—and when you're also tired from making decisions all day. That's when you may be most vulnerable to requests from organizations soliciting donations or vulnerable to scams, even if you think you're savvy.

Set your phone to switch over to "Do Not Disturb" during those hours to send all calls to voicemail without bothering you. Not only will it help you avoid uncomfortable solicitations, it takes away that decision about whether to answer the phone at all. Then, make sure the family and friends you talk with most often are on a "favorites" list so you'll hear the calls that you look forward to taking.

Index

About the Author

Lisa Rowan is a writer and editor based in St. Petersburg, Florida. She is a staff writer at *Lifehacker*, where she covers personal finance for the "Two Cents" vertical. Prior to that, she was a senior writer and on-air analyst at *The Penny Hoarder*, where she wrote more than five hundred personal finance–related posts and launched the "Dear Penny" advice column syndicated by the *Tampa Bay Times*. A graduate of the University of Maryland and Georgetown University, her work has appeared in *Retail Dive*, *The Washington Post*, *Family Circle*, *CityLab*, and the *Washington City Paper*, among others.